D1539934

SIR EDWARD DE
2nd Baronet
by Sir P. Le

Sir Edward Dering, second baronet, from the painting by Sir Peter Lely

House of Lords Record Office Occasional Publications No 1

The Diaries and Papers of Sir Edward Dering Second Baronet 1644 to 1684

Edited by Maurice F. Bond

London
Her Majesty's Stationery Office

HOUSE OF LORDS RECORD OFFICE
OCCASIONAL PUBLICATIONS

1 *The Diaries and Papers of Sir Edward Dering, Second Baronet, 1644 to 1684*
edited by Maurice F. Bond (1976)

2 *Divisions in the House of Lords, 1685 to 1857, an analytical list*
compiled by J. C. Sainty, Reading Clerk, House of Lords
and D. Dewar, formerly a Clerk in the House of Lords
(*in the press*)

3 *Handlist of records relating to Private Bills, 1794 to 1830*
compiled by H. S. Cobb, Deputy Clerk of the Records
(*in preparation*)

For further details of these and other House of Lords Record Office publications
application should be made to the Clerk of the Records, Record Office,
House of Lords, London SW1A 0PW

Typographic design by HMSO

ISBN 0 11 700364 6*

Preface

Since 1870 a detailed calendar of the Parliamentary records preserved in the Victoria Tower at the Palace of Westminster has been in course of publication. In addition, following the establishment of the House of Lords Record Office in 1946, a series of brief *Memoranda* has been issued, in many of which particular classes of documents are listed or described. For some time, however, a need has been felt for an intermediate type of publication, more substantial than the *Memoranda* and less elaborate than the Calendars. The result is the 'House of Lords Record Office Occasional Publications' of which the present edition of the papers of Sir Edward Dering is the first. It will be followed by two further volumes, already fairly well advanced in preparation, an analysis of Divisions in the House of Lords between 1685 and 1857, largely based on a detailed investigation of the Manuscript Minutes of the House, and a Handlist of Private Bill records for the important period from 1794 to 1830.

The *Occasional Publications* may in this way progressively represent periods subsequent to that of the latest Calendar volume (1714-1718), and also deal with any important groups of documents of pre-1718 date acquired since the existing Calendar volumes were published. It must be emphasised, however, that the most useful immediate indication of source material relating to both Lords and Commons available to students in the Lords Record Office remains *The Guide to the Records of Parliament*, published by Her Majesty's Stationery Office in 1971, together with the subsequent *Annual Reports* of the House of Lords Record Office (issued in the *Memoranda* series) which contain full lists of accessions. It is hoped that the *Guide*, the Calendar, the *Memoranda* and the *Occasional Publications* between them will be effective in bringing to the attention of still more students and members of the general public the considerable range of untapped sources for the history of Britain, America and the Commonwealth preserved in the Victoria Tower at Westminster.

Maurice Bond
Clerk of the Records

November 1975

Contents

Illustrations

 * *For further references concerning the portraits, see p. 5 below.*

Abbreviations

Abbreviation	Full title
ABı	Sir Edward Dering's First Account Book, 1680-1683 (calendared on pp. 105-33)
AB2	Sir Edward Dering's Second Account Book, 1683-1684 (calendared on pp. 135-51)
AC	*Archaeologia Cantiana* (1858-)
Al Cant	J. and J. A. Venn, *Alumni Cantabrigienses* (Cambridge, 1922-7)
Blake MSS	Manuscript collections of Philip Blake, Esq., of Beechwood Park, Nenagh, co. Tipperary
BL Add	British Library Additional Manuscript
BL Stowe	British Library Stowe Manuscript
CC Comp	*Calendar of State Papers Domestic, Committee for Compounding with Delinquents, etc.* 1643-1660, 5 pts., ed. E. Green (1889-93)
CJ	*Journals of the House of Commons*
CP	*The Complete Peerage . . . by G.E.C., revised . . .*, 13 vols. (1910-59)
CSPD	*Calendar of State Papers Domestic, Charles II*, ed. E. Green, etc., 28 vols. (1860-1947)
CSPI	*Calendar of State Papers relating to Ireland, Charles II*, ed. R. P. Mahaffy, 4 vols. (1905-11)
CTB	*Calendar of Treasury Books*, ed. W. A. Shaw, 32 vols. (1904-62)
DCP	Sir Edward Dering's Diary and Commonplace Book 1656-1662 (calendared on p. 158)
DNB	*Dictionary of National Biography*, ed. L. Stephen and S. Lee, 21 vols. (1885-1900)
DS Corr	*The Dering-Southwell Correspondence*, Report of the National Register of Archives, ed. S. P. Anderson (1971)
Finch	Holograph annotations by Daniel Finch (later Second Earl of Nottingham) of a journal of proceedings in the House of Commons. Leicester County Record Office, Finch MSS, Political Papers 37
G	Anchitell Grey, *Debates of the House of Commons, from 1667 to 1694*, 10 vols. (1763)
Gardiner	S. R. Gardiner, *History of England from the accession of*

<table>
<tr><td></td><td>*James I to the outbreak of the Civil War, 1603-1642,* 10 vols. (1883-4, etc.)</td></tr>
<tr><td>Haslewood</td><td>*Genealogical Memoranda relating to the family of Dering of Surrenden-Dering* [probably printed 1876] containing items reprinted from *Archaeologia Cantiana,* x (1876)</td></tr>
<tr><td>HB1</td><td>Sir Edward Dering's First Household Book, 1648-52 (calendared on pp. 155-6)</td></tr>
<tr><td>HB2</td><td>Sir Edward Dering's Second Household Book, 1652-85 (calendared on pp. 156-7)</td></tr>
<tr><td>Henning</td><td>*Parliamentary Diary of Sir Edward Dering 1670-1673,* ed. B. D. Henning (Yale University Press, 1940)</td></tr>
<tr><td>Hist Coll</td><td>Historical Collections in the House of Lords Record Office</td></tr>
<tr><td>*HL MSS*</td><td>*Manuscripts of the House of Lords,* new series, vols. i-xi (1900-62)</td></tr>
<tr><td>HLRO</td><td>House of Lords Record Office</td></tr>
<tr><td>HMC *HL MSS*</td><td>Historical Manuscripts Commission, *The Manuscripts of the House of Lords,* appendices to Reports of the Commission, 13 vols. (1870-94)</td></tr>
<tr><td>KAO</td><td>Kent Archives Office</td></tr>
<tr><td>Larking</td><td>*Proceedings principally in the County of Kent in connection with the Parliaments called in 1640 and especially with the Committee of Religion appointed in that year,* ed. L. B. Larking (Camden Society, Old Series, vol. lxxx, 1862)</td></tr>
<tr><td>*LJ*</td><td>*Journals of the House of Lords*</td></tr>
<tr><td>*OPH*</td><td>'Old Parliamentary History', i.e., *The Parliamentary or Constitutional History of England,* 24 vols. (1751-61)</td></tr>
<tr><td>*Ormonde*</td><td>*Calendar of the Manuscripts of the Marquess of Ormonde* (new series), Historical Manuscripts Commission, 8 vols. (1899, etc.)</td></tr>
<tr><td>PD</td><td>Sir Edward Dering's Personal Diary, 1673-1675</td></tr>
<tr><td>*PH*</td><td>*Parliamentary History,* ed. W. Cobbett and T. C. Hansard, 36 vols. (1806-20)</td></tr>
<tr><td>Pl D</td><td>Sir Edward Dering's Parliamentary Diary, with annexed sheets, 1675, etc. (see pp. 57-103, below)</td></tr>
<tr><td>*Return*</td><td>*Return of the names of every member returned to serve in each Parliament,* pt. i (House of Commons Sessional Papers, 69 (1878)</td></tr>
<tr><td>Sainty</td><td>J. C. Sainty, *Treasury Officials* (1972)</td></tr>
<tr><td>Witcombe</td><td>D. T. Witcombe, *Charles II and the Cavalier House of Commons 1663-1674* (Manchester University Press, 1966)</td></tr>
</table>

Introduction

Sir Edward Dering,[1] second baronet, was the head of a family that for centuries had been settled near Lydd, in Dengemarsh, a property of Battle Abbey. Among the men of Dengemarsh employed in building the Abbey in the early 12th century were 'Dering Pionius' and 'Dering'.[2] The earliest connected ancestor of the family was Thomas Dering of Dengemarsh,[3] who was father of John of Westbrook, near Lydd (d. 1425). Westbrook, which was apparently the Dengemarsh property, remained in the family until sold by Sir Edward C. Dering, 8th baronet. John of Westbrook, by marrying the heiress of John Haute of Pluckley, acquired the estate with which the family was thereafter identified. The name Surrenden-Dering was bestowed upon the capital messuage there by Dering's father.[4] Marriage with the heiresses Alice Bettenham of Pluckley and especially Margaret Brent of Charing and Willesborough brought further additions to the estate.

Several members of the family had achieved more than local fame. John Dering, a monk of Christ Church, Canterbury, supported Elizabeth Barton, the nun of Kent, and was executed at Tyburn in 1534. Edward Dering (c. 1540-1576), the Puritan and outspoken Divinity Reader at St Paul's, was described by Archbishop Parker as 'the greatest learned man in England',[5] and Richard Dering (d. 1630), organist to Queen Henrietta Maria, was a composer of lasting reputation.[6] Anthony Dering (1558-1636) was knighted in 1603 while Commander of the Tower of London. His son Edward was elected Member of Parliament for the Cinque Port of Hythe in 1625[7] and represented Kent in the Long Parliament.[8] His subsequent career as a politician has

---

[1] The name was (and is) usually spelled thus by members of the family, but contemporaries in the 17th century frequently wrote 'Deering'. Edward was a much-favoured Christian name. Of the 12 baronets since 1627 eight have been named Edward, which in six instances was their only Christian name. This has led to occasional confusion, increased by the fact that the second baronet's half-brother, also Edward, was knighted.

[2] *Chronicon Monasterii de Bello* [ed. J. S. Brewer] (1846), 13, 15.

[3] F. Haslewood, *Genealogical Memoranda relating to the family of Dering of Surrenden-Dering* (1876), reprinted from *Archaeologia Cantiana*, x (1876), 327-51. I am most grateful to Mr Blake for drawing my attention to the genealogical origins of the Dering family.

[4] who also built the mansion at Surrenden-Dering (in the 1630s), which was burnt down in 1952 (see illustration 32 in R. Strong, M. Binney and J. Harris, *The Destruction of the Country House* (1974)).

[5] *DNB*

[6] Sir George Grove, *Dictionary of Music and Musicians*, 5th ed., ii (1954), 671-2.

[7] *Return*, 467.

[8] *ibid.*, 490.

frequently been described.[1] It began notably; he had been knighted in
1619 and created a baronet in 1627. 'Distinctly Protestant without
being Puritan', he moved the first reading of the Root and Branch bill
in 1641, but then defected from the Parliamentary cause,[2] opposing the
Grand Remonstrance and, after raising a regiment of horse on behalf
of the king, was at the siege of Coventry.[3] The siege failed and by the
time of Edgehill, Dering was seeking to make his peace with Parliament,
becoming the first person in England to petition to take the Covenant.[4]
He died on 22 June 1644, a month before the Commons confirmed a
composition payment of £1,000 for his confiscated estate.[5] The first
baronet's political reputation remains equivocal, but his scholarship
has proved more enduring. He collected charters and other documents
on a vast scale, and compiled careful and elegant records of Kentish
arms and monuments. As an antiquary he worked with Hatton, Shirley
and Dugdale, and Dugdale spoke with enthusiasm of Dering—'a most
compleate gentleman in all respects, and an excellent Antiquarye.'[6]

Dering's estate passed on his death in 1644 to his eldest son Edward,
the second baronet, to whose diaries and papers the present volume
entirely relates. Among them is an autobiographical note compiled in
1680.[7] Unfortunately, two folios of this have been destroyed, but the
remaining text provides a brief but useful outline of the second baronet's
life from 1625 to 1661 and from 1669 to 1680. He was born on 12
November 1625, at Surrenden, the son of Sir Edward and his second
wife Anne Ashburnham. His christening was delayed three weeks in
the hope that the Duke of Buckingham, a distant relation of his mother,
would be able to attend. As Edward Dering himself commented years
later, that expectation failed; he added that the 'first misfortune I had
was the loss of that prudent and virtuous mother' (in 1628). He noted
as a further misfortune that his father then married again—and there is
little evidence that he had any particular affection for his step-mother.
The unhappiness of his childhood was intensified at school (one master

---

[1] e.g. by S. R. Gardiner in *DNB* and by J. Bruce in Larking, *op. cit.*, pp. v-li. Some of the
factual material on which such biographies have been based will be re-considered in a
forthcoming study of the first baronet by Mr Blake.

[2] Cf. the detailed account of Dering's behaviour by D. Hurst, 'The Defection of Sir Edward
Dering, 1640-1641', *Historical Journal*, xv (1972), pp. 193-208. Dering's own editions of his
speeches (1641-1642) and his other publications between 1641 and 1644 are briefly listed in
DNB and itemised in the BM *General Catalogue* (1967), sub 'Dering'.

[3] His son Edward accompanied him, see p. 109 below.

[4] Larking, 1; *CJ*, iii, 390.

[5] Larking, li; his heir Edward was admitted on 22 August 1644 to his estates without
being required to pay the composition, *CJ*, iii, 603.

[6] C. E. Wright, 'Sir Edward Dering: A seventeenth-century Antiquary and his Saxon
charters,' in *The Early Cultures of North-West Europe*, ed. C. Fox and B. Dickins (Cambridge,
1950), 371-393. Cf. also L. B. L[arking] 'On the Surrenden Charters', *AC*, i (1858), 50-65.
The collections after passing to his descendants were partly acquired by Thomas Astle
in the 18th century and Sir Thomas Phillipps in the 19th century.

[7] See for the matter in this paragraph pp. 108-10 below.

was 'a barbarous tyrant') but then matters began to mend. At Cambridge he clearly showed more than average ability. He observed, 'I kept my act publiquely in the schooles (a thing not very usuall for fellow commoners to do) and tooke my degree of Bachelor of Arts.' Then, from 1644 to 1646, he pursued his studies in France, and, until 1647, in the Middle Temple. Dering remarked that he had profited from his work—'my owne sedentary inclinacions and my father's encouragement and example having encouraged me to it.'[1] A turning point in Dering's life came with his marriage in 1648 at the age of 23 to Mary Harvey, daughter of Daniel Harvey of Coombe in Croydon, a native of Folkestone, a prominent Turkey merchant and brother of Dr William Harvey, the discoverer of the circulation of the blood.[2] In the course of their 36 years' notably happy marriage they had 17 children, of whom five boys and five girls survived infancy, and entries in Dering's various diaries and account books suggest that care both for his children and for his more distant relatives was the first claim on his attention and resources.[3] In the last resort he lived within his family rather than in political or literary circles, although it is noticeable that his family connections were of substantial political significance.

This fact Dering himself strongly emphasised in the autobiographical notes. Mary's elder sister Elizabeth had two years earlier married Heneage Finch, a barrister of the Inner Temple, son of the Speaker of the Commons, Sir Heneage Finch, and grandson of the Elizabeth Heneage who had been created Viscountess of Maidstone and then Countess of Winchilsea in her own right. Inclusion within the Finch circle became of crucial importance. When Heneage Finch, by then Earl of Nottingham and Lord High Chancellor, died in 1682, Dering wrote of their 'tender and uninterrupted friendship of 34 years continuance, cultivated and improved all that time by constant and familiar conversacion, and by a perpetuall succession of all good offices and instances of kindness.'[4] These good offices, as Dering's diary and papers show, often brought him into the inner consultations of the Court party, and were strengthened by the almost identical outlook

---

[1] See p. 109 below. Dering entered Sidney Sussex and then Emmanuel Colleges, graduating in 1642/3 (J. & J. A. Venn, *Alumni Cantabrigienses* (Cambridge, 1922), ii, 36). Dering was also entered at the Middle Temple on 3 December 1641 (C. H. Hopwood, *Middle Temple Records*, ii (1904), 917).

[2] Mary had previously been forcibly married at the age of 13 to William Hawke of Hastingleigh, near Canterbury, a cousin, but the marriage was dissolved in the Bishop's Court (cf. the Case for Opinion, KAO U350 and the further detail in Henning, xii, fn. 9).

[3] The genealogical table prepared by Mr Philip Blake which is included at the end of this volume illustrates Dering's family relationships.

[4] pp. 138-9 below; cf. the life of the Earl of Nottingham by John, Lord Campbell (*Lives of the Lord Chancellors* iii (1845), 378-426) and a more dispassionate evaluation by D. E. C. Yale in his edition of *Lord Nottingham's Chancery Cases* (1957), especially xxiv. *A History of the Finch Family* was compiled by Bryan I. Anson (1933). Lord Chancellor Nottingham is remembered in Campbell's phrase as 'the father of equity', and in Dryden's description, 'with Moses' inspiration, Aaron's tongue' (*Absalom and Achitophel*).

shared by the brothers-in-law; intense devotion to the Crown, avoiding undue commitment to individual ministers or groups; and a deep sense of loyalty to the social and family background in Kent.

Immediately after his marriage, however, Edward Dering's connection with the rich Harvey family was more important for him than the Finch relationship.[1] He and his wife passed the years from 1648 to 1652 in his mother-in-law's house (Carlisle House, Lambeth Marsh) 'on free cost', moving for a time to Daniel Harvey's house near Croydon, then to a rented house near the family estates at Pluckley in Kent. They lived 'as private and unobserved as [they] could in respect of the times.'[2]

A further result of Dering's marriage was that he was introduced to some of the musical and literary circles of the time.[3] His wife had attended Mrs Salmon's school at Hackney where she had become the friend—'one of the best friends'—of Katharine Fowler, later Katharine Philips, who was known as 'the matchless Orinda'. Dering may not have become a member of Orinda's society, 'the Official Order of Friendship in the Kingdom of feminine sensibility', but he was given a pseudonym as 'the noble Sylvander', and when in 1651 William Cartwright's poems were published one of the prefatory poems was by Dering.[4] Then in 1655 when Henry Lawes, the musician, published his *Second Booke of Ayres* they were dedicated to his pupil Mary Dering and contained four poems[5] by her husband, which she had set to music.[6] When Dering and Orinda found themselves in Dublin at the same time in 1662, she to argue her Irish claims before him as Commissioner, it was he who wrote the epilogue to her play, *Pompey*.[7] The play was performed before the Governor's Court, and Dering's verse now appears in full in the printed *Calendar of State Papers Domestic*.[8] Recently, an important manuscript of Orinda's poems has come to light, which is

---

[1] As noted on p. 2 above Dering's mother had died when he was three; his step-mother, Unton lived until 1676, but was not always on good terms with him (in one of three vigorous letters to him preserved in KAO (U1107 C20-2) she demanded the family pictures and denied that she owed money on her pearls).

[2] p. 110 below. It was worth noting, however, that Dering took some part in local affairs. On 7 February 1655 he wrote from Coombe to James Brockman, that he was 'ingaged to attend our high Sheriffe' the following week at the Southwark Assizes (see p. 157 below).

[3] I am extremely grateful to Dr Mary Hobbs for drawing my attention to Dering's friendship with 'Orinda' and Henry Lawes and discussing the relevant sources with me.

[4] Cf. P. W. Souers, *The Matchless Orinda* (Harvard, 1931), especially 44, 59, 60-9.

[5] 'And is this all?', 'What, one poor kiss?', 'In vain, Chloris, you design', and 'When first I saw fair Doris' eyes.'

[6] W. M. Evans, *Henry Lawes, Musician and Friend of Poets* (Oxford, 1941), 150, 190, 202-3 (on p. 202, however, the second baronet is confused with his father).

[7] Concerning *Pompey* and Orinda's other verse, see Edmund Gosse's essay 'The Matchless Orinda' in his *Seventeenth Century Studies* (1882), 203-230. Cf. also Dame Veronica Wedgwood, *Seventeenth Century Literature* (1950), 78, 91, 122. Orinda later addressed a somewhat obscure poem 'To Sir Edward Dering (the Noble Silvander)' in reply to a poem of his entitled 'Dream and Navy' in which Dering had written of the 'Fleet he trafficked with, which sails in my sight, and Anchors in my Arms.' (Souers, *op. cit.*, 69-70).

[8] *CSPD*, 1663-5, 114.

entirely in Dering's hand and includes two unpublished poems and variant readings.[1]

Orinda died at the age of about 34 in 1664 but Dering's membership of salons seems to have continued; on a page in his small personal notebook he jotted down the classical pseudonyms of a group of twelve women in 1673 and a further group of 20 for 1674.[2] At the end of his life one of the pigeon-holes in his bureau at Surrenden was for 'poetica' as well as 'medica'.[3]

Dering, like other members of his family, believed in maintaining careful family records;[4] he began to make entries in 'Household Books' almost immediately after his marriage in 1648[5] and some of the early entries document his efforts to preserve a record of it in a more striking way. In the first year he commissioned a portrait of his wife.[6] A little more than a year later Peter Lely painted portraits of them both[7] and in what proved to be the last year of their marriage the portraits of each of them were again painted, Edward by Godfrey Kneller and Mary by Edward Hawker.[8]

During the twelve years of Dering's married life before the Restoration his circumstances seem to have been 'comfortable'.[9] His second Household Book[10] shows that while his father, in the whole of his life, had added just on £6000 worth of lands to the family estate,[11] the second

[1] Sotheby & Co., *Catalogue of the Celebrated Collection of Manuscripts formed by Sir Thomas Phillipps, 28–9 June, 1965*, 94. I am most grateful to Mr P. J. Croft for this reference.

[2] PD, f. 140 v.   [3] p. 151, below.

[4] Richard Dering had kept a memorandum book entitled 'A booke of divers necessary remembrances' from about 1570 to which his son Sir Anthony and his grandson Sir Edward, the first baronet, had made additions (Sotheby & Co., *Catalogue of the Celebrated Collection of Manuscripts formed by Sir Thomas Phillipps, 28–9 June, 1965*, 31). To the antiquarian compilations of the first baronet reference has already been made.

[5] Calendared below, pp. 155–6 (HB1). Some extracts from this book were published by E. F. Rimbaud in *Notes and Queries* (1850) pp. 161–2.

[6] From Cornelius Neve (*fl.* 1637–64), some of whose portraits survive at Petworth House and at Knole (cf. *DNB sub* Neve) Dering noted '23 Dec. 1648, paid Mr Le Neve in part for my wife's picture, £3' (HB1, f. 41). '28 April 1649, paid Mr Le Neve the remainder due for my wife's picture, £3 4s'. (*ibid.*, f. 42v.)

[7] '8 April 1650, paid Mr Lelly for my wife's picture, £5' (*ibid.*, f. 48v). '21 April 1651, paid Mr Lelie for my picture £5, paid him for my wife's picture, being larger £10 (*sic*) (*ibid.*, f. 62v). Le Neve's portrait (a miniature) of Edward is now in the possession of Mr Cholmeley Harrison of Erno Court, Co. Leix; Lely's portrait of Edward is at Parham, Pulborough and is reproduced here as the frontispiece by permission of the late Hon. Mrs Clive Pearson.

[8] '15 October 1683, paid Mr Knellar for my owne picture, £8.8.4.' (HB2, 27). '18 October 1683, paid Mr Hawker for my wife's picture, £15' (*ibid*). Hawker (*c.* 1640–*c.* 1723) succeeded to Lely's studio and was made a poor knight of Windsor. Kneller's portrait of Edward is in the possession of Mr Philip Blake by whose kindness it is reproduced as Plate II; a later copy, dated 1687, belongs to Lord Brabourne and is hung in the County Hall, Maidstone. Hawker's portrait of Mary is in the possession of Lord Brabourne, with whose permission it is reproduced here as Plate III.

[9] Henning, xii.   [10] HB2, calendared below, pp. 156–7.

[11] 'Lands bought by my father' HB2, pp. 59–63. On balance, however, the first baronet disposed of more than he acquired; in 1636–7 he sold over £7000 worth, and in 1639 he gave extensive lands to his half-brother Henry, and to Lady Unton's son, Edward ('Lands sold by my Father', HB2, 38–9).

baronet, after selling some lands in 1646 to pay his debts on coming of age,[1] between 1647 and 1656 spent over £6000 on lands in Ousden, Pluckley and other Kentish villages, the main property settled to himself, his wife and heirs consisting of some 266 acres.[2] In 1671 Dering noted £14,461 as the 'Totall of what I have paid to clear the estate and to enlarge it.'[3]

When Dering married, his annual expenses for some years amounted to about £450; then between 1652 and 1660 they rose erratically to about £1,300. Between 1665 and 1673 they varied up to a maximum of £2,400. In the last years of his life (1681-4) his annual expenses were between £2,200 and £3,400.[4] Annual receipts from his estate in the 1650s consisted mainly of rents between £500 and £900, with varying sums for timber and small sums from his farm produce, his whole income normally totalling £600 to £1,500.[5] To some extent he later turned from land to investment—by 1681 his rents were much less (between £137 and £365 in a year)—and interest on investments ran from £100 to £500, but in his last years his principal reliance was on office, notably on his employment as Commissioner of the Treasury, which brought in between £1,200 and £1,920 a year.[6] In April 1683, at the age of 58 and realising how insecure his tenure at the Treasury might prove, he worked out a scheme for cutting expenses on wages, wine, firewood and books—and also his wife's personal expenses—in order to save £900 p.a.[7] In general, his accounts from 1657 onwards suggest careful house-keeping within the limits imposed by the need to maintain a large family and live up to steadily rising standards.

With the Restoration of the King in 1660, Dering at the age of 34 entered public life. Five days before the demise of Parliament, an Act had been passed for settling the Militia, and amongst the Commissioners of the Militia named in it was Edward Dering.[8] Almost immediately after this, he was elected as one of the two Knights of the Shire for Kent,[9] and he participated actively in what he himself described as 'the happy worke of our restitution to our ancient lawes.'[10] Professor Henning notes that in the Convention Parliament, Dering was 'named for 22 committees. . . . He had a hand in framing the bills which abolished feudal

---

[1] 'Lands sold by my selfe' HB2, 41-2.

[2] 'Lands bought by my selfe' HB2, 64-5.   [3] HB2, 69.

[4] In a year of considerable expense, from Michaelmas 1680 to Michaelmas 1681, out of a total of over £3,300 spent, Dering disbursed £761 on running his household, £84 on his own personal expenses and £111 on his wife's, £708 on his children (one of whom went to sea), £300 on his daughter Katharine's portion and wedding clothes, £60 on building, £567 on debts, and £396 on other expenses.

[5] The Commons had been informed on 27 July 1644 that his father's estate was worth £800 per annum or thereabouts (*CJ*, iii, 572).

[6] The foregoing section is based on the accounts kept by Dering in HB1 and HB2.

[7] AB2, 154.

[8] C. H. Firth and R. S. Rait, *Acts and Ordinances of the Interregnum*, ii (1911), 1433.

[9] The *Return* has no entry, but see *PH*, iv, 4; see also DCP, p. 158, below.

[10] p. 37 below.

dues, fixed a revenue for the King, settled the militia, and began the settlement of the church.'[1] In addition he was a member of the committee of elections and privileges.[2]

The brief Parliamentary diary Dering compiled in 1660[3] (as has been seen) was not the first of the sequence of his surviving diaries. Previously Dering had kept entry books or 'household' books for accounts, births, deaths and marriages, purchase and sale of lands, itineraries, etc., and between 1656 and 1662 he had compiled a manuscript, part diary, part commonplace book.[4] But he was not yet an experienced diarist. His parliamentary diary for 1660 is in many ways an unpractised piece of work. After regular entries for the business of the Commons on 16 days, there is a gap for the next 12 days' sittings, and thereafter scattered entries, concluding on 15 August 1660. There is nothing to represent the further sittings to 13 September, or those after the adjournment between 6 November and 29 December (when the Convention Parliament was dissolved). Some gaps were due to Dering's absence from London (e.g. 7-16 July),[5] but others occur when he was in his place in the Commons (e.g. 17 July onwards).[6] He was clearly jotting down what interested him when he had an opportunity, and doing so in a paper volume without covers, title page or any other marks of a diary intended for permanent preservation or frequent consultation.[7]

An analysis of the contents of his Convention diary reveals certain characteristics of his later and more developed diaries. On the third sitting day Dering entered at length the 'rule of proceedings' in cases of double returns of members by a constituency, and after only three weeks as a member of the House he attempted to sum up in 13 clauses the general orders followed in debates. How Parliament worked; what were its established rules and precedents; matters such as these became an abiding interest for him, and many of his subsequent interventions in Parliamentary debates concerned apparently minor points of procedure. Next, unlike most Parliamentary diarists, Dering was more interested in business done and in the general tenor of debate than in the individual speeches, although he selected key speeches for brief summary. And again he is somewhat unusual in including notes on committee work in 1660. He did not report any speech of his own in the Convention Parliament, but at two points he provided details concerning the 'bill for ministers' in the passage of which he clearly took some part as a member of the committee.

Although Dering thus had participated with some assiduity in the

[1] Henning, xiii.
[2] p. 35 below.
[3] pp. 155-71 below.
[4] p. 158 below.
[5] HB1, 273.
[6] *ibid.*
[7] Apart from what is noted in the Commons Journal, some of the proceedings of the Convention Parliament are recorded in the *Parliamentary or Constitutional History of England from the earliest times to the dissolution of the Convention Parliament* (1763) xxii, 210-495, and xxiii, 1-101.

work of the Convention Parliament between 25 April and 29 December 1660, he did not become a member of the new Parliament (which met on 8 May 1661) nor was he given any public office. In his autobiography Dering merely remarked that he 'thought of nothing more than setling my selfe quietly at home, to governe my small fortune and many children as well as I could.'[1] He lived at Surrenden House[2] and began to enjoy the state that fitted a well-connected country gentleman. Yet there had been some talk of Dering continuing as a Member of Parliament. One correspondent on 17 December wrote to him to say that though several people were proposed for the next election, he thought some would not stand in competition with Dering.[3] In fact, however, although Dering's fellow Knight of the Shire for Kent, Sir John Tufton, was again elected, Dering was replaced (on 18 March) by Sir Thomas Peyton, bart.[4] Professor Henning surmises that Dering may have 'been given notice of other employment in store for him.'[5]

The employment when it came was in Ireland. Dering notes in his Household Book for 21 May 1662, 'I began my journey from my owne home towards Ireland',[6] though he did not leave London until 5 July, boarding ship on 26 July with the Duke of Ormonde[7] and the Duchess, and reaching Dublin on 28 July.[8]

On 18 July 1662 the King had instructed the 'Lord Deputy', i.e. the Duke of Ormonde, to appoint Dering and six others (three of them judges) Commissioners to execute the Act of Settlement.[9] The purpose of the Act was to give the force of law both to the Declaration of 30 November 1660 concerning the allocation of lands in Ireland and to the Instructions annexed to the Declaration in the Statute Book.[10] Between 1660 and 1662 an original group of 36 Commissioners had achieved practically nothing; the work of the new group of 7 was correspondingly exacting. It soon became clear how complicated their enquiries would prove. On 17 October 1662 the Irish Council proclaimed that the closing date for claims was altered from 29 September

---

[1] p. 111 below.

[2] Surrenden had been the Dering family seat since the 15th century (see p. 1).

[3] Alexander Burnet of Hythe to Dering, NRA *Report 4363*, 108.

[4] *Return*, p. 524. For Dering's connection with Tufton and Peyton, see the pedigree at the end of this volume.

[5] Henning, xiii.   [6] HB2, 275.

[7] James Butler, 12th Earl of Ormonde and Ossory, 1st Duke of Ormonde, who had been appointed Lord Lieutenant of Ireland on 21 February 1662.

[8] HB2, 275.

[9] *CSPI*, 1660-2, 577. Dering's fellow Commissioners were Henry Coventry, Sir Richard Rainsford, Sir Thomas Beverley, Sir Edward Smith, Colonel Edward Cooke and Winston Churchill. Except for tendering an oath, three were to form a quorum, either Coventry, Dering, Cooke and Churchill, or Rainsford, Beverley and Smith. Coventry was replaced in 1663 by Sir Allen Broderick; cf. *CSPI*, 1663-5, 65, 87 and the directions for a new quorum, 87.

[10] 14 & 15 Car. II, c. 2, *Statutes at Large passed in the Parliaments held in Ireland*, ii (Dublin, 1786), 239-348.

1662 to 1 April 1663;[1] and in fact Commissioners continued to work for an additional six years. The law fixing the period of the original court (14 & 15 Car. II, c. 2 (Ireland)) was interpreted as bringing the hearings to an end on 21 August 1663. A second court of claims was appointed under section 159 of the Act of Explanation, 1665 (17 & 18 Car. II, c. 2 (Ireland)), which named Sir Edward Smith, Sir Edward Dering, Sir William (*sic*) Churchill and Edward Cook as Commissioners for the execution of the Act of Explanation and of such parts of the Act of Settlement 1662, as were in force. This second court sat until January 1669.[2] They were described by Clarendon as 'gentlemen of very good extractions, excellent understandings, and above all suspicion for their integrity, and generally reputed to be superior to any base temptation',[3] but their work inevitably aroused violent passions, as Clarendon himself acknowledged. The Commissioners 'rendered themselves as generally odious to the Irish', and the Irish Commons were greatly offended by the Commission's tenderness for the claims of Papists.[4] The Commissioners proceeded undeterred, for there was no appeal against their judgments and the King fairly consistently supported them.[5] They found it difficult to come to unanimous decisions, the common saying being that three (Rainsford, Beverley and Churchill) were 'for the King', i.e. for the so-called innocent Catholics, three (Smith, Dering and Cooke) for the English (Protestant) interest, and one (Broderick) for himself.[6] The Earl of Orrery told Viscount Conway in 1666 that Dering and the other Commissioners 'carry themselves very justly and obligingly to the English.'[7] Ormonde strongly approved of Dering; he told Lord Arlington[8] in 1667 that he considered Dering 'an able and loyal servant . . . knowing and active in business.'[9] With this Arlington apparently

---

[1] *CSPI*, 1660-2, 603-4.

[2] The then active Commissioners, Churchill, Dering, Broderick and Cooke, returned to England on 21 January 1669 (*CSPD*, 1668-9, 163). I am most grateful to Dr J. G. Simms for his guidance over the work of the Courts, which is to be dealt with in his introduction to the forthcoming edition of the records of the Second Court of Claims (see p. 159 below).

[3] Clarendon, *Life and Continuation of his History of the Great Rebellion* (1827), ii, 51.

[4] *ibid.*, 59, 60.

[5] 'The King was very tender of the reputation of his commissioners', *ibid.*, 62.

[6] Robert Lye to Joseph Williamson, *CSPI*, 1663-5, 231. How far this was true may be doubted. Dr Simms points out in his forthcoming introduction to the work of the Court of Claims that Broderick was 'active in promoting the interests of Catholic claimants' and Dering himself told his son-in-law in May 1673 that the Duke of York's 'good offices' towards him (Dering) may have been due to his own 'personal kindness to them of that persuasion' (*DS Corr*, p. 3). Dering together with Smith and Cooke admittedly opposed the King in the Marquess of Antrim's case in 1663, wishing to proceed 'by the evidence'—Dering commented 'Better never judge than precipitately judge' (*CSPD*, 1663-5, 218).

[7] 17 July 1666, *CSPI*, 1666-9, 158.

[8] Henry Bennet, 1st Earl of Arlington, Secretary of State, 1662-74.

[9] 26 March 1667, *CSPI*, 1666-9, 331; on 15 June Ormonde told Arlington that Dering was 'of excellent parts and proportionable industry and integrity . . . (with) more than ordinary knowledge of the affairs of this Kingdom' (*ibid.*, 377).

agreed, and Dering was ordered to be sworn of the Irish Privy Council in April 1667.[1]

Whilst Dering was helping to settle Irish claims he worked closely with Arlington, the two men exchanging letters of mutual deference.[2] Each had something to gain. Dering for instance was receiving the profits of some unallocated Irish lands,[3] and sought favour for his son-in-law, Sir Robert Southwell (who became Clerk to the Privy Council in Ireland) together with the reversion of the auditorship of the Irish Exchequer for himself.[4] Arlington was anxious that the claims in Ireland of his own friends and dependents should receive ready acceptance by Dering and his fellow-commissioners; Arlington began one letter to Dering 'Sir, when you see my name at the botome of a letter to you, you may conclude I have something to ask of you.'[5] Dering and the other Commissioners must have received many requests for special favours,[6] and Dering was probably not alone in seeking a *quid pro quo*. Sir Thomas Peyton in 1666 asked for consideration for a cousin of his, Captain Stephen Hales,[7] and as a letter of Arlington's shows, Peyton was at the same time trying to obtain a seat for Dering in the Commons—this time the Cinque Port of Winchelsea.[8] Mutual bargaining, however, was not always a consideration, and one correspondent told Dering 'how generously' he had been treated by him although 'I never performed anything to you or your relations that merited your care.'[9]

The varied papers of Dering relating to his service as Commissioner are calendared below;[10] they include some letters, hitherto unprinted, in the Stowe Manuscripts and certain of Dering's own minutes of proceedings in the Court of Claims.[11] The texts of the latter, by kind permission of the Irish Manuscripts Commission, are to be published as an appendix to the forthcoming edition by Dr Simms of the Court of Claims record now in the Public Library of Armagh, and are not therefore printed here *in extenso*. The somewhat fragmentary documents show that Dering as Commissioner took full notes as business proceeded,

[1] The King to Ormonde, 20 April 1667, *CSPI*, 1666-9, 347.

[2] e.g. Arlington to Dering, 10 March 1668, BL Stowe 745, f. 7 and Dering to Arlington, 29 November 1666, BL Stowe 744, f. 139 (p. 163 below). From Clarendon's fall in 1667 until about 1675 Arlington was in close relationship with Dering's brother-in-law Finch.

[3] BL Stowe 744, f. 67.

[4] See pp. 164-5 below; for the grant of the reversion see p. 164, fn. 2, below, and *CSPI*, 1666-9, 483. The reversion passed to Dering's son, Charles, who served as Auditor and was a success at it.

[5] Arlington to Dering, 3 November 166(6), BL Stowe MS. 744, f. 136.

[6] The Earl of Anglesey's letter of 18 April 1668 is a good example of flattery and urgency, mixed with an element of bribery in a postscript ('I hope I shall secure your timber bill out of the remains of seamen's wages . . .') BL Stowe 745, f. 16.

[7] Peyton to Dering, 16 February 1666, BL Stowe 744, f. 101.

[8] Arlington to Dering, 20 March 1666, *ibid.*, f. 105. The attempt failed, Arlington telling Dering that the Duke of York (Warden of the Cinque Ports) 'was engaged before I spake to him of it' (*ibid.*).

[9] (?) Sir Francis Fowkes to Dering, 15 November 1667 (*ibid.*, f. 157).

[10] pp. 159-66.   [11] pp. 159, 166.

often on the standard loose folded sheets on which he noted down much contemporary business (bound registers he usually reserved for formal records written at leisure). His notes are purely factual; no current or subsequent annotation indicates comment or judgment, except that here as elsewhere Dering sometimes underscores facts or arguments.

When Dering's work in Ireland came to an end in January 1669 he had no immediate prospects of further office, although as he remained sworn of the Irish Privy Council his advice was likely to be sought on Irish matters. Soon after his return to England, however, he heard that he was to be appointed as one of three Commissioners of the Privy Seal.[1] The Lord Privy Seal, John Robartes, 1st Lord Robartes (later 1st Earl of Radnor) succeeded Ormonde as Lord Lieutenant of Ireland in 1669,[2] and although Robartes remained technically Lord Privy Seal the Commissioners executed the office. Dering commented that he had not 'made the least application' for the post as commissioner,[3] but his name may well have been advanced by Ormonde in the course of whatever discussions accompanied Robartes's appointment. Dering showed restrained enthusiasm; the office brought him £650 a year, but living in London was expensive. He decided however, that 'the honour of so great a trust, my desire to serve the King and to give some countenance to my children who now began to grow up' made him very willing to accept the employment.[4]

The work of the three commissioners of the Privy Seal, Sir Thomas Strickland, Robert Millward, and Dering, concerned the execution rather than the initiation of policy. They were responsible for issuing warrants for payment, and one of their docquet books, throughout in Dering's hand, enumerates 388 warrants issued by them between 22 September 1669 and 23 December 1670.[5] Most are purely financial: for the Treasurer to pay the royal jeweller £6,000 for two diamonds, or to pay £150,000 for the use of the Navy; some are administrative, for the Archbishop of Canterbury to grant letters of administration to the executors of the late Queen Mother, for a pardon to John Sharpe for killing George Whitfield, or for a grant to the Earl of Bedford of the Covent Garden market.[6]

Work such as this at the Privy Seal can hardly have taxed Dering's administrative ability, but it gave him a close view of some aspects of the financial administration of the country, and he worked at it with his customary assiduity. In July 1671 he told Southwell that he had not

[1] The Royal Warrant was dated 10 September 1669 (*CSPD*, 1668-9, 487) and the order to deliver the Privy Seal to the Commissioners was made on 30 October (*ibid.*, 514).

[2] In March 1669 the King announced he intended appointing Robartes, but Lord Ossory was to be obeyed as Lord Deputy until Robartes arrived (*CSPI*, 1666-9, 704); Robartes was leaving for Ireland on 29 August (*ibid.*, p. 784).

[3] p. 111 below.   [4] *ibid.*   [5] See p. 167 below.

[6] *Manuscripts of J. Eliot Hodgkin* (1897), HMC, 15th Report App. ii, 8-16, *passim.* Other docquet books, but not in Dering's hand, are preserved in the Public Record Office.

had a holiday for six years, and had only been able to leave for Surrenden because Judge Millward, his fellow Commissioner, had arrived in
London.[1] From time to time, moreover, Dering was present at Treasury
meetings,[2] and he became a member of the Committee of Irish Lords
in May 1670,[3] discussing for instance on 11 May the arrangements for
the Irish Civil List.[4] Dering was thus concerned, in however limited a
way, with the work of Charles's ministry. To his duties as Commissioner
and Irish Privy Councillor in 1670 were added those of member for
East Retford borough,[5] an election which he attributed to the favour of
the Duke of Newcastle[6] and Dering continued to sit for East Retford
during the succeeding eight sessions of the Pensionary Parliament.[7]

A week after his election to Parliament in 1670, Dering began to make
diary entries for each day's proceedings. He seems to have started this
quite casually, using a book into which he had already entered 24 years
earlier (on 28 August 1648) an abstract of Sir Thomas Browne's
'Pseudodoxia epidemica' of 1646 (ff. 5-14v), followed by a summary in
French of 'L'Examen des Esprits' (ff. 15, 15v),[8] and, in Latin, a summary
of the controversy between the Pope and the Venetian republic in the
years 1605-7 (ff. 17-19). At the end of the volume he arranged a list of
famous modern battles in England, France and Italy down to 1515 in
calendar form under months. This manuscript was bought by the
British Museum at a sale at Puttick's on 12 June 1858 (lot 630) and is
now BL Add 22,467. The Parliamentary entries on ff. 20-129 were
edited and published *in extenso* by Professor Basil Henning as *The
Parliamentary Diary of Sir Edward Dering 1670-1673* (Yale University
Press, 1940). The text provides important additional information to that
contained respectively in the Commons Journals and in Anchitell
Grey's Diary. The first part of Dering's diary concludes on 20 March
1671, although the House continued to sit, and almost undoubtedly
Dering continued to attend. In the manuscript a blank leaf follows
(ff. 101, 101v) before Dering pursues his Parliamentary diary with an
entry for 4 February 1673, then continuing until 3 November 1673.
Apart from noting his own speeches he does not comment on his position
as a Member, but during the period he seems to have established
himself as a judicious and hardworking member of the Court group.[9]

Meanwhile, in 1673 Dering's service as Commissioner had been
abruptly ended by the handing of the Privy Seal on 22 April to the Earl
of Anglesey. A week before, on 16 April, the Treasurer, Arlington, had

[1] *DS Corr*, 2, Dering to Southwell, 1 July 1671.
[2] e.g. on 11 March 1670 (*CTB*, 1669-72, i, 385).
[3] He was present at a meeting on 2 May 1670 (*CSPI*, 1669-70, 121).   [4] *ibid.*, 429.
[5] He was returned on 8 November 1670 (*Return*, 526).
[6] p. 112 below.
[7] He was subsequently returned for the Cinque Port of Hythe on 14 February 1679
(*Return*, 539), 8 August 1679 (*ibid.*, 545), and 11 March 1681 (*ibid.*, 551).
[8] See pp. 167-8 below.   [9] Henning, xiv-xv.

informed Dering that the King took the commission away 'not out of any displeasure to us, or dissatisfaction to the administration of it as now it is, but that as he had put the treasurie not longtimes so now he thought best for his affaires to put the privy seale also into a single hand.'[1] The King then seemed unable to face Dering, and on Dering's attending him at court 'said it was some mistake.' Two days later the King received him and expressed his 'favourable intentions' towards the three commissioners, but as Dering noted in his diary 'mentioning nothing in particular for us.'[2] Looking back on his loss of office seven years later, Dering still felt resentful that his 'two brethren' were immediately given pensions of £400 a year, more than half the income from the office itself, whilst 'no such thing was done for me, nor anything else during my Lord Clifford's time.'[3] Clifford (who had been Lord High Treasurer since November 1672), Dering scathingly described as the 'factotum' and self-righteously commended his own behaviour— 'who never knew what it was either to pray or pay for court favours (the two most prevailing topicks in our time)',[4] though his letters reveal some vigorous machinations to obtain a suitable post for himself. Through his son-in-law Robert Southwell he persuaded Heneage Finch to influence Speaker Seymour,[5] who as a result sought a commissionership of the plantations for him, which Dering preferred to a commissionership of the Navy or a mere pension.[6] Sir John Banks moved the Chancellor for a place for him in the Customs House, but nothing came of it[7] and Dering gave up 'all farther sollicitation', commenting to Southwell that the King was unwilling, and concluding that 'if the favour of the Chancellor, Treasurer, Duke of Ormonde, Earl of Arlington and Attorney General cannot obtain for him [Dering] what Father Patrick did for Sir Thomas Strickland, and Sir Robert Carr for his brother Milward, it is high time surely for him to write a Non Ultra to his pretences at Court, and to sit down in patience and enjoy his innocence and ill fortune as well as he can.'[8] Dering was doubly distressed; he became conscious of the enmity of the then all-powerful Clifford; and he realised that without public employment he needed to reconsider his whole way of life. Eventually, on 29 September 1673 he entered a long 'Reflexion necessaire sur la condicion de mon estat' in his personal diary.[9] He foresaw 'a considerable alteracion in my affaires,

---

[1] PD, f. 3v.

[2] *ibid.* Dering's copy of Arlington's mandamus to Strickland and himself to deliver in the Privy Seal to the King, dated 19 April 1673, is BM Stowe 745, f. 71.

[3] p. 112 below. The pension was eventually secured in October 1673, just after Clifford's resignation (see p. 14, fn. 2 below).

[4] p. 112 below.   [5] *DS Corr*, 3, Dering to Southwell, 22 June 1673.

[6] *ibid.*, 4, Dering to Southwell, 21 July 1673.

[7] *ibid.*, 4, Dering to Southwell, 4-5 August 1673. Dering hoped Finch would also speak to Danby and the King and suggested that 'Sir Robert Croke's clerkship of the pipe is the only good office . . . not already disposed in reversion' (*ibid.*).

[8] as summarised in *DS Corr*, 5.   [9] PD, ff. 36v.-45v.

and the plenty I have hitherto lived in.' There was no way in which he could improve his estates, 'there being no opportunitie either of draining or flouding or building or digging of mines as tin lead or coale;' but in his own systematic analytical way he proceeded to list five personal and as many as 24 practical means of improving his financial situation. He must practise 'generalle frugalitie'; he must 'keep more at home'—the expenses of his travels were 'intolerable'; and on his estate he must try to establish a lime kiln, a windmill, a malthouse and a tile kiln. He would like to grow cherries and make cherry-brandy; or introduce the making of serges, druggets or fustians. He sadly commented, however, that these last projects were 'of vast expense and doubtful success'. The twenty-fourth aim was 'the most reasonable, to obtain some compensacion from his majestie for the loss of my employment.'

The appointment of Thomas Osborne, Viscount Osborne, on 19 June 1673 as Lord Treasurer, however, led to a change in Dering's fortunes. Dering seems to have become a close associate of the new Treasurer (who was created Viscount Latimer on 15 August 1673 and Earl of Danby on 27 June 1674), and noted in his diary on 21 October 1673 that 'I went to wait upon my Lord Latimer Lord Treasurer of England, to whom I had been very much beholden,'[1] and subsequently he received the pension which had been refused him.[2] Dering's general views on policy coincided with the Treasurer's; the two men were courtiers and churchmen, hostile to dissenters and papists, but with no ultra-protestant fervour against Rome. The Declaration of Indulgence they had each disliked; and Clifford's pro-papist policy they had opposed. The Treasurer, on coming to power, quickly formed a circle of associates; Viscount Ranelagh, the Irish Vice-Treasurer, Viscount Conway, an Irish Commissioner of Customs, and Edward Seymour, Speaker of the Commons, together, as Professor Browning has pointed out, with 'Lady Conway's numerous relatives of the Finch family.'[3] Heneage Finch on 9 November 1673 became Lord Keeper, and from then on the Treasurer, the Keeper and Speaker Seymour 'regularly worked in unison.'[4] Of this inner circle Dering became a dependent, and it is possible to trace in his personal diary a sequence of laconic but significant entries which indicate that, from being a political outcast in April 1673, he had, by the autumn of that year gained the confidence of the dominant trio.[5] On 21st October he waited on the Treasurer as has been noted; in November he dined successively with the Treasurer (on the 14th), the Keeper (on the 15th), the Duke of Ormonde (on the 16th) and with the Keeper again (on the 17th). There

[1] PD, f. 50v.　　　　　　　　　　　　　　　　[2] e.g. *CTB*, 1672-5, 256, 302, etc.
[3] A. Browning, *Thomas Danby, Earl of Danby and Duke of Leeds*, i (1951), 118.
[4] *ibid.*, 119.
[5] See the relevant entries in PD, under the dates mentioned.

were similar sequences of dinners in January and March 1674. In July Ogle, Ailesbury and Finch visited him; on 20th January 1675 he recorded that he went 'with my Lord Keeper to attend my Lord Treasurer, who had with him only my Lord Ogle, where he had some discussion.' Two days later he noted 'This day again my Lord Keeper and I dined just with my Lord Treasurer and Lord Ogle and Mr Cheyney; and dined at Wallingford House[1] in private, nobody being suffered to come into us where we continued till past fower.' The climax came on 25th February 1675 when 'my Lord Keeper carried me with him to my Lord Treasurer, with whom we sate nobody else coming in, from fower o clock till eight, discussing of many things but chiefly in relacion to the sitting of parliament intended to be 13 Aprill next.' Dering clearly did not come to these inner conclaves as a political leader; he was a useful speaker in the Commons, but he contributed little to the formation of opinion; he was a respected member of the Kentish gentry but unknown to the general public. What he most obviously provided was administrative experience and considerable knowledge of Parliamentary procedure, although it may be that he also undertook investigations and drafted memoranda which went unrecorded in the diaries.

The great majority of the entries in Dering's diary for 1673-75 do not in fact suggest the life of a political leader at all. Long sections are devoted to the negotiations for marriages of his family; frequent entries record his attendance at the Justices' meetings at Ashford and at the Assizes in Maidstone; and his abiding interest in religion is reflected in discussions with Peter du Moulin[2] and with Dr Nicholas Gibbon.[3] He told Gibbon —who was evolving a theological system of his own—'that it would startle all men to put to a new catechisme after 1600 yeares', thus admitting we had 'been all this while mistaken in the grounds on which we did believe it.'[4] Dering declared that the theologian of 1675 must not only say a new doctrine was true, but that it was 'absolutely necessarie', for every novelty took off from the reverence owed to antiquity, i.e. to church tradition.[5] Gibbon's doctrine of the Holy Ghost he dismissed as being 'not easily reconcileable to the Athanasian creed'[6]— Gibbon riposted that the creed itself 'was a noveltie'.[7] Dering ultimately rested on church authority as it existed: 'the government, that is the order of Bishops, being divine and unalterable', though he admitted

---

[1] Wallingford House, once the home of George, Duke of Buckingham, was the official home of the Treasurer in Westminster. It occupied the site of the present Admiralty building in Whitehall (*Survey of London*, xiii (1930), 112).

[2] Calendared on p. 54 below.

[3] Also calendared on p. 54 below. Nicholas Gibbon, the younger, D.D. (1605-97) was Rector of Corfe Castle, 1660-97 and in 1653 had published *A Summe or Body of Divinity Real* which Richard Baxter described as a 'contrivance of a very strong headpiece, secretly and cunningly fitted to usher in a Socinian Popery' (*DNB*).

[4] PD, f. 91v.   [5] *ibid.*

[6] *ibid.*, f. 93.   [7] *ibid.*

that rites, ceremonies and vestures were variable.[1] Dering recorded Gibbon's version of a dispute in Charles II's presence about bishops' lands.[2] Bishop Duppa,[3] who took part in the discussion, eventually conceded that these were not held 'by divine institucion', at which 'the King seemed extremely pensive and melancholy and leand back against the wall a great while not saying a word.'[4]

From this lengthy theological entry in his personal diary Dering abruptly turned to the repayment of a debt to himself, and a visit with Finch to 'a play at court called Callisthe'.[5] Dering although out of office was clearly enjoying a varied life as courtier, politician, county gentleman and scholar, and it was during this period too that he appears to have been associated with the salons of ladies noted in his personal diary for 1673 and 1674.[6] It remained for him to obtain some place in the King's service that would reflect the favour in which he clearly stood with the King's ministers.

The first stage towards this came with Dering's vigorous participation in the work of the Commons during the spring session of 1675, and it is to this session that his third surviving Parliamentary diary relates. The diary, printed below *in extenso*,[7] shows him recording not only the events of the days' sittings, but also, once more, various private conferences with ministers. The Parliamentary diary of 1675 seems never to have been written into any bound volume; as it survives today it consists of 19 sheets, each folded once to form 4 pages of uniform quarto size. In addition to dating his entries Dering has numbered each folded sheet at the head.[8] Preserved together with these diary sheets were 18 further folded sheets, a number of them uniform in appearance and relating to the same session, others[9] on paper of different size, and concerning varying dates up to and including 1680. One folded sheet[10] is a brief Parliamentary diary for March 1677.[11]

Slight variations in ink and handwriting suggest that the Parliamentary diary sheets of 1675 were written up almost immediately, perhaps on the same day as the sitting, although on some occasions a group of two or three days was described at the same time.[12] Dering's aim later in life was certainly to make daily notes of the sittings[13] and in the Par-

[1] PD, f. 94.   [2] *ibid.*, ff. 95, 95v.

[3] Brian Duppa (1558-1662) Bishop of Winchester, 1660-2 and Lord High Almoner.

[4] *ibid.*, f. 95v.   [5] *ibid.*, f. 96.

[6] *ibid.*, f. 140v.   [7] pp. 57-103.

[8] With the exception that the first sheet is missing and the second is unnumbered. It should be added that Dering mis-numbered sheet '19' as another '18' and then '20' as '19'.

[9] e.g. Pl D, ff. 57-8, a speech concerning the Popish Plot, and *ibid.*, ff. 67-8, a draft bill to protect dissenters.

[10] *ibid.*, ff. 72-3.   [11] printed below, pp. 180-2.

[12] e.g. to take an extreme case, the entries for 18-21 May 1675 were written continuously as a single section, pp. 87-8 below.

[13] In October 1680 he came to the Commons from his office at the Treasury so late 'and tired out commonly when I came hence, I tooke no notes at all though there were many things very remarquable.' (p. 120 below).

liamentary diary of 1670-73 the appearance of very many of the daily entries suggests that the notes were turned into a diary narrative before he went to bed.[1] The day's entries in each of the Parliamentary diaries of 1670-73 and of 1675 were written continuously with occasional (but extremely few) amendments and were probably based on brief notes, jotted down at the time, of divisions, motions, etc., and on drafts he may have prepared for his own speeches. The way in which Dering presents a broad picture or summary of a day's business rather than an itemised series of speeches or points suggests that his basic notes were few and his principal source his memory. The 1675 sheets are written so neatly that it is unlikely that he intended re-entering them in a bound volume, as he had entered the 1670-73 diary.

By comparison with that diary and, still more, with Anchitell Grey's detailed and thorough diary for 1667 to 1685, Dering's Spring 1675 diary is relatively brief and unspecific. It has value, however, in at least three ways. Firstly, as has been indicated, it includes entries concerning ministerial discussions which throw light on the political groupings of the day. Secondly, it provides notes on sittings for certain days omitted by Grey, notably for 13 to 17 April 1675. Thirdly, it rather naturally provides full synopses of Dering's own speeches—24 in all—twelve of which are abbreviated by Grey and the remaining twelve wholly omitted, while Dering's supplementary sheets enable a very full reconstruction of three of the speeches,[2] vividly indicating the style of Restoration oratory in the Commons. In addition, the occasional comments on procedure[3] are of value in understanding how in fact a House functioned which, unlike the Lords, had no systematic sequence of Standing Orders. Dering had in 1660 begun his effort to grasp and rationalise the customary rules of Parliamentary behaviour[4] and by 1675 he was an acute and learned observer of procedure.

During the session Dering was nominated to 28 committees, including those concerned with relations between the two Houses. Dering at the start of the session had contributed the idea that two special bills concerning popery might be useful in keeping the House busy,[5] distracting it from business unwelcome to the ministry, and he seems to have belonged to an inner group which from time to time included Sir Charles Wheeler, Sir Richard Wiseman, Sir Philip Musgrave, Sir Joseph Tredinham, Mr Peregrine Bertie, Sir John Bramston, Sir Humphrey Winch, Mr Cholmondeley, Mr Cheney and Lord Alington.[6] He was thus a 'link man' between small meetings of a ministerial type and the meetings of leading Commons members.

The original plan to divert attention from Danby to popery was one

---

[1] See also p. 16, fn. 13.
[2] pp. 168, 175-9 below.
[3] e.g. pp. 71, 86-7, 89, 90, 100-1 below.
[4] pp. 42-3 below.   [5] pp. 61-2 below.   [6] pp. 62, 63 below.

of the features of the session, but, as it turned out, a minor one, since the attempted impeachment of Danby foundered in a mass of technical detail. Three days after the opening—on 16 April 1675—Tredinham and Dering raised the question of popery, moving for a committee to inspect the penal laws against popery, though Dering characteristically urged that the House should prevent the growth of papists in future 'rather than to punish them that are allready in it.'[1] In fact a committee of the whole house was moved and matters of religion were 'spoken to and fro', the next day an anti-popery bill being decided on. The following week (on 21 April) Dering spoke at considerable length in order to deter the Commons from agreeing to a register of papists; he was 're-solved not to pull downe my house till I had another to put my head in'[2] —if men formally registered as papists the government would have to make up its mind whether the penal laws were to be enforced, repealed or revised. When the Test Bill came from the Lords Dering welcomed it and discounted criticism by Colonel Titus.

In two other respects, concerning the demand for recall of British subjects serving abroad in foreign countries and during the impeach-ment proceedings against Danby, Dering gave the ministry still stronger support. The diary includes one of his longest texts of his own speeches—that on the 2nd article of the impeachment on 30 April—in which he sought, with some success, to discredit three witnesses against Danby before they were heard.[3] With the diary is the separate text of his speech of 10 May on the recall of British subjects. This is a vigorous defence of the King. The French, Dering asserted, were now on the defensive and there were more British fighting for the Dutch than for the French. But the main issue concerned the King's honour; if that were lessened the House might 'raise a Spirit' it could not lay when it would. The standing of this country abroad would be damaged if the King's message concerning recall was voted unsatisfactory.[4]

An effective (though accidental) diversion from the attacks on the King and ministry began on 5 May with the first discussion of the Shirley *versus* Fagg case.[5] Dering took an active part in this; it appealed to his feeling for precedent and procedure. He thought of himself as belonging to the 'moderate party'; four of his speeches survive on this subject, and in that of 28 May he reminded the House that the Lords' appeal jurisdiction had stood for 55 years, that 'the mischiefs we had suffered all this while had not been very grievous to the publique.' The Commons had asserted their right; the Lords would now 'proceed with more caution than with lesse.'[6] Dering's was the key ministerial speech,

---

[1] p. 62 below.   [2] p. 67 below.
[3] pp. 75-6 below.   [4] pp. 175-8 below.
[5] in which the Commons challenged the right of the Lords to hear appeals from Chancery, unsuccessfully as it turned out (cf. the relevant MSS calendared in App., pt. ii of HMC 9th Report, *passim*).
[6] pp. 92-4 below.

and he was seconded by Henry Coventry, the Secretary of State, by Sir William Coventry and by others. He failed, however, to achieve a delay in the matter, and subsequently took up an attitude more hostile to the Lords. As a member of a conference with the Lords on 3 June, he observed that Anglesey, Lord Privy Seal, 'delivered their Lordships sense in very high words;' in the Lords' arguments 'there was more of words and noise than reason and argument.'[1] The next day he became involved in a conflict with the Speaker, by telling the House that they could not send for the lawyers concerned in the case while the Courts of Justice were sitting. The Speaker 'tooke me downe and said it was much other wise.' Dering accepted the rebuke—'I sate down with it'—but observed in his diary that no instance was known which supported the Speaker's argument.[2]

Dering had actively supported Danby and his colleagues in this session of Parliament. He consequently looked for some reward over and above the pension he had extracted with difficulty from the Crown in 1673. He was not altogether certain that Danby would continue in favour, but he told Southwell on 28 June 1675 that on Danby's survival his own prospects would be determined one way or the other.[3] In September he imagined he could not obtain 'an Irish sinecure worth £1,000'—he was not prepared to hold an active post in Ireland, as he was 'too old to transplant.'[4] He told Southwell, however, that he was ready to serve those in London who were farming the Irish custom for a much lower salary and this he asked Southwell to discuss with Sir James Shaen and Sir William Petty.[5] Nothing came of it immediately but from 1680 onwards he moved into the centre of the negotiations by the Crown with Shaen and others for the renewal of the farm.[6]

The reward for support ultimately bestowed by the ministry on Dering in 1675 was that of Commissionership of Customs. The Customs were a principal source of royal revenue. From 1604 until 1671 (except under the Long Parliament) they had been farmed; from 1671 they were directly administered by commissioners, six being named on 26 September 1671, and granted salaries of £2,000 a year.[7] On 22 February 1673 an additional commissioner was appointed and the further Customs Commission of 22 December 1675 likewise was for 7 commissioners, each commissioner having a salary of £1,200 p.a.[8] Dering's patent of appointment was dated 8 January 1676.[9] He was retained as

---

[1] pp. 99-100 below.   [2] pp. 100-2 below.   [3] *DS Corr*, 6.
[4] *ibid.*, 8.
[5] *ibid*. For Shaen see p. 25, fn. 7 *et seq.*
[6] p. 118 below.

[7] *CSPD*, 1671, 505; *CTB*, 1669-72, 935. Seven were subsequently appointed in 1673 and Professor Browning writes of 'the seven much-envied Commissioners of Customs, with salaries of £2,000 each [of whom] five were members of Parliament.' (Browning, *op. cit.*, i, 171).

[8] *CTB*, 1672-5, 71, 869.   [9] p. 114 below.

commissioner by subsequent appointments, the warrants for which were dated respectively 31 October 1677 and 31 January 1679,[1] and on 25 March 1679 Southwell commented that Dering 'adheres to the Customs' in official changes then occurring.[2] In fact, however, the next day a warrant was issued to appoint Dering and four others Commissioners of the Treasury in place of Danby,[3] and a week later the King revoked Dering's appointment at the Customs.[4]

Dering's service as a Commissioner of Customs has not left substantial trace among his papers apart from the minutes for 9 November 1677.[5] The supervision of the collection of customs must have been work for which he was fully competent; efficient and economical administration was the aim of his master, Danby, and the fact that in April 1679 Finch had sought to have Dering made Chancellor of the Exchequer[6] suggests that he proved successful at the Customs, as does more positively his appointment (on Danby's fall) as one of the Commissioners of the Treasury—in some sense to continue Danby's work there. When Dering went to the Treasury his first 'considerable' achievement included the reduction of the number of Commissioners of the Customs from seven (at which number it then stood) to five, and by this he commented in his diary the King saved £6,000 p.a.[7]

The Customs did not overload Dering with work in the years between 1675 and 1679, and several additional forms of employment came to him as marks of increasing power and success. On 22 July 1675 he was appointed a Commissioner for recusants' lands in Kent;[8] and on 23 September 1677 a warrant was issued to name him and others Commissioners to enquire into abuses in the Mint,[9] but what he seems to have considered of greater significance was his election as Governor of the Company of Merchant Adventurers, the Hamburg Company. He had extensive mercantile family connections[10] and considerable administrative experience in Ireland and the Privy Seal Office. With his hopes in 1675 of an office such as that at the Customs, he must have seemed an ideal choice to the Hamburg merchants. In July 1675 Dering told Southwell that he had been named as a candidate, but as it was only worth £150 p.a. it would not 'content' him, nor would it settle his claims on the King, since the governorship was wholly in the disposal of the Company.[11] Eventually, however, in September 1675 he

---

[1] *CTB*, 1676-9, 769, 1219.
[2] Southwell to Ormonde, *Ormonde*, iv, 501.
[3] *CTB*, 1679-80, 4-5.
[4] *ibid.*, 12.
[5] pp. 182-3 below. [6] Browning, *op. cit.*, i, 197, fn. 1.
[7] p. 115 below.
[8] *CTB*, 1672-5, 788.
[9] *CTB*, 1676-9, 751.
[10] through his relationship with the Turkey merchant Sir Daniel Harvey, and his father-in-law, Daniel Harvey. His half-brother Edward was himself a Hamburg merchant.
[11] Dering to Southwell, 20 July 1675, *DS Corr*, 7.

accepted it but as he had 'really no desire to ingage in a trust'[1] the Company undertook to elect a deputy 'to ease me of the greatest part of the trouble.'[2]

The period during which Dering was at the Customs from December 1675 to 1679 included five sessions of Parliament. Throughout these years Danby continued as Lord Treasurer, and Heneage Finch, already Lord Keeper, became Lord Chancellor on 19 December 1675, remaining in that office until his death on 18 December 1682. Dering as Finch's brother-in-law was close to the ministry, and continued to attend the Commons fairly assiduously, but he does not seem to have been in the centre of affairs.[3] From 1675 Danby's relations with the Chancellor did not improve, and Dering was Finch's man in the last resort both by relationship and conviction.

It is likely that Dering kept separate Parliamentary diaries for the sessions between 1675 and 1679, for he referred in April 1680 to 'blew bookes' in which he had entered 'all parliament business'[4] but all that are known to survive are his notes for days in 1677,[5] drafts of a bill against popery[6] and the texts of speeches made in 1678 concerning the Duke of York and the Popish Plot.[7] In his autobiographical note he made a passing reference to the dissolution in January 1679,[8] no more. Grey's *Debates* and the Commons Journal, however, indicate that Dering was an active member of the Commons. Appointment to 31 committees in 1677 with widely differing purposes suggests frequent attendance and two of his eight recorded speeches that year were obviously of major importance, the one advising the House to 'leave treaties to the King,'[9] the other defending the bishops against accusations of popery.[10]

During the session of 1678 Dering's standing in the House increased. Twelve of his speeches are recorded by Grey, and on 4 February 1678 he was named as Chairman of the Grand Committee on Supply. On 6 February he desired to be excused 'by reason of my unskilfulness in so great a matter, which required [he said] a person of greater authority than I am.' He was also suffering from some form of indisposition, but in spite of this he continued as Chairman until 8 February; and at other dates he was chosen Chairman of the Committee of the Whole House on Navy and Army estimates, of the Grand Committees of

---

[1] PD, f. 115.   [2] *ibid.*
[3] Dering's autobiography passes over 1677 as a period of mainly domestic interest (p. 114, below).
[4] ABi, p. 19.   [5] pp. 180-2 below.
[6] pp. 188-90 below.   [7] pp. 184-8 below.   [8] p. 115 below.
[9] In this speech on 6 March 1677 Dering spoke immediately after Daniel Finch and echoed his sentiments, adding an admission that the French fleet was 'terrible in the Indian and Mediterranean seas' and commenting that 'what cost the Roman Eagle twenty years to fly over, he [Louis XIV] makes but one year's work of.' (G, iv, pp. 197-8).
[10] On 20 March 1677, when the House was discussing a bill against popery and to provide for the education of the Duke of York's children, 'we would worship the God of our fathers' was Dering's cry (*ibid.*, p. 295).

Supply and of Ways and Means, and was almost daily appointed to individual Select Committees on Bills. He seemed for a time in 1678 to have been accepted as a guide on business perhaps second only to the Speaker. When the House 'sat silent' on 2 May it was Dering who urged it to work, as he again did a little later, on 30 October. The only politically significant contribution made by him was on 7 May for the removal of Lauderdale from office. He spoke twice in an attempt to avert an Address to the King except along innocuous lines, and in particular he appealed to the House's sense of justice: 'We never judge a man without hearing him. We never did it before; I never remember it.' Dering did not object to an impeachment process; but he did object to arbitrary condemnation. However, by 137 to 92 the House was against him. On the whole his interventions were not partisan; he seemed to be feeling his way towards the position of 'elder statesman' from that of Danby's disciple.[1]

The Popish Plot gave Dering excellent opportunity to act the elder statesman. He was totally convinced of the existence of a plot and was appointed to the Committee to translate Coleman's papers,[2] himself participating in the translation.[3] He preserved with the 1675 diary two interesting drafts for the energetic speech which he delivered on 16 November (reported by Grey). In it he warned the House that time was elapsing. If they did not take action against popery there was 'nothing to do but to dig our own graves, and lie down in them.'[4] In the draft speech he added the reminder that they were 200 to 1 against professed papists, and the exhortation not to be afraid to suffer 'a degree of martyrdom' as had Sir Edmund Berry Godfrey.[5] In an earlier speech, also preserved with his diary (but not reported by Grey), he was prepared to urge that the Duke of York should retire 'at some reasonable distance from London.'[6] The Journals of the House show that on several occasions in November Dering made report to the House as chairman from committees dealing with the Papists Bill, and from the Conference held with the Lords.[7]

Together with his texts of speeches on popery Dering preserved two schemes in his own hand for 'heads for bills against popery'—one of these[8] being a shorter and less developed form of the other.[9] The essential provisions were for the registration of papists, together with their lands, and the exclusion of papists from 30 miles around London,

---

[1] It is noticeable that Dering seems not to have spoken in defence of Danby when impeachment was discussed. Dering appears in the list of supporters drawn up for Secretary Williamson or Danby in May 1678, but not in a list of court members drawn up by the opposition. In 1679 he is again counted a firm courtier (Browning, *op. cit.*, iii, 111-20).

[2] On 28 October 1678, *CJ*, ix, 523.

[3] G, vii, 434.   [4] pp. 184-8 below.

[5] *ibid*. Godfrey's murder at some date between 12 and 17 October 1678 had been the main incident in the early stages of the Popish Plot.

[6] p. 184 below.   [7] *CJ*, ix, 546, 547, 548.

[8] pp. 188-9 below.   [9] p. 190 below.

with a provision for all papists to be forced to hear one sermon a year 'for their conversion'. The proposed removal of papists from London received definitive legislative shape in the bill introduced into the Lords on 31 March 1679 which was subsequently considered and amended in the Commons, but failed to reach enactment.[1]

During the sittings of the Commons in 1678 Dering is recorded by Grey as having spoken on 17 occasions; nine court members made more speeches—the Chancellor of the Exchequer for instance making 74— but other active courtiers such as Philip Warwick spoke on 13 occasions and Winston Churchill on five only.[2] A similar count during the 1675 and 1677 sessions reveals 30 speeches by Dering against 55 by Richard Temple and 41 by Charles Wheeler, but 11 by Warwick and none by Hanmer.[3] During these years of active attendance in the House, Dering was clearly one of the more frequent speakers.[4]

In March 1679 Danby resigned the Treasurership and Dering became one of five Commissioners of the Treasury.[5] 'I were never more surprised at anything than the newes that I were to be one, having not made the least application', Dering commented in his autobiography.[6] He ascribed his appointment to the recommendation of Sidney Godolphin, a man to whom he had never 'spoke one word'.[7] Dering's standing in the Commons, his experience both in Ireland and as a Customs Commissioner, and, not least, his diminished dependence on Danby, were probably all factors in the choice. The King had already turned to him as an Irish expert, for in August 1678 he had placed a bill for the settlement of Ireland in the hands of Lord Chancellor Finch and of Dering, described by the Irish Lord Chancellor Boyle as 'most versed in the former Acts of Settlement and Explanation'.[8] In the course of October Dering dealt with objections and amendments proposed to the bill and his conduct of this business was a foretaste of what was to be his principal concern at the Treasury—provision for the future taxation of Ireland—although the Irish bill itself was 'absolutely laid aside' by January 1680.[9]

[1] The bill was received from the Lords on 3 May 1679 (*CJ*, ix, 611) and passed with amendments on 21 May (*ibid.*, 626).
[2] Browning, *op. cit.*, iii, 118-19.   [3] *ibid.*, 94-6.
[4] At the end of 1675 Dering had drawn up his own list of 'such publique acts as were before the House of Commons or another place' (pp. 179-80 below), which suggests that he tried to keep a general watch on the whole of Parliament's activities during a session.
[5] The first Lord was Arthur (Capel), 21st Earl of Essex; the remaining Commissioners were Laurence Hyde, second son of Clarendon (subsequently 1st Lord Hyde, and in 1682, 4th Earl of Rochester), Sir John Ernle and Sidney Godolphin. On 21 November 1679 Hyde became 1st Lord and Essex was replaced by Sir Stephen Fox. This commission remained unchanged until 24 April 1684 (J. C. Sainty, *Treasury Officials, 1660-1870* (1972), 18). Dering's own surviving papers as Commissioner which are calendared below (pp. 190 ff.) mainly concern the renewal of the farm of Irish taxes, but include an estimate of the revenue and expenditure of England for 1679 to 1680 in Dering's own hand and various diary entries for 1683 (pp. 139-50 below).
[6] p. 115 below.   [7] *ibid.*   [8] *Ormonde*, iv, 191.
[9] E. Lanesborough to E. Ossory, 18 January 1680 (*Ormonde*, v, 268).

Dering, as has been seen, was proud that his first work at the Treasury in 1679 was to help reduce the number of Commissioners at the Customs, the Excise and Appeals to five in each case.[1] In addition, he and the other Lords of the Treasury set their faces against granting reversions and any offices under them 'for any other terme but during the King's pleasure'. Dering observed that they had thus lessened their own power (i.e. of patronage).[2]

The Parliament elected in February 1679 did not contain more than 30 or 40 members on whom the Court could rely continuously.[3] The Duke of York's succession was considered a chief encouragement to the Popish Plot and on 15 May a bill to exclude him from the Crown was introduced, but when Parliament was dissolved on 14 August 1679 it had not become law. Danby was imprisoned, but otherwise 'the balance of success had on the whole been with the King.'[4] Dering's position as an anti-papist and a staunch royalist was an awkward one and his part in the work of the Commons in 1679 was not spectacular; although appointed to several key committees he was not chosen as chairman; and the four speeches recorded in Grey were of small political importance.[5] That on 12 March, however, showed his command of precedent concerning the election of Speaker.[6]

Parliament sat again on 21 October 1680, but Dering not unfairly dismissed its work as concerning 'disputes and proposalls in discourse which came to nothing at last.'[7] Moreover, he found daily attendance at the Treasury as well as membership of the Commons unusually tiring, and he 'tooke no notes at all'.[8] He was concerned with the reconciliation of dissenters and supported the bill for 'uniting His Majesty's Protestant Subjects' to the Church of England,[9] which reached the Committee stage, but then lapsed.[10] (A similar bill was ordered on 26 March 1681, but made no progress.)[11] Dering preserved his own draft of a parallel bill 'for the ease of dissenting protestants', dated by him 'November 1680', which in the event had no greater success.[12]

This bill clearly exempted dissenters from the penalties incurred by papists for non-conformity and should have been sufficient evidence of Dering's anti-popish sentiments. During the time he was forwarding his bill, however, he was subjected to attack in a pamphlet by Ezekiel Tonge, printed by Janeway, as 'an active and seditious Papist'.[13] What

[1] p. 20 above. [2] pp. 115-16 below.
[3] D. Ogg, *England in the Reign of Charles II*, ii (2nd ed., 1956), 586.
[4] *ibid.*, 590.
[5] 11 March, 12 March (G, vi, 429, 436) and 14 May, 26 May (G, vii, 275, 342).
[6] G, vi, 436.
[7] p. 120 below. [8] *ibid.*
[9] *CJ*, ix, 645, 681, 686.
[10] *ibid.*, 687, 695. [11] *ibid.*, 711.
[12] pp. 194-6 below, and references given there.
[13] G, vii, 433-4 gives Dering's speech of complaint on 9 November at length.

had happened was that letters he had translated for the use of the House in the previous session were mistakenly thought to have been written by him. Sir John Knight gave his testimony 'to Dering's zeal for the prosecution of the Plot. He translated those Letters faithfully [which] he stands now accused of having received from the Internuntio'.[1] Eventually, after Janeway the printer had been examined,[2] the storm blew over, and on 16 November the House resolved 'that all the reflective parts of the Pamphlet upon Sir Edward Dering, a Member of this House, are false, scandalous and libellous'.[3] Ezekiel Tonge's detailed defence of 16 November of his own innocence in the matter to Sir Thomas Clarges is preserved in the Stowe MSS,[4] together with a letter of abject apology to Dering 'as you judg it my error and my misfortune'.[5] An original manuscript petition of Samuel Lee and others to the Commons praying for discharge from their confinement by the House Dering subsequently preserved among his own papers.[6]

The farm of the revenues of Ireland had been granted to Sir James Shaen[7] and ten other contractors for the period from Christmas 1675 to Christmas 1682. During 1680 the renewal of the farm came under discussion and Dering was inevitably involved in the negotiations both as a Commissioner of the Treasury and as an Irish Privy Councillor. He recorded in his Account Book a meeting at the Treasury Chamber on 15 September 1680 presided over by the King[8] and in February 1681 the King issued instructions to the First Lord of the Treasury, Laurence (later Lord) Hyde, to Daniel Finch (later Lord Finch), First Lord of the Admiralty, and to Dering to draw up proposals 'for the improvement of his revenue in Ireland'.[9] Ormonde observed to his son in March that Shaen was 'much hearkened to in the Treasury' and that new proposals were under way—he objected to the secrecy being observed.[10] On 20 May Hyde, Finch and Dering went to see the King at Windsor, to explain their proposals to him, 'none else present but Mr Edward Roberts' (the agent of Sir James Shaen).[11] Dcring noted that the

---

[1] *ibid.*, 434.
[2] G, vii, 1-3, which includes Dering's speech of expostulation: 'if there be the least suspicion upon me, I am ready to lie at the Door of the House, and to be trod on, as in the primitive times.' From his baptism he had never deviated from the protestant religion in which he had been bred by his father. He added in connection with the printing of the libel: 'As for the Printing-trade, it is like robbing, not altogether done for malice, but for reward.'
[3] *CJ*, ix, 654.
[4] BL Stowe 746, f. 35.
[5] *ibid.*, f. 40.
[6] KAO U350.
[7] Shaen served as Surveyor-General of Ireland, in that capacity receiving records of the Courts of Claims (*Liber Munerum Publicorum Hiberniae* (1824), pt. ii, 56). He had been made an Irish baronet in 1662; but was heartily disliked by Ormonde (cf. *CSPI*, 1660-2, 278, 316, 560, 578, 680, etc. for details of his posts).
[8] p. 119 below.
[9] p. 120 below.
[10] Ormonde to Arran, 31 March 1681, *Ormonde*, vi, 23-4.
[11] p. 127 below.

proposals were brought 'into a system fit for his Majestie's knowledge'[1] and the King obviously approved the outline.

On 1 June Dering gave a brief but interesting account in his diary of a council held at Windsor dealing with the farm.[2] A counter-proposal of the Earl of Arran 'coming below the present rent of £240,000 p.a. was soon rejected'.[3] Then, as Dering noted, the King brought a second proposal 'out of his pocket' which he thought was better[4] (the proposal drawn up by Roberts and approved by Hyde, Dering and Finch). Some counsellors present disliked it and the King decided to delay the matter and speak privately with the proposer and one or two others.[5] This he did in the Treasury Chamber on 8 June when the (unnamed) proposer attended and the explanation of the proposal made to Hyde and Dering was read and approved. The King then ordered a warrant for the contract which would reserve approval of the Trustees to him as well as the modelling of the army.[6] On 21 June the Treasury Lords officially informed Ormonde that a contract for a new farm had been ordered.[7] Ormonde complained to Secretary Jenkins that he did not know who the proprietors were.[8] Although Lord Lieutenant, he was not told and on 14 September Ormonde declared bitterly that he could not understand Treasury communications because he was kept in ignorance of the negotiations.[9]

Ormonde knew in general, however, what it was about—in June Arran had described it to him as part farm, part management, part project; £270,000 p.a. was to be paid, with an advance of £80,000 of which £60,000 was to reimburse the present farmer (he felt Shaen's finger was 'too clear in the matter').[10] The Council referred Ranelagh's appeal to the Irish group. Arran considered Hyde and Dering to be privately managing the new undertaking but 'Mr Roberts is a main engine in the business'.[11]

Detailed negotiations for the new farm continued in the autumn, Ranelagh leading an attack on it, Hyde asking the Irish Lords to wait and hear the other side.[12] Arran told his father there were 500 sheets in the contract.[13] On 9 November Ranelagh's objections were ordered to be given to the contractors—Edward Seymour asked 'who were they?'[14] On 21 November Roberts appeared as their agent and various calculations were referred to the Auditors.[15] In December it seemed the

---

[1] p. 127 below.
[2] pp. 127-8 below.
[3] 'en ridicule' as Arran felt (Arran to Ormonde, 4 June 1681, *Ormonde*, vi, 75).
[4] p. 127 below.
[5] p. 128 below.
[6] *ibid.*
[7] *CTB*, 1681-5, 185.
[8] Ormonde to Secretary Jenkins, 2 July 1681, *SPD*, 1680-1, 342.
[9] Ormonde to Arran, 14 September 1681, *Ormonde*, vi, 153.
[10] Arran to Ormonde, 11 June 1681, *ibid.*, 81.
[11] Arran to Ormonde, 30 July 1681, *ibid.*, 114.
[12] *Ormonde*, vi, 205, 206, 210, 213-4.
[13] *ibid.*, 216.
[14] Arran to Ormonde, 12 November 1681, *ibid.*, 225.
[15] Arran to Ormonde, 22 November 1681, *ibid.*, 236.

Auditors could not agree on their report but various clauses were being changed (some notes of the Irish Committee's discussions on 20 December were preserved by Dering).[1] By 24 January 1682 the contractors were reported as saying they would have given £10,000 not to have meddled with the farm;[2] the new Secretary of State, the Earl of Conway, noted on 4 February that the King wanted the revenues of Tangier included in the contract,[3] and on 18 February it was reported that a scheme for a general bidding was being prepared.[4]

Dering's papers show him continuously supporting and guiding the contractors[5] and, it seems likely, being encouraged by the King in doing so. Charles for long was in favour of the proposals, then only turned against them early in 1682—after eight months' discussions including '22 several dayes of examinacion' in the King's presence. Dering was on the losing side, and proposals for alternative farming and for management did not come from him; his personal diary after recording the King's (abortive) authorisation of a warrant on 8 June 1681[6] does not give any further detail concerning the Irish revenues. By 8 August 1682 the proposed farm was laid aside[7] and eventually, on 25 October, a warrant was issued to the Duke of Ormonde for a Commission to manage the Irish revenues.[8]

The Irish project had brought Dering into close contact with the King and it seems that it was Dering rather than Hyde or the other Commissioners who had been organising the whole scheme. Its failure was very much Dering's failure. He had had against him the still very considerable power of Ormonde, the doubts of various Lords of the Council and the shifting views of the King. But Dering emerged unscathed from the incident and continued in power as Treasury Commissioner to his death. The degree of his personal authority with the King, and incidentally of his own courage, is clearly indicated when in December 1683 he disagreed with Charles concerning the King's legal control over Irish lands vested in him by the Acts of Settlement and Explanation,[9] Dering pursuing his own interpretation of the situation with vigorous independence against that held by the King.

The management of the Irish farm negotiations was as delicate and complex work as the settlement of the Irish land tenure in the 1660s had been. Dering now was twenty years older, and the task probably

1 Arran to Ormonde, 7, 10 December 1681, *Ormonde*, vi, 252, 254, and pp. 202-3 below.
2 Arran to Ormonde, 24 January 1682, *ibid.*, 300.
3 Conway to Ormonde, 4 February 1682, *ibid.*, 307.
4 Longford to Ormonde, 18 February 1682, *ibid.*, 314.
5 See, e.g. the submission drafted by Dering probably in February 1682, pp. 205-6 below, and the paper concerning the final submission of July 1682, pp. 206-8, below.
6 p. 128 below.   7 *CSPD*, 1682, 341.
8 *Ormonde*, vi, 418; *CTB*, 1681-5, 617-8. There were five commissioners led by Francis, Earl of Longford.
9 See p. 147, below. Eventually Dering lost this particular battle, but defiantly reiterated his own opinion in his diary entry for 17 January 1684.

exhausted him. He noted in April 1682 as one of his misfortunes 'the perpetuall and not yet ended trouble of the Irish farm'.[1] By 1682 his health was clearly deteriorating; he was 57 and since 1675 had suffered severe attacks of the stone, which he recorded, together with the elaborate advice of various doctors.[2] In his later years he was also becoming increasingly anxious about his finances. He had inherited an estate heavily in debt; much of this he cleared, but his extensive family, including 17 children, had involved a considerable drain on his resources. His careful accounting summed up the situation in 1680 in terms of three decades thus:[3]

	Expenses	*Receipts*
1648-1658	£9,303	£8,774
1658-1668	£12,594	£11,930
1668-1679	£20,160	£19,285

Dering concluded that 'my expence hath been very great and my way of living very free'. His position at the Treasury he considered uncertain; and his four younger sons were still unprovided for.

During the last three years of his life Parliament was only in session for 7 days, from 21 to 28 March 1681, and then at Oxford in order to escape the influence of the London mob. Dering, no longer attempting to prepare separate Parliamentary diaries, noted down the business in his account book and included detail for the sittings of 25 and 26 March—he does not seem to have spoken himself. On 28 March, as he observed, the Parliament was dissolved 'so soudainly, that only his Majestie was in his robes, but not any one of the Lords. Nor was the sword of state there'.[4]

By November 1683 he felt old age was 'now neare hand or rather in truth come allready'[5] (he had made a second will on 24 February 1683).[6] He felt more cheerful, however, his stone had ceased to plague him, and various entries in his Account Book for 1684 show him attending his office at the Treasury, enjoying the company at a drawing room at court, and jotting down detailed accounts of the severest frost he had ever experienced, and of the bull-baiting and ox-roasting on the Thames which accompanied it. In March 1684 he concluded that the past year had been 'happy and fortunate', and in the following month he celebrated his 36th wedding anniversary surrounded by friends, children and grandchildren, commenting that 'all I shall say upon this occasion is, that after 36 years I believe we are not weary of one another, nor our children weary of either of us. Benedictum sit nomen domini nunc et in secula.'[7] There came a second fit of gout in May 1684; on 9 June he made what proved to be his last diary entry—concerning his

---

[1] AB1, 135; see also his comments in October 1681, pp. 129-30 below.
[2] AB1, 22. [3] *ibid.*, 19. [4] p. 125, below.
[5] AB2, 197. [6] pp. 208-10, below. [7] AB2, 214.

son Daniel's success as commander of a frigate.[1] Then on 17 June Dering developed a fever; at first he persisted in going to the Treasury but then took to his bed, and on being told he would not recover, sent for the beer his nurses had been denying him, 'for since I must die I will die playing the good fellow in small beer.'[2] On 24 June Dering 'went away without the least groan or sign to the great amazement of all'.[3]

He was buried in the family vault at Pluckley Church on 28 June 1684,[4] and on the south wall of the Lady Chapel his life was succinctly commemorated.[5] Four of his public offices were enumerated: he was *Unus ex arbitris Confiscatimum (Vulgo) Clameorum In Hyberniam Delegatis (Ubi etiam a secretis conciliis)*; then in England he was successively *e custodibus Privati Sigilli*; *Deinde e Praefectis Aerarii*; and in addition he was *Praeses item Commercij Hambergensis*. When elected to Parliament he had worked there *Cum diligentia et fidelitate*. The dry restraint of the inscription is untypical of funerary monuments of the epoch; only in the introductory sentence was a wider claim made for Dering, that he was *Plurimis honestissimisque Reipublicae*, a eulogy more characteristic of the age but one which his papers and diaries do much to justify.

[1] AB2, p. 220.
[2] Henning, xvii, quoting HMC, *Egmont*, ii, 139.
[3] *ibid.*, xviii.
[4] Haslewood, 12.
[5] The inscription is given in full in Haslewood, 20.

Editorial Note and Acknowledgements

In the text which follows documents preserved in the House of Lords Record Office (with a few indicated exceptions) have been transcribed in full. The original spelling and grammar have been retained, but punctuation and capitalisation have been modernised and abbreviations extended. Editorial matter or comment which has been added is printed between square brackets. Documents in other custody have been calendared, but where material of direct Parliamentary or political interest is included, a full text of those sections is appended to the calendar. Inevitably the entries concerning Dering's family life and his complex accounts have had to be omitted—amongst them extensive entries in the Dering Account Books—but a fairly clear dividing line has usually been apparent, and it is to be hoped that in due course Dering's estate and personal records will receive the detailed treatment they merit.

The central documents which led to the preparation of this volume are Sir Edward Dering's Parliamentary diary of 1675 and the political papers ancillary to it, acquired by the House of Lords Record Office in 1971 (Phillipps MS. 29698). Professor Basil Henning's invaluable edition of Dering's earlier diary of 1670-1673, published by Yale University Press in 1940, had drawn attention to Dering's skill as a diarist and his eye for the details of Parliamentary procedure; the newly-acquired papers in the House of Lords added substantially to our knowledge of the Parliament of Spring 1675 and led to a quest for any other Dering material that would enable a fairly complete picture of Dering's Parliamentary and political life to be compiled. Gratitude is due to the owners and scholars who helped in seeking out and making available this material. In the first place Mr Philip Blake, a descendant of the Dering family and the owner of Dering portraits and documents, gave most generously of his time and expert guidance in the preparation of this volume. He made available from his own collections two key records, the Second Household Book and the Personal Diary; he read and commented on the complete text of the volume and, above all, he has contributed to it a pedigree of Dering which demonstrates the complex inter-relationship of the Dering, Harvey and Finch families. I would also like to express my deep gratitude for the encouragement given by the late Sir Rupert Dering, 12th and last baronet, to the preparation of this volume.

I am much indebted to Dr Felix Hull and to the Kent County Archives Office for permission to calendar and in many cases print *in extenso* Dering documents preserved in that office. The remainder of the material appearing in this volume is printed by kind permission of the Keeper of the Public Records, and the Board of the British Library, respectively. Many scholars have assisted me in dealing with the quite broad range of subjects with which Dering was concerned and I would like in particular to thank Professor Basil Henning, Dr H. Horwitz, Dr Mary Hobbs, Dr Robert Latham, Dr J. G. Simms, Miss Sonia Anderson, and my colleagues, Mr J. C. Sainty, Mr H. S. Cobb and Mr D. J. Johnson at the House of Lords for their help and guidance most generously given. The preparation of the index, as well as a great deal of transcription, typing and proofreading, was the work of Mrs Joan Wise, then a member of the Lords Record Office, and I know she would wish to join me in thanking Mr J. P. Ferris and the staff of the History of Parliament Trust for their assistance during the preparation of the index. Finally, thanks are due to Mr David Napthine of the Graphic Design Division of Her Majesty's Stationery Office, for the help he has given in designing not only the present volume but also the recently issued *Guide to the Records of Parliament*.

Maurice Bond

November 1975

I

THE PARLIAMENTARY DIARY
OF SIR EDWARD DERING

25 April to 15 August 1660

Kent Archives Office, U 275 05; photocopy in the House
of Lords Record Office, Historical Collections, 85/13

The Parliamentary Diary of
Sir Edward Dering, 25 April to 15 August 1660

Note that the dates which are usually set in the margin of the text of the MS in slightly varying styles have here been standardised and printed centrally.

[f.1]   *Wednesday, 25 April*

The parliament began at Westminster. Dr Reynolds preaching first at St Margaret's church, from thence the members went to the parliament house and immediatly chose Sir Harbottle Grimstone baronet their Speaker. He tooke the chaire just at 3 quarters past eleven.

Then we named Mr Jessop clerke, Mr Darnell assistant to the clerke, Mr James Norfolke serjeant at mace to the house.

Two masters of the [Chancery] came from the house of Lords to tell us their Lordships had agreed upon Monday next to be a day of humiliation, and desired our concurrence, which was soon graunted, and Mr Calamy and Dr Gawden appointed to preach before the house at St Margaret's, to which two, upon the motion of Mr Hamden was added a third, Mr Baxter.

Ordered that no new businesse should be heard after twelve.

[*CJ*, viii, 1]

Thursday, 26 April

Some offered to question our owning the house of Lords upon an occasion, as not knowing how farre they would joine with our ends. But it was thought, that it was a good step to the King's admission the admission of the Lords, and the doore being open and no force to restraine them it was thought infallible that all the young Lords would come in, and not be excluded by the opinion of those 12 Lords did first set alone. And so it proved, for Thursday some, Fryday many and Tuesday after, very many others came into that house.

The Commons proceeded to name a committee of priviledges, as they allwayes do, but with great noise and indecent clamorous confusion, which they say is allwayes usuall at the naming that committee. At last there were named about two hundred,[1] of which I were one, and we were ordered to set [f.1v] Tuesdays, Thursdayes and Saturdays in the afternoones.

The house also then gave thankes by their Speaker to Generall

---
[1] *rectius*, 158 (*CJ*, viii, 2)

Monke, for his great services by which he had so highly deserved of the nation, and to Collonell Ingoldsby for his late service in taking prisoner at Daventrey Collonell John Lambert, which was indeed of very great consequence to the peace of this Commonwealth.

It was said in the house by Serjeant Glin that at naming of the committee of elections every member might name two. Others allowed it, but not to name two together.

None are refused of any committee that are named, but when the committee is sufficient, it may be said there is enough and restraine the naming any more.

[*CJ*, viii, 2-3]

Friday, 27 April

A petition from Mr Berkead to be restored to his place of serjeant at mace to the house, which he had by ordinance of Lords and Commons, and also by the Great Seale in 1646. This was referred to a committee, and to enquire of the demerits of the person as well as his right, and report both together.

My brother Finch speaking against the petition, and mentioning that this was not the place he sued for because we were not that house of Commons to which he served in 1646, for that was in the time of King Lords and Commons, which we were not so happy to be, gave occasion to Collonel King to move that since the foundations were questioned they might be examined and searched into and that we might take in hand the settlement of the government, which was assented unto, and my brother Finch moving that since the debate was solemne and important, and the fast was on Monday, the devotions of that day might prepare us for the next, and we might adjourne till Tuesday, which was assented to, and proved very usefull to good purposes.

[f.2] ## Saturday, 28 April

The committee of priviledges sat in the parliament house, and by order of the house dispatched first the double returnes, which we ended in Thursday and this Saturday. Our rule of proceeding was that w[h]ere any more was returned by the lawfull officer, he should set till the merits of the cause was heard, upon the petition of any complaining p[etitioner]. But if two were returned by the lawfull officer, then neither to set till the cause decided. Nor did we admit at this time any evidence at all of the merits of the cause, although sometimes we were told there were witnesses at the doore, but reserved them entire.

1. Ruled that the mayor was the lawfull officer in mayor townes, where there were no sheriffes.

2. That the mayor might returne himselfe, although no sheriffe can.
3. That he is the proper officer against whom the penaltie lyes by the statute Hen.[*blank*][1] and to whom the sheriffe ought to direct his precept.
4. That a returne by the mayor under his seale manuall and his hand, may be a good returne.[2]
5. That a returne without the hand and seale of the mayor, but under the common seale of the towne and his name in the body of the indenture, may be good.

Upon which two considerations we adjudged the returne from Great Bedwin in Wiltshire a double returne, and that none of the 4 burgesses returned could set till the election determined.

Sir Walter Saint John ⎱ by one indenture ⎰ Mr Robert Spencer
Sir Ralph Hare[3]   ⎰   ⎱ Mr Gape
                                             by another

[*CJ*, viii, 3-4]

Tuesday, 1 May

This day began the happy worke of our restitution to our ancient lawes.

Mr Annesley, Lord President of the Councell of State, delivered in a letter from the King directed to the Lord Generall Monke, to be communicated to the Councell of State and the officers under his command, brought by Sir John Greenvill. Another letter directed to the house of Commons was read. These were both dated the 4th Aprill at Breda, and brought thence by Sir J.Greenvil.

Mr Morris, Governour of Plimouth, a kinsman of the Generall, began after the reading of the letters with a set and elegant speech to persuade us of the King's goodnesse and our happinesse in him,[4] which was seconded by my brother Finch with his usuall eloquence, and all the house soon moved by their arguments and example and the generall inclination to make very dutifull reflexions upon his Majestie's letter.

The resolves were to send immediatly an answer to his Majestie's gracious letter expressing the great and joyfull sense we have of his Majestie's favour and goodnesse and that we would speedily take into consideration his Majestie's proposals.

Resolved that his Majestie's letter and declaration should be printed and published together with our votes (moved first by Collonell Jones).

Resolved that the house do set againe in the afternoon, contrary to the first order, but desired by the Lords.

[1] Parliamentary Elections Act, 1444, 23 Hen. VI, c. 14.
[2] Items 4 and 5 are bracketed by Dering in the left margin.
[3] *sic*, but Sir Ralph Verney in *CJ*.
[4] G. Davies, *The Restoration of Charles II, 1658-1660*, 342, although quoting Dering's diary entry, describes the speech as by Monck himself.

Resolved that the summe of fifty thousand pound be sent to his Majestie with all expedition.

Resolved that a jewell of £500 value be given to Sir John Greenvill as a marke of honour from this house.

[*CJ*, viii, 4-8]

[f.3]   *Wednesday, 2 May*

My brother Finch, Arthur Annesley president, Sir Anthony Ashley Cowper etc., sent down to the city to borrow the money of them for present advance. They borrowed of them £100,000, halfe for the King and halfe for the present occasions of the army. The security given them is a taxe through the nation at £70,000 per mensem to begin at midsummer next and to continue for three moneths. The city also sent the King a present of £1000(o)[1] and £2000 for the King's servaunts.

Memorandum, agreed that all matters of money must move originally from the lower house, and though the ordinance for the assessment is not valid till the Lords have concurred yet it was not thought fit so much as to acquaint them with it, till the thing was brought into an ordinance heare, and fit to be presented to them.

This morning taken up with severall debates about a conference with the Lords, or a free conference, and a reconference, which Sir Walter Earle mencioned and others had never heard of.

The Lords sent us word they had appointed the Earle of Manchester one of the commissioners of the Great Seale. Our answer was we would send an answer by messengers of our owne.

The usuall returne, when we will lay it quite aside.

[*CJ*, viii, 8-9]

[f.3v]   *Thursday, 3 May*

Sir John Greenvile was called in to receive the thankes of the house and notice of the jewell.

We fell upon the proposicions of his Majestie, and voted a committee about 40[2] of which I were one and to whom all the long robe were added, to draw the billes upon the King's letter. It was [*blank*][3]

Afternoon.

I were at the committee of elections. The cases were [*sic*] Wiccomb in Bucks.

[*CJ*, viii, 9-11]

---

[1] deleted.   [2] of 56 (*CJ*, viii, 11.)
[3] the letter is printed in *PH*, iv, 28-30.

[f.4]   *Friday, 4 May*

The Lords having sent us word that they intended to send six of their members with the letter they intended in answer to the King's letter, we found ourselfes obliged to send twelve of ours, it having been allwayes the custome to send double their number, and they to appoint their owne number

The president[1] moved that the case being now but to carry a letter, and indeed two severall letters, he thought we were not tied to double theirs, but carried against his opinion.

My brother Finch, chairman of the committee for drawing the billes upon the concessions, brought in first a bill for confirming of this present parliament, by the King's consent though not called by his writ, de quo postea.

[*CJ*, viii, 11-12]

Saturday, 5 May

The number of 12 being agreed upon to be sent, and the way to be by writing every member twelve names in a paper, this day we delivered in our papers, putting them into two glasses carried about by the 2 clarkes.

The house being first told by 4 appointed for that purpose, viz.

Lord Howard	Sir Henry Yelverton
Sir Henry Cholmeley	Major Generall Browne

The number of the house was 408, beside Collonell Ludlow, who would give in no paper.

Resolved that all processe and other proceedings should be in the King's name.

Resolved that Easter terme to the two last returnes, viz. the 28 day of May, should be put off and that there should be no trialls at barre this terme.

[*CJ*, viii, 12-14]

[f.4v]   *Monday, 7 May*

The committee brought in the names of the 12 chosen by the major (part—*del.*) number of the votes, for the businesse of reckoning the votes were a worke of ten houres.

The 12 chosen to go with the letter to the King were[2]

1 Arthur Annesley, later 1st E. of Anglesey, who in February 1660 had been chosen president of the council of state; there was no Lord President of the Council until 1679 (see entry for 1 May, above).
2 Dering gives 11 names; the 12th was Sir Horatio Townsend (*CJ*, viii, 15).

Sir George Booth	Lord Falkland
Sir Anthony Ashley Cowper	Sir John Holland
Lord Bruce	Denzell Hollis
Lord Fairfax	Lord Castleton
Lord Herbert	Sir Henry Cholmeley
	Lord Mandevile

[*CJ*, viii, 14-16]

Tuesday, 8 May

This day the King was proclaimed in usuall manner, with as much ceremony as the shortnesse of time would permit.

[f.5] The same day ordered that the seale of the Commonwealth, viz. that with the crosse and harpe, and the same stamp of moneys should be used till new could be made.

That the State's armes should be taken downe and the King's set up, and accordingly the State's armes in [*blank*] were taken downe by Mr Prin and burnt in a bonfire before Lincolne's Inne gate.

Resolved also that his Majestie should be desired to make a speedy returne into his dominions and to the exercise of his kingly office.

Resolved that the proportion of taxes should continue upon the severall counties as it stood in the last assessment and not as it was in 1648 and 1649, but that it should be no president for future taxes and assessments.

Resolved that henceforward the moneys to be raised for the publique occasions of the Kingdome should be by the way of subsidyes.

[*CJ*, viii, 16-18]

[f.5v] ## *Wednesday, 9 May*

Resolved the messengers should go toward his Majestie on Fryday next.

Instructions for them agreed upon.

The billes for indemnity, confirmation of proceedings of civill justice and religion read the first time. That of religion being brought in by the sub committee and not by the chairman of that committee nor ever seen by him, was much spoaken against as irregular, and indeavoured to be thrown out upon that occasion, and at last retained for the reputacion of not casting out the first bill that came in of religion, and besides any private member may bring in a bill.

[*CJ*, viii, 18-20]

Thursday, 10 May

Thursday was a thanksgiving day, but the house sat in the afternoon. A conference then with the Lords, to persuade them to admit of the armes of the Commonwealth to be used in the King's name and stile for the most urgent affaires of the Kingdome till farther convenience might give one of the King's owne appointing. But the Lords consented not, although the damages suffered for want of a Great Seale be very great and allmost insupportable.

[*CJ*, viii, 20-22]

[f.6]   ## *Friday, 11 May*

The letter to the King delivered by the Speaker to Denzell Hollis: (and the—*del.*) sealed with the Speaker's private seale. Complaint made that £7,900 collected by the charity of severall men for the reliefe of the poore protestants in Piedmont, was taken away by the rump parliament to pay the souldiers. Much was indeavoured to lay it upon the members then sitting but some then and now sitting saying they were against the taking it away, it was at last resolved to lay it upon the excise, to be paid by £2000 per mensem.

The rest of the day taken up with the bill of assessment.

[*CJ*, viii, 22-4]

Saturday, 12 May

First the bill for the assessment was read the second time and the payment agreed to be the 1 August.

The bill of indemnitie and oblivion read the second time. Which done, Mr Prin brought in a narrative conteined in a journall booke kept among the parliament rolles of every dayes proceeding of the high court of justice, January 1648.[1]

Divers of the present members being named in the list were desired to speak for themselves, which they did with much detestation of that horrid fact:

1. Collonel Richard Ingoldsby   4. Collonel Fagg
2. Collonel John Hutchinson   5. Collonel Morley
3. Collonel Lassells   6. Sir Thomas Wroth

The three last were put in commission without their knowledge, and had once answered to their names in the painted chamber, and then

---

[1] This was the record presented by Say to the Commons on 12 December 1650 (cf. *HL MSS* xi (1962), xviii-xix).

41

avoided the service. Lassells had been often at their meetings but was not at the sentence. The two first had signed the sentence, but Ingoldsby in a manner forced by *the protector*[1] Oliver Cromwell, who set his owne seale to Ingoldsbye's name, Ingoldsby refusing and saying he had done to much allready, and that he did repent. Hutchinson said he had gone according to his opinion and judgment, that he had purchased but £5 per annum, and all of them begging the mercy of the King and of the house.

The last was John Lenthall, sonne of the old Speaker, who saying his name was put in without his knowledge, fell upon expressions that we must fixe our eyes upon the beginning of the warres, not upon the last act, and that he that first drew his sword upon the King committed as great offence as he that cut off his head. These words gave so great offence, to Irby, Bulkeley, Northcot, Earle and the old parliament men, that he was called to the barre, and first kneeling, after standing up, received by order of the house from the Speaker, a very severe reprihension. The house upon this occasion not rising till halfe an hower past fower.

[*CJ*, viii, 24-5]

[f.6v] Orders of the house occasionally mencioned

1. That when two arise to speake, the Speaker is to direct whom he thought first up, and the other to set downe.
2. If two rise up and one preferred to speake, and the other set downe, he that set downe hath no preaudience of any one that can after that rise up before him.
3. If any one will speake to the orders of the house, he is to be heard before any one that will speake to anything else.
4. If any one will speake to the orders of the house, he may interrupt him that is speaking to another thing.
5. None must come crosse one that is speaking.
6. None must speake but while the mace lyeth upon the table.
7. None should stand up in their places but he that speaketh so.
8. At naming committees, it was said that every one may name two.
9. None that is named of a committee is to be refused.
10. At the first reading of a bill, none usually speake to it, but they that would have it cast out.
11. He that reporteth, should stand at the seat neare the barre at the left hand, and report aloud.
12. He that bringeth in a bill should bring in a breviat for the ease of the Speaker.

[1] These two words are underlined.

12. [*sic*] Regularly no bill should be read above once in one day. The contrary sometimes practised in cases of great importance.

[ff.7, 7v, blank]

[f.8]   *Monday, 14 May*

The house proceeded in the bill of indemnity. (My brother Finch—*del.*) The Lord President beginning the discourse after much had been said to proceed first with the members of the present house, and that laid aside, by the president, who advised first to agree upon the number that should be excepted out of the pardon of life, which he said might be seaven. My brother Finch made a speech for moderation to be used, Mr. Gering [Gewing] for severe and full justice. My Lord Generall that they might not exceed six. Mr Prin, that they might be twelve. After long debate the number seven agreed to be excepted out of pardon for life of those that sate upon the King 27th January, when sentence was past. But because we did not know which of them would be fixed on, order given to the serjeant to secure them all if he could, and all officers civill and military to be assisting to him.

Mr Prin then made an invective against William Lenthall as the most criminall of all others. My brother Finch relieved him from the pro[mp]t censure of the house likely enough to have fallen upon him.

Then order was given to secure Broughton, Phelps, Cooke, Dendy serjeant at mace, and Cornet Joice, the two executioners of the King if they could be knowne, and one Matthewes that said he was himselfe the executioner and had three hundred pound for it, although it is thought he did not do it.

Order also given to summon Robert Danvers, alias Villers, alias Lord Purbeck, to attend tomorrow morning to give accompt of those (words—*del.*) that he had moved Collonell Eyres to speake to Oliver Cromwell that he the said Villers might do the execution upon the King, which Collonell Eyres had said in the last parliament.

[*CJ*, viii, 25-6]

[f.8v]   *Tuesday, 29 May*

The King came into London. Between 6 and 7 the house of Commons attended him with their Speaker at the Banquetting House, where we all kissed his Majestie's hand.

[*CJ*, viii, 48-9]

43

Monday, 4 June

The house of Commons tooke the oaths of allegeance and supremacy and I among others. The Marquesse of Ormond as Lord High Steward administred it to some and then left commission with them to give it to the rest. This was the first time I ever tooke it.

[*CJ*, viii, 53-5]

Tuesday, 5 June

I kissed his Majestie's hand.

Friday, 8 June

Fryday before Whitsunday. The King touched those that were sick of the disease called the King's evill, about 100 in number. The [*sic*] Among which my beloved Heneage[1] was one. Benedicat Dominus.

[*CJ*, viii, 58-9]

[f.9, blank]

[f.9v]   *June*

The names of his Majestie's councell new sworne.
  The Lord Generall Monke
  The Lord Marquisse of Hartford
  Lord Marquisse of Ormond
  Sir Edward Hide, Lord Chancellor
  Earle of Southampton
  Earle of Leicester
  Earle of Lindsey
  Earle of Manchester
  Earle of Norwich
  Lord Viscount Say
  Lord Roberts
  Lord Wentworth
  Denzell Hollis
  Arthur Annesley
  Sir Anthony Ashley Cowper
  [1] Dering's fourth child (b. 1653).

44

Sir Edward Nicholas
Sir William Morris } secretaries

Lord Colepeper

[f.10] The names of those excepted out of the generall pardon.

John Lisle
William Say
Thomas Harrison
John Jones } These are excepted for life
Thomas Scot
Cornelius Holland
John Barkstead

William Hulet
Hugh Peters }

Andrew Broughton
John Cooke }
Edward Dendy

The twenty excepted for penalties not extending to life

1. William Lenthall
2. Sir Henry Vane
3. Oliver Saint John
4. William Burton
5. John Desborow
6. Sir Arthur Haslerigg
7. John Blackwell
8. Richard Deane

[9, 10, omitted]

11. Collonell Daniel Axtell
12. Serjeant Keeble
13. Charles Fleetwood
14. Christopher Peek, alderman
15. John Pine esq
16. John Lambert collonell
17. Major Creed
18. Phillip Nye } ministers
19. John Goodwin
20. Collonell Ralph Cobbett

[*CJ*, viii, 60-8]

[f.10v]   *Tuesday, 12 June*

Tuesday in Whitsunweeke. My brother Henry married Mistress Damaris Peake, eldest daughter to Mr Peake of Canterbury.

Sunday, 17 June

Trinity Sunday. I went to the King's Chappell at Whitehall where was the common prayer according to the rubrick. The reading psalmes were sung to the organ, as the hymnes also and doxologie. The litany was not read, nor usuall to be but on Wednesday and Fryday (I thinke). The Bishop, Warner, Bishop of Rochester, preached upon the words, so

45

teach us to number our dayes that we may apply our hearts unto wisedome.

The King and his two brothers present.

Tuesday, 19 June

My wife went into Kent by water to Gravesend, thence this night to Cosinton and intendeth tomorrow for Pluckley. With her went poore Heneage,[1] but with so great a paine in his head, as I know not how he will be able to endure the journey, though contrived as much as possible to his ease.

[ff.11,11v, blank]

[f.12]   ### Saturday, 7 July

I went into Kent, taking post horses to Rochester, and there my owne so coming the same night to Pluckley.

Thursday, 12 July

I went to Eastbridge and agreed with Henry Philpot to take the land and house there for three yeare from Michaelmas next at £212 per annum. Excepted out of this demise, two pieces called Chappell leaze and Bowles wyre, with other agreements.

Saturday, 14 July

I came from Pluckley to my cousin Smith at Chart Sutton.

Monday, 16 July

I came from thence to London, and at three of the clock went to the committee of religion, which sat till ten at night, and had candles brought in and twice blowen out by those that would not have them brought in, but at last were continued, and after some passion, the committee agreed in a vote, to discontinue the committee till 23 of October. And in the meane time to desire his Majestie to assemble such a number of divines as he thought fit to advise about church discipline.

[1] cf. entry for 8 June above.

[f.13] (Thursday—*del.*) *Saturday, 21 July 1660*

I received a commission from the Earle of Winchelsey to be one of the deputy Lieutenants in the county of Kent.

There were five in all:
Sir Thomas Peyton
Sir Roger Twisden
Sir Edward Hales
my selfe
Sir John Tufton

Wednesday, 25 July

It was thought fit to add three more[1] in respect of the weight and number of the occasions, and extent of the county. These three were pitched upon:
Richard Spencer esq
Sir Norton Knatchbull
Sir Anthony Aucher

Thursday, 26 July

Joined with the colledge of physicians at the anniversary feast instituted by Doctor Harvey and the invitation running Epulo philaestesio Harveyano. Dr Cox made the oration.

The same day I signed a bond of £300 to Captain Anthony Nowers for the payment of £159 10s on the [*blank*] day of January next.

Memorandum, this money was received by my cousin Christopher Dering and he had it all, and is first in the bond. I am but surety for it.

[f.13v]   *Saturday, 11 August*

Afternoon, we finished the bill for ministers at the committee, adding some provisos for securitie of those who had paid:
1. Their tithes to the ministers for the time being.
2. And for payment of arreares of fifths and for continuance of fifths, but nothing said of subscription.
3. And that all presented to the triers and refused without lawfull cause should be esteemed incumbents.
4. And that all who since the 25 December last had voluntarily re-linquished or yielded up their livings should not be restored, and all bargaines made by the present incumbent to yield up the living at Michaelmas to the sequestred to stand.

[1] *sc.*, as deputy lieutenants for Kent.

The same day in the evening my sweet niece pretty Moll Finch was buried at Sandersted. She died at Comb Thursday the 9th about 9 at night of an inflammation of the lungs or inward squincy.[1]

Sunday, *12 August*

Mr Calemy preached before the King at Whitehall.

Monday, *13 August*

We went over all the amendments and alteracions made by the Lords in the act of indemnitie. The clause which condemned Vane, Haselrigg, Lambert and Axtell for life as also Croxton, Waring, Wybert and Blackwell, we dissented to, preserving the first and for other penalties not extending to life, and (disabling—*del.*) dismissing the other.

Collonell Hacker we consented to be put in for life, and Sir Gilbert Pickering and Thomas Lister we consented to absolve.

The sixteen we had subjected to future penalties we consented to punish no otherwise than by rendering them incapable of future employment.

[f.14] Those twelve who had come in upon the proclamacion and had by the Lords been excepted for life, we did not agree with the Lords.

Those that are allready dead, and excepted by the Lords for life, we did not agree.

Concerning pardoning crimes in Ireland, we did not agree to the Lords.

All that gave or signed sentence in any illegall high court of justice to be disabled of bearing any office civill or military.

Afternoon

At the committee for sales.

Voted not to go by way of mortgage.

Voted to make generall rules for all purchasers and not to distinguish souldiers from others.

At the committee for the King's revenue.

Voted by the committee, that the revenue fit to maintaine the royall dignitie was twelve hundred thousand pounds per annum.

That the house should be moved to desire the King that no leases should be good if made by him for longer than one and thirty yeares or three lives, nor such as reserved lesse to the King than one full third part of the improved value yearly.

Every seaman in the fleet royal to cost the King £4 a month, reckon 14 moneths to the yeare. In this all charges are included.

[*CJ*, viii, 117-9]

---

[1] Mary Finch was second daughter of Sir Heneage Finch, Dering's brother-in-law.

[f.14v]   *Tuesday, 14 August*

We sent up the bill of indemnity with our agreement or disagreement to the Lords' amendments.

We received from the Lords the bill of judiciall proceedings, with severall alteracions.

We read the (bill for reli—*del.*) amendments to the bill of ministers. We began to debate the amendments to the bill for ministers and that of judiciall proceedings, but finding the debate long, adjourned till tomorrow.

The bill for Austin Skinner to cut off the entails of Tulsham Hall in Kent setled on Austin Skinner sonne to William Skinner (This da—*del.*) read yesterday and ordered to be ingrossed.

The bill for Sir Robert Dallison to cut off part of his estate this day read and committed.

The bill for making good colledge leases made by the master and fellowes de facto, read.

Afternoon

At the committee of (sales—*del.*) stating publique debt.

8 Lords and 16 Commoners went into the city to borrow £100,000 toward the present disbanding the army upon credit of the poll bill, but sans succes.

[f.15] Exceptions to the bill for setling Ministers.[1]

1. That ordinacion by presbiters without a bishop is not only tolerated for the time past, but goeth without observacion of the temper of those times, and is not restrained for the future, nor so much as discountenanced, but left equally estimable to the auncient episcopall ordinacion.

2. That the right of presentacion in the King is not preserved, those especially which he hath disposed of since he came into England, which is not fit for us to presse him to restraine.

3. That the word waiving, being a little uncertaine, should be left out, Dr. Hacket's case, and only the word resignation to continue.

4. The word constant refusall is in as relating to baptisms, and leaving it out at the eucharist.

[*CJ*, viii, 114-20]

[f.15v]   *Wednesday, 15 August*

An act for making Covent Garden a parish church and endowing it.
An act for encouragement of navagacion.
An order for prohibiting exportacion of wooll and fuller's earth.

---

[1] The (second) bill for the settling of Ministers in their Livings was reported on 14 Aug. and amendments were read, *CJ*, viii, 120. See also the entry for 11 Aug. above.

An act for continuing the excise bill 25 of December next, read twice. Pargeter and Alderman Atkins left out of the commissioners of excise and Wingate put in.

The amendments to the poll bill read and consented unto, all but the additionall names for Cornwall.

Consideracion of the poore maimed souldiers in Ely house.

The bill for Durham to be enabled to send burgesses to the parliament sent up to the Lords.

Afternoon

At the committee of sales, nothing at all done or resolved on, nor any question put.

At the committee for the forest of Deane. Sir John Winter gave accompt that he had hired of the King in 1640, 18,000 acres, part of that forest, at £16,000 per annum for 6 yeares, and £1,950 per annum afterwards: The timber in it was 61,500 tun of which fit for shipping in 9,000 trees, 15,000 tun

Loads of wood were 157,000

(He was—*del.*) Timber then estimated at 9s. per tun.

He paid £10,000 fine and held it but a yeare and halfe.

[f.16] The committee for the Earle of [Hert]ford to be restored to the title of Duke of Somerset, met, and the Lord Herbert sonne to the Marquess of Worcester produced a pattent under the Great Seale by which his father is made (Earle—*del.*) Duke of Somerset.

[*CJ*, viii, 120-2]

2

THE PERSONAL DIARY
OF SIR EDWARD DERING

29 March 1673 to 24 September 1675

Collections of Philip Blake Esq., MS F

Sir Edward Dering's Personal Diary
29 March 1673 to 24 September 1675

ff. 1-7
29 March-25 April 1673. Diary entries including those relating to Dering's loss of office (ff. 3v-7, see below, p. 55), and to the settlement of Ireland.

ff. 7v, 8
'Things to be done this Easter or Midsummer terme, 1673' (with subsequent annotation).

f. 8v
3 May 1673. Notes on an Irish Committee meeting.

ff. 9-13
5-7 May 1673. Entries mainly concerning the arrangement of a marriage between Charles Bargrave and Mr Buckford's daughter.

ff. 13v-15
8-14 May 1673. Marriage of Dering's daughter Mary and Thomas Knatchbull; payment of the marriage portion.

ff. 15v-17v
15-23 May 1673. The Bargrave marriage contract; Dering's tallies on the customs; viewing the lands at Barham.

f. 18
Note of subsidy payable on his lands, May 1673.

ff. 18v-19
24 May-3 June 1673. Miscellaneous entries.

ff. 19v-20
'Things to be done this Midsummer Term' [1673] (with subsequent annotation).

ff. 20v-25
4-18 June 1673. The Bargrave contract; the customs tallies; appearance as witness in the Rolls in Arnold v. Percivall et al.; the arrears due to Dering of his salary.

ff. 25v-26
Account of money owed to him and by him, 1 June 1673.

ff. 26v-27
20-28 June. Miscellaneous entries.

f. 27v
'A note of my stock this 24 June 1673'.

ff. 28-34v
2 July-26 Sept. Purchase of lands; the Bargrave contract; attendance at assizes and sessions; proposed marriage between Lord Colepeper's daughter and Dering's son; three monuments set up in Pluckley church; sale of hops, etc.

ff. 34v-36
30 Sept. 1673. Meeting with Peter du Moulin.

ff. 36v-45
'Reflexion necessaire sur la condicion de mon éstat', with a list of 'such things as may be beneficiall by way of improvement . . .' (see Introduction above, pp. 13-14)

[ff.45v-49 blank]

ff. 50-55v
16 Oct. 1673-17 Jan. 1674. Meeting of the Commons, 20 Oct., etc. (see p. 55 below); the Bargrave contract; death of Mr Justice Millward.

ff. 56-60
1 Feb.-24 April 1674. Entry into trust with Lord Keeper Finch; the assizes, etc.

ff. 60v-61
Debts owed, 10 April 1674.

ff. 61v-77
1 May-30 July 1674. Debts owed by Edward, his half-brother, to Sir Robert Viner; assizes, etc.

ff. 77v-78
'A Note of my stock and crops with the value', 24 August 1674.

ff. 78v-102v
6 Aug., 1674-24 July, 1675. Meeting of Parliament, 10 Nov. 1674 (pp. 55-6 below); meetings with ministers; discussions with Dr Nicholas Gibbon 'about his system of divinitie'; proposal that Dering should take charge of the young Lord Lexington; prorogation of parliament.

ff. 103-104
Notes of stock and crops, 20 July 1675.

ff. 104v-115v
28 July-24 Sept. 1675. Cousin Wilkinson's case at Maidstone assizes; marriage proposal between second Lord Lexington and a daughter of Lord Ogle; appointment as governor of the Merchant Adventurers (see pp. 20-1 above), etc.

ff. 121v-135
Abstract of accounts, 1665-1673.

f. 137v-138
Account with Cousin Millward, 1672-1673.

f. 138v-139
Account with Henry Philpot, 1672-1674.

f. 139v
Account with Henry Filby, 15 Oct. 1673.

f. 140v
Lists of classical pseudonyms, 20 Sept. 1673 and 20 Sept. 1674.

[f.5v]   *Saturday, 19 April 1673*

This evening about six at night, I received a note from my Lord
Arlington to waite upon the King and to deliver up the seale.[1] Sir Thomas
Strickland being at Hampsted, I were forced to go alone to Court which
I did about 8 this night, and sending in word that I waited without
according to his Majestie's command signified to me by my Lord
Arlington. The King presently called for me in and went into his closet
whether I followed him.

He there told me he had now resolved to dispose of the Privy Seale
into a single hand as he had done the Treasurie. That he was very well
satisfied with our carriage in it, and should be mindfull of us with the
very first opportunity, and many expressions of his favourable intentions toward us, but mencioning nothing in particular for us, and after
such replyes as did become [me] to make to such gracious expressions, I
left the seale in his hands which he presently locked up in his closet.

[f.50]   *Monday, 20 October 1673*

We met at the parliament house. The Speaker came at halfe an hour
past ten. The Black Rod was expected as soon as he, for it was known we
should be prorogued that day.

As soon as the Speaker was come the house cried to the chair to the
chair; which he making no haste to do, some said if he would not take
[f.50v] the chair, another should, Mr Powle saying, if he would not take
the chaire he would speake to him where he was, he was forced to take
the chaire. When immediatly Mr Powle moved that an addresse might
be made to the King that the intended match of the Duke of Yorke
with the Princesse of Modena might not be consummated. This was
seconded by Coll.Birch and followed by Sir Thomas Clarges and Sir
Robert Howard, and voted without much opposicion, that the privy
councellers of the house should acquaint his Majestie that it is the
humble desire of the house that the said intended match may not be
consummated. Soon after, the Black Rod was at the doore, and we
being called up to the Lords' house were prorogued to the 27 instant.[2]

[f.83]   *Tuesday, 10 November 1674*

This day the parliament met according to the prorogacion made the
24 February last.[3] In our house there was nothing done or said, the
Speaker not taking the chaire till the Black Rod was at door, as indeed

---

[1] The Mandamus, annotated by Dering, is BL Stowe 745, f. 71.
[2] See the fuller entry for this day in *PD*, 149-151.
[3] cf. *CJ*, ix, 314.

he ought not to do upon a prorogacion, because it being a new session can not take beginning till the King by himselfe or by his commission hath given a beginning to it and opened it.

In the Lords' house[1] was only performed the ceremonie of admitting some new Lords, some by creacion, viz. the Duke of Lauderdale made an English earle; some by promocion, as the Viscount Latimer, Lord Treasurer, as Earle of Danby, the Lord Baron Powis as Earle of Powis; and some by discent, as Lord Gray of Warke by his father's death, since the last session. The Lord Norris had his writ, but did not come to house.

[1] cf. *LJ*, xii, 650-1.

3

THE PARLIAMENTARY DIARY
OF SIR EDWARD DERING

13 April to 5 June 1675

House of Lords Record Office Historical Collections, 85/1

The Parliamentary Diary of Sir Edward Dering

13 April to 5 June 1675

Tuesday, 13 April

The house met at halfe an houre past ten the Black Rod being come to the door. The Speaker took the chair. When returned he read the King's speech to us, but for my Lord Keeper's, who indeed had not given him a copie, and he said he could not remember it, but must referr himselfe to the gentlemen of the house who were there.[1]

After some pause, Sir Thomas Meeres moved that we might proceed to name our committees, as was usuall in beginnings of parliament.

Sir Baynam Thogmorton said there was something first to be done, which was to give his Majestie thanks for his gracious speech, seconded by Secretary Coventry. This was opposed by Sacheverill, my Lord Cavendish, Mr Russell and many others, Mr Powell, Mr Waller, Sir John Coventry, Sir John Mallott, Garway, Sir William Hickman. The reasons they gave that

1. It did justify the ministers in all they had done since our last adresse if we gave thanks now,
2. that they did not desire the severe execucion of the lawes against papists which is the chief part of the speech, Sir John Mallet,
3. that it would preclude all debate concerning the altering or amending the laws for religion if we gave thanks for the execution those which are

After allmost 3 hours' debate, the Question was put for adjourning the debate.

The Yeas who went out were 91
The Noes who staid in were 180

And soon after they came to a resolve to give the King thanks for his gracious expressions in his speech for preserving the established religion and our properties [f.1v] according to law, and for calling us together at this time for that purpose, which last clause was added by Sir Robert Howard.

A bill then read for indowing of small vicaridges.

Then we proceeded to name the 3 grand committees of (trade—*del.*) religion, grievance, and courts of justice and afterwards to grant writs for the vacant places by death or promocion, and then nominated our committee of election.

It was moved by my Lord Ogle and seconded by my selfe that the writs should go out for the countie and citie of Durham, which seemed allowd by the house, that my Lord Keeper might send them out, with-

---

[1] The Lord Keeper's speech is printed *in extenso*, *LJ*, xii, 653-5.

out order of the house, but at the rising of the house Mr Sacheverill moved that that business might be referred to the committee of elections, which was so ordered.

Tuesday in the afternoon the committee of election sat and appointed severall days for hearing.

[*CJ*, ix, 314-6; Finch, *sub* 13 April 1675]

Wednesday, 14 April

Mr Sacheverill told us of 3 records he had found and examined in the originalls, which he desired might be read: 2 Richard II, 26 Edward III, 4 Henry IV. All very materiall, and the first, as he conceived, an act of parliament of high importance, being that no parliament should be dissolved or prorogued till all bills and peticions are answered.

The house ordered the records themselves to be brought to the house the next day.

The Speaker told us of a letter he had received from Sir John Pretti-man, a member of parliament, who was in restraint in the King's Bench.

The house ordered the marshall of the King's Bench [f.2] to bring his prisoner to the barr of house of Commons to morrow morning with the cause of his committing, for they would not order his discharge because he might be in for felonie or treason for ought appeared.

After this they fell upon the Duke of Lauderdale, that we had last session voted him a person obnoxious and dangerous to the govern-ment, [that he was now—*del.*] and made an address to remove him from the King and court, that he was still there, and returned from Scotland in triumph, and since made a peer of England, and £3,000 per annum pencion bestowed upon him.

This was aggravated by Sir John Coventry, Sir Tho. Littleton, Mr Powell and others.

After the Question, urged for a second addresse to be made to the King against him.

Many preferred the way of impeachment to the Lords, of which mind were [*blank*] and Sir William Coventry. Sir Thomas Lee replied he thought, we could not go that way because the offence we complained of was pardoned by the late act of indemnitie.

Sir William Coventrie upon comparing the time, being satisfied it was so, said he recanted his opinion and waved the way of impeachment.

Mr Secretary Coventry, Lord Anchram and Mr Demahoy spoke to excuse and denay but Anchram confest the words were spoken, which the house ref[l]ected upon. Much more spoken concerning common fame, which was agreed to be a good cause for [f.2v] Quest[ion]ing any man but not for condemning him, but the Question being earnestly preferred and the Speaker ready to put it, I stood up and moved as well as I could, as indeed I was divided between my care of the justice and of the honour of the house so I (entered on—*del.*) went not about to justify him, but only to say that there was this difference between our last vote and this, that he was then absent, and at such a distance as we could not send for him, being then in Scotland; that if he had been heare we would doubtless have heard him as we did the Duke of Buckinghamshire and Lord Arlington; that now he is hear, if he do desire we could not fairly refuse it; that the consequence of that were to[o] great and might reach every man there; that to retract our vote without hearing any cause for it were as unreasonable on the other side. and therefore I moved they would go on with what they intended, only inverting the method of it; that whereas other gentlemen had moved they should first make their vote that he was obnoxious and dangerous to the commonwealth and then intended to order a committee to draw up reasons for it, they would please to order the committee first to bring in their reasons and then proceed to the vote afterwards; that by this meanes he would have an opportunitie to be heard if he desired and then he would either give us satisfaction to what lay upon him, or we might proceed upon addresse in such a way as might suit both with our honour and our justice.

[*CJ*, ix, 316-7; Finch, *sub* 14 April 1675]

[The folded sheet numbered '2' by Dering is missing; it probably included diary entries for the latter part of 14 April and the beginning of 15 April.]

[f.3]   *Thursday, 15 April [concluding an account*
of a meeting at Hampden House[1]]

3[2]

after this informacion finding nothing in all this which could justly render my Lord Treasurer obnoxious to any censure in parliament we agreed to divert it if we could, and that the best way of diverting it was to ingage the house in other businesse; that the best businesse to be gone upon for the Kingdome and the (most—*del.*) likeliest also to ingage the house warmely in it, was matter of religion, and severall things and methods of argument being proposed, my Lord Treasurer asking my opinion, I concurrd with it, so that we did not interest the nonconformists in the matter, nor yet came to such a particular way as

---

[1] Hampden House occupied the site of the present Downing Street. The Duke of Buckingham and Danby had each lived there previous to its demolition by Sir George Downing in 1683 (*Survey of London*, xiv (1931), c. 9).

[2] This number and subsequent numbers placed centrally represent Dering's original numbering of his folded sheets.

might be disgusted but to open the door to the dispute in which I did not doubt but they of the other side would fall in to the debate. This being resolved, it was concluded Sir Joseph Tredinham should begin the mocion and I should second it, and the rest should then keep it up till the day was spent.

Fryday, 16 April

This morning after some ordinarie business done Sir Joseph Tredinham began accordingly and after that I did second him, making a generall discourse of the necessitie of doing something upon it, of the reasonable-nesse of doing something at this time, the King's inviting us to it, the people's expectacion of it, our own giving the King thankes for calling us together at this time for that purpose, and after a pretty long discourse concluded with my hopes that some worthy gentlemen of the house had so well ripened and digested their thoughts as they had something to present us with about it. If not, I moved that in the first place they would appoint a committee to inspect the penall laws against poperie and report us the state of them as they now are, and what defects they did observe in them.

I confined my mocion to poperie, as thinking the whole businesse of religion too great a work [f.3v] for a short session as this was like to be, and therefore we should looke to secure ourselves against what was the greatest danger and the most formidable enemie of it, which were the papists.

That if that were yet to large we might restraine ourselves to a consideracion of a more spedy way of conviction which was that which was most wanting, and that it was my desire chiefly to prevent the grouth of them for the future rather than to punish them that are allready so.

This discourse was well enough liked by the house, and then Sir Charles Wheeler stood up and made a speech of an hour long of great circumference of discourse, offering us very many things which he thought necessarie to be considered in matter of religion, and at last mencioned the case of our King's marriage and the educacion of the children as protestants.

This was presently taken up, and prest hard by Sir Thomas Clarges, Sir Thomas Littleton and Mr Powell, that Sir Charles Wheeler should be comanded to draw such a bill.

Sir Edmund Jennings said it was no reason that one member should be obliged to such a taske which would prove hard enough for us all, the whole house, and at last Sir Charles Wheeler said he wondered they should think of beginning in the first place with what he mencioned in the last, and that he did not intend any act for that purpose. So that going off, it was moved the house would turne themselves into a committee of the whole house to consider of matters of religion. [f.4] Which being done, and Sir Thomas Meeres in the chair, much was spoken to and fro and little resolved but that we should proceed in the debate the next day, which was very well for our purpose.

[*CJ*, ix, 317-8]

Saturday, *17 April*

At first, a bill for continuing an act for exporting of leather, now near expiring, was tendered by Sir John Bramston, with many farther and new things in it. Mr Jones said it was a greater tax than £70,000 per mensem on the Kingdome, but it was read once, and ordered to be read again in a full house.

Then the Speaker left his chair and we proceeded on the consideracion of religion and resolved one bill should be brought in for hindering papists from sitting in either house of parliament.

That another bill should be prepared to prevent growth of poperie, that therein should be a considerable reward for any would discover a popish priest, that it should be paid by all that did remain in the house where the priest did officiate. That he should be deemed a priest who did say masse or did officiate heare, or in any part, of the office of a priest according to the rite and use of the church of Rome, or had been seen so to do beyond the seas, unless such priest have been since reconciled to the church of England, and that these votes should not prejudice the lawes now in being against popish priests.

Such was the expression though very imperfect.

Then we adjourned the debate till Tuesday.

[f.4v] Saturday night we had a meeting again at Hamden house, where my Lord Treasurer was, and told us he would be there every night about 8 of the clock while the parliament did sit, and should be glad to meet us there. There met Mr Peregrine Bertie, Sir John Bramston, Sir Richard Wiseman, Sir Humphrey Winch, Mr Cholmondley, Mr Cheney, my Lord Alington and my selfe.

[*CJ*, ix, 318]

Sunday, *18 April*

I dined at Lambeth at the consecracion dinner of Dr Brideoke to be Bishop of Chichester, and Dr William Floyd to be Bishop of Landaffe. The consecracion sermon preached by Mr Sharpe, Chaplain to my Lord Keeper.

That night we met again at Hamden house, where we agreed that if the bill for making levying of (treason—*del.*) money otherwise than by act of parliament to be treason should be brought in the next day, as we expected, it would not be safe to endeavour to throw it out the first reading: which is hard for any bill, but more hard for a bill which bore the pretence of the publique good, and which had the last session past up to ingrossment, but rather to speake only to the weightinesse and importance of it, and to get what time we could for the second reading.

And if the mocion of recalling the King's forces out of France should be started, that it would not be possible to over beare it, or resist it, and therefore better to let it passe. Both which was agreed upon.

[f.5]   4

I then told my Lord Treasurer that there were 2 bills which would find us businesse enough for this session, and yet be extremely gratefull (to—*del.*) both to the house and to the nacion in generall, and that it was usefull that they should come from his frends. That they may see they do mind the publique good. And that was the bill for a registry of deeds of land, and a bill against brandy.

Monday, 19 April

A bill for preventing the sending the subject prisoner to Ireland, Scotland, Guernsey, Jersey or any foreign part where Habeas Corpus doth not run, presented by Sir Thomas Lee and read the first time.

A bill for graunting Habeas Corpus where any one is committed, presented by Sir Eliab Harvey and read the first time.

A bill against exportacion of wooll, read the second time and committed.

A bill for preventing the levying of money otherwise than by act of parliament or for longer time than it is graunted by act of parliament, presented by Sacheverell and read the first time. Sir William Hickman moved for the second reading on Fryday, but upon debate ordered to be on Monday next. Memo. in this bill of Habeas Corpus there were some penalties which ought not to be, for bills ought to be brought in with blanks to be filled up by the house, or at least by the committee after the second reading. The Speaker told us of this, but then with a pen dashed it out at the table. I took notice of it at the doing that it was the first time I had seen a bill mended upon the first reading, but I said nothing to it. But next day Sir Thomas Meeres did reflect upon it. The Speaker said it had been often done. Sir Thomas Meeres denied, and the Speaker replied no farther, and I believe he was in the wrong. [f.5v] After this Sir Thomas Littleton began a set speech against the growing greatnesse of the French,[1] how dangerous and formidable he was, what enlargement he had made of his empire in Flanders, Germany, Alsace, the Franch Comte and elsewhere, now threatning all

---

[1] *sc.*, King.

Secelie, but concluded that he did not say this to ingage us in a warr with France, but only to forewarn us, that we might not at least lend our owne hands to raise him so high, and therefore that an address should be made to the King to call home his forces that are now there.

Secretarie Coventrie moved that we should forbear this address, for it was not in the power of the King to call those home, they were now under the King of France his pay, and he might hang them if they should come away.

Secretarie Williamson said that it was under consideracion allready and some care was taken in it last night that the King of France was in no such grandeur as was apprehended, that he had got but two tounes by this warr and they had cost him fourscore millions of money, and that the King of (France—*del.*) Sweden had now interposed to procure from the Emperor good condicions for the protestants in Hungarie.

Sir William Coventrie replied upon them, that it could not be thought that our minesters would let so many thousand of his Majestie's subjects go over without making condicions for them. If they had done so, they deserved to be questioned for it.

That otherwise they were sold to perfect slaverie, if they could not returne when the King commanded them, and they desired it.

[f.6] That the case of the protestants in Hungarie was very remote. He would be glad to hear there were as much care taken for them in France.

That if it be not safe to provoke the King of France now that he hath so many enemies in the field, what would it be when he shall have gained a victorie or made a peace. That this could be no breach of articles nor just cause of warr, but would rather keep of the peace, by strengthening the hands of the confederats against him.

Sir Thomas Meeres and others to the same purpose, and so it was voted.

Garaway desired that a representacion might be drawn up of the state of this Kingdome in reference to France, but this went off, as it was fit it should, for there is so little difference between a publique representacion by parliament, and a remonstrance that I were not plea[s]ed with the mencion of it.

[*CJ*, ix, 318-9; G, iii, 1-9]

Tuesday, 20 April

1. The bill for Sir Francis Compton read and committed.
2. The bill for repairing of churches read and committed.
3. A bill tendered by Sir Philip Warwick for preventing the increase of new buildings about Westminster read and long debated, and the whole sense of the house going for a bill of this nature, yet they

voted this bill to be withdrawn and a committee appointed to bring in a new bill for that purpose.

I think that what offended them was the power of licencing, reserved to the King.

[f.6v] Then we entered upon the debate of priviledge in the case of Sir John Prettiman who is in custodie in the King's Bench upon execucion for debt and taken in time of prorogacion.

The arguments in this case were very many and the debate held very long. Prescidents there were none directly in the case. The case of Thorp in 31 Hen. 6, taken in execucion in time of prorogacion and not delivered, though at that time Speaker of parliament, was all that could be found, and that being 220 years agon, and nothing like it ever since, and done by the power of the Duke of Yorke and under colour of the King's debt, to remove him and put a better man for this purpose in his place, he then designing to claim the crowne, was no great proof of a right.

That we have allways taken the law to be otherwise, especially since the statute of King James.

That there is no materiall difference, between being in execucion and being in prison (of—*del.*) in meane processe, and this last was allowed, why not the first.

That it is no reason, the countie or borough should loose their representatives. If it be said, they must look who they employ, it is answered that private men may as well look who they trust.

[f.7]   5

That the best men of estates might be excluded by this meanes, for by common practice a man chargeth what he will in personall actions, suppose £40,000 though the debt be not £200. Then they may stand not only upon good baile but freemen of the city or corporacion, which few men can get.

No doubt but they had a thought, that the time might come when the King might committ some member, as he had done Elliot and others, tertio Caroli, and they would have a prospect how to get out.

At last the Question being put for agreeing with the committee. The Noes that went forth were 67. The Yeas who staid in were 143. So they ordered Sir John Prettiman should have his priviledg and the serjeant should go with his mace (*deletion*) to fetch him to his service in the house.

[*CJ*, ix, 319-20; G, iii, 9-15]

Wednesday, 21 April

The bill for repairing churches read and committed.

The bill for exportacion of leather read and committed.

The house turnd into a grand committee to consider of the businesse of religion. The greatest debate about a register or no register for the papists. Sir William Coventrie spoke against it: Sacheverill, Garaway, Temple, Weld, etc. for it. Toward the end of the debate, and the Question ready to be put, I desired before they put that Question for a register, those gentlemen who were so much for it would clearly open what they intended by it. For all the discourse being of a voluntarie register that papists should come in and register themselves, I could not yet see but it must be either useless or dangerous, uselesse if they meant to keep on foot the penall laws now in being against the papists, and dangerous if they did not. [f.7v] Uselesse if they did, it being most apparant that no man would discover himselfe a papist if by so doing he should subject himselfe to the penalties of the laws, they being no lesse than praemunire, disabilitie to bear offices, and even high treason itselfe, according to the severall statutes.

On the other side, if they meant to repeale all the laws if a papist by boldly owning himself such, should be free thereby from all penalties all incapacities whatsoever, if the oathes of allegeance and supremacie, the late test by act of parliament made and provided must all be laid aside. It was then the greatest encouragement to turne papists that ever was. It was not warranted by the power given by the house, which was to consider how to prevent the growth of poperie, not how to encourage it, and secure it. That if ever we should be so unhappie as to see this house disposed to countenance papists, it must begin where we begin, that is in repealing the laws against it. I had reason therefor humbly to move them to consider well before they did this thing, and that they who were for it, would clearly tell us what ease they meant to give to those who should register themselves, and what lawes they intended to repeale, what penalties to continue and what not, for till I knew that, I could not give my vote for a register, being resolved not to pull downe my house till I had another to put my head in, nor [f.8] not to alter at one breath so many and so important lawes, till I knew what we should have in the roome of them.

This I think helpt to lay aside that question concerning the register, and the committee did rise ordering to move the house that a bill should be brought in upon the heads allready agreed on the 2 days before: adding only a clause to hinder discharges of indictments upon the attorney generall's nolle prosequi.

The house being sate, that was agreed.

Then Mr Powle offered an accompt from my Lord Lauderdale's committee, which was read, being the confession of one Dr Burnet against my Lord Lauderdale,[1] which was read though after one of the clock and the debate of it adjourned to Fryday.

[1] cf. Finch, 21 April 1675.

In the afternoon the house went up with the Speaker to Whitehall to present the vote of the house that his Majestie would be pleased to call back his forces out of the service of the French King. To which his Majestie answered, it was a matter of great weight, and he would consider of it and give them an answer.

[*CJ*, ix, 320-1; G, iii, 15-9]

[6]

[f.9]   *Thursday, 22 April*

This day we read Mr Sacheverill's records again, but there appearing nothing in them we laid them aside.

Sir William Coventrie delivered in a bill that no parliament man should heareafter beare any office at home nor be sent embassador abroad. If he did accept any, then his place in parliament to be void and a new writ to issue, but that he might be chosen again, (if—*del.*) with an excepcion for the offices of deputy lieutenants, justices of Peace, and commission of sewers.

This was read the first time and upon a question for the second reading the house divided. The Yeas went out and were 88. The Noes staid in, 67. So it was carried for a second reading but that to be in a full house, after ten a clock.

[*CJ*, ix, 321-2; G, iii, 19-24]

Fryday, 23 April

This day we sat till halfe an hour past 3. The businesse concerned the addresse against the Duke of Lauderdale drawn up by Mr Powell and Sir Thomas Littleton. Which being read, and part of it voted to stand, it was moved by Sir Robert Thomas that Dr Burnet, who had intimated he could say something in this businesse, might be called in. Which he was. He being desired to tell his knowledge, first desired the judgment of the house whether he ought to discover what he heard in private discourse with my Lord, [f.9v] and he being withdrawn, and the sense of the house running to heare him, as it allways will doe where there is newes in the case, he was called in again, and there told us that in September '73 he was with my Lord Lauderdale and talking of the declaracion in matters ecclesiastical. He said my Lord asked him if Scotland would assist the King if he should desire it. Burnet answered he thought not. My Lord replied, he thought they would, and the coming into England would invite many. Burnet telling him they at that distance could not well see into matters heare, particularly how it came that the King should publish his declaracion and afterwards declare he would stand by it, and then presently recall it, my Lord replied Hinc illae lachrymae, they have all deserted the King. This was the substance of what he said in 3 times coming in, yet saying once that the words did not relate to the declaracion. When the words were to be wrote downe and the clerke fumbling much in taking them, and the house not agreeing upon it, was desired he might write them downe himselfe, but then whether at the table or at the barr or in the lobby. At last it was agreed he should be called in to (what—*del.*) heare what the clerke had wrote and have a pen given him at the barr to mend it. And that being done he was called in and saying the paper was not right taken, he tooke the pen and without saying a word immediately wrote [f.10] that my Lord said hinc illae lachrymae, they have all deserted the King but my selfe and my Lord Clifford. Next, this being laid together, that this was upon descourse of the declaracion for religion, that the army was raised in (the—*del.*) Scotland at the same time, that my Lord was desirous the army should march into England, and that for some purposes in which my Lord Clifford and he were agreed though others seceded, that is to maintain that declaracion by force, made such an impression in the house, and indeed a surprize by the soudainesse of it, that no man did open his mouth afterward in behalf of my Lord, but they put the question for the addresse and for another day to consider farther of this matter informed by Burnet, and carried both without the least opposicion.

[*CJ*, ix, 322-3; G, iii, 24-33]

Saturday, 24 April

This day Mr Pepys by order gave us accompt of the state of the Navy, of the severall ships and force, that upon the whole of ships, about 20 guns a ship, we were 45 below the number of the Dutch and 4 below the French.

That being a little dilated upon and referred till Tuesday next to consider.

It was moved by Sir Thomas Littleton that some care might be taken to prevent the antecipacions and farming of the customes [f.10v] and that we would vote that it should not be done, that being indeed the revenue appropriate to the defence of the sea. It was a little opposed, but Sir Robert Howard proposing that it might be by way of addresse to the King, and that seconded by Sir William Coventry and not opposed by any to any purpose, it so past.

That an humble addresse be made to his Majestie that no farther anticipacion or charge be laid upon the customes of England or Ireland, it being to the disservice of his Majestie and the Kingdome.

[*CJ*, ix, 323; G, iii, 34-40]

Monday, 19 [rectius 26] April

After some private bills read, at ten of the clock the house being pretty
full, the bill for making it high treason to levy money otherwise than by
act of parliament was read and committed. The objections against this
bill are many and great and unanswerable and it was much wondered
that it past so easily to the committment, and nothing said against it.

But the truth was that at a meeting the night before between Sir
Charles Wheeler, Sir Richard Wiseman, Sir Philip Musgrave, Sir
Joseph Tredinham and myselfe and some others, I were of opinion that
we should let it passe in that manner.

1. For it is agreed by all of us that this is a very ill bill and can never be
   made good.
2. That it was to no purpose to dresse those cucumbers that we resolved
   to throw out of doores.
3. That the worst time to attempt throwing out a bill of four times we
   have to offer at it, is when it comes to be committed, because
   every thing is said against any part of it, is an argument for the
   committing it not for rejecting it, for if the scope of it be good, every
   part of it may then be allowed.
4. That if we should speak against the penalties of high treason in it,
   and they should then change it for a praemunire, it would reconcile
   many to the bill, who are now frighted at the name of high treason,
   and yet the bill would still be a very ill bill.
5. That if we set to it now one effect must follow, either to heat the other
   partie or to discourage our owne, as we did or did not carry the
   question, both which were inconvenient, especially considering that
   the Question about getting money for increase of the Navy was
   to come on the very next day to which it was fit to reserve our
   forces entire.

And these reasons prevailed, and it was resolved accordingly, and it
was committed, and not one committee named by our side.

[f.11v] Then Mr William Russell began a speech against my Lord
Treasurer concluding, after a generall exaggeracion of crimes and
misdemeanours, that he thought it fit to impeach him to the Lords.

Then Sir Samuel Bernardiston tendered a paper containing a charge
of high crimes and misdemeanours against my Lord Treasurer in 7
articles, which being read at the table, Mr Powle stood up and desired us
(then—*del.*) the house to proceed upon them to impeach my Lord
Treasurer, for he was ready to prove the articles.

Much was said to urge the house to proceed immediatly, but that
seemed unreasonable, for they who could prove it might be supposed
not to have their testimonies ready. So it was resolved to proceed the

next day, allthough that day was appointed for consideracion of the state of the Navy.

The main question was whether they who offered the impeachment should be obliged to produce the proofes to the house, or whether upon their undertaking the proofs, it should be sufficient for us to send up an impeachment.

The practice in my Lord Clarendon's case was so. To which it was answered, that was in case of treason where we could not be too secret nor too speedy in what concerned the King's person, for witnesses once knowne might be diverted, but in misdemeanour, which this is, the reason was otherwise, and so had the practise been in my Lord Mordaunt's case. And that when an impeachment was carried up to the Lords not the single [f.12] honour of those who have undertaken it, but the honour of the whole house is ingaged in it, and therefore we ought to know upon what good grounds we go.

All my Lord Treasurer's friends were for having the proofes produced to the house, and so it was carried.

That night we met at Wallingford house with my Lord Treasurer, and heard what answers he could give to every particular, which are to my thoughts very satisfactory.

[*CJ*, ix, 324-5; G, iii, 40-9; Finch, 26 April 1675]

Tuesday, 27 April

This day we proceeded upon the first pattent objected against my Lord Treasurer, which was that of Mr Monteney, Treasurer of the Excise. A long debate of it, and at last we came to a vote that we saw no ground from that pattent to impeach my Lord.

In the afternoon was at the committee of elections. The case between Sir Lionell[1] Jenkins and Mr Hales which had depended above two years before the committee, the house having forborne to heare it because most of the time of this sitting Sir Lionell had been abroad at Collon and so could not be summoned.

Mr Hales objected, 1, want of notice of the time of election, keeping out some which offered their votes and were refused, and building two houses for the towne and putting two poor children apprentices. All which was clearly answered by Sir Lionell Jenkins and his election adjudged good.

[*CJ*, ix, 325; G, iii, 49-56]

[f.12v] ## *Wednesday, 28 April*

This day we proceeded again upon the first article against my Lord

---
[1] *sic*, for Leoline.

Treasurer, but on another pattent which was to one Mr Kent as receiver of the excise. The pattent was opened, and appeared to be done at the desire of Sir Stephen Fox, to enable him the better to pay the King's forces which he undertakes to do. That the Chancellor of the Exchequer was acquainted with the progresse of it and approved the substance of it though he put a caveat against it at the Great Seale. Sir John Duncomb was in the house and gave an accompt of it, but said he had moved the King as to what he thought unreasonable in it, and was to be heard there upon it.

For my Lord Treasurer it appeared:

That he had no benefit at all by this pattent.

That he had acquainted the King with it and the Chancellor of the Exchequer with it.

That it past every word under the King's attorney's hand.

That it was past but during pleasure, that so it might be recalled when ever anything did appear in it illegall or inconvenient.

After long debate coming to the Question it was hotly disputed whether the Question should be that heare was ground for impeachment against my Lord Treasurer

or—This pattent was illegall and contrarie to the course of the Exchequer.

The first was desired by my Lord Treasurer's friends and indeed much the most proper question

[f.13]   8

for we had no consideracion of the pattent of it selfe but it was brought in merely as evidence against my Lord Treasurer, and voting the pattent illegall advanced nothing at all against my Lord Treasurer, who was not (to—*del.*) supposed to know the law, but was discharged if he had the advise of the King's learned counsell in it. But on the other side, the condemning it as illegall, did arraigne the King's counsell and the Lord Keeper who had past it, and this without hearing, so that by voting it illegall, we condemned those we had not heard, and did nothing at all to the person before us. And it was said that (But after a—*del.*) the condemning the pattent as illegall did in some sort reflect upon my Lord Treasurer, though they said they intended it not. Whereas the clering my Lord Treasurer did in no sort justify the pattent, which we offered to take into consideracion as soon as my Lord Treasurer's articles were over.

But by wrangling and obstinacie, and it maybe because we thought my Lord Treasurer's partie strong enough, they gained the putting that Question. But that being consented to, it was moved by Sir Thomas Lee to amend the Question and to leave out the word illegall. When presently Mr Garaway steps up and desires those words of being contrarie to the course of exchequer might be left out, and that being seconded, it then became a question again which of the two amendments (had— *del*.) should bee put at (last the words—*del*.) [f.13v] at last it was agreed the Question should be whether these words

contrarie to the course of the Exchequer should be part of the Question

and the house being divided the

Noes went forth and were 181
The Yeas staid in were 105

so those words were left out.

Then the word illegall was put, whether that should stand in the Question, and carried without division, it should not.

Then the Question was, what was become of the Question, there being now nothing left of it but those words This pattent is —. Some would have gone to the former question, this being now lost being become no sense. Others said when any words were put out, the next question is, for words to be put in their place, to which it was said it must be of words which had been formerly debated, but not alltogether new. Mr Stockton moved, After the word is might be added — a good and lawfull pattent. At last Mr Cheney helped us out by adding This pattent is — not a sufficient ground of impeachment against my Lord Treasurer. And so it past.

And then we past a vote upon the whole first article that there was not matter in that article to ground an impeachment upon against my Lord Treasurer.

[*CJ*, ix, 326, G, 57-51[1]]

[f.14]   *Thursday, 29 April*

This day we proceeded upon the bill for granting of Habeas Corpus which was committed.

Then we came upon the bill tendered by Sir William Coventry for to enact that if any parliament man did heareafter accept any office his place in parliament should be void, and a new writ should go out to chuse another in his place, with only a proviso that he might be chosen again if the people pleased.

There were not many that spoke for this bill but very many against it.

Upon the accompt of the injustice it did to all members of parliament to deprive them of the King's favour.

The inequality of letting them who have them keep them, and exclude others from the same freedome.

The unreasonablenesse to place all the offices of the Kingdome into the hands of the Lords.

1 vol. iii of Grey has duplicated pagination for 49-64, then proceeding to 81.

But especially upon the reproach it cast upon all men that no man could faithfully serve the King and yet discharge his duty to his country, for if this bill passe, all men must think that to be the sense of the parliament.

[f.14v] It came at last to a question whether the bill should be committed and upon the Question the Yeas went forth, 113

The Noes staid in, 145

The next question the Speaker said ought to be for rejecting the bill, but Sir Thomas Meeres said it ought to be for engrossing. The Speaker said that might hold where the debate before was between ingrossing and committing, but not where all the debate was for casting it out.

So it was carried to reject the bill.

An order was made to summon my Lord Mayor of London, Sir Robert Viner to give evidence to morrow, and 4 more, against my Lord Treasurer. This was at the desire of Mr Powle and Sir Samuel Barnardiston.

At the rising of the house it was (agreed—*del.*) offered by Sir John Hanmer, that some others might be ordered to attend as witnesses for my Lord Treasurer, but that would not be granted, they urging that they were in the nature of a grand jury which were to receive evidence for the King but not against him. I thought it not best to insist upon it, but leave it to the hearing rather than to discover who my Lord's witnesses were and so we adjourned.

[*CJ*, ix, 326-7; G, iii, 51-8; Finch, 29 April 1675]

[f.15]   9

Friday, 30 April

Sir George Downing took occasion to open the mischief we suffered by the French trade, saying that the 4 commodities of wine, brandy, silk stuffes and linen, any one of them brought more into England than all we carried thither could pay for, so that we lost in money by that trade at least £800,000 per annum, which must of necessitie quickly beggar us. And refered it to a committee to consider and report the state of the trade of England with France.

Sir Samuel Barnardiston opened to us that the decay of our cloth trade was from the act prohibiting the importing of Irish catell, which had put that kingdom of increasing their stock of sheep, which is done to that degree that now there is more wooll bred in England and Ireland than all Europe can consume, and so it must be a danger, but the house did not much shew inclinacion to repeale that act.

Then we had the Mayor of Canterbury before us and five of his brethren upon their knees at the barr. They had been sent for in custody upon a complaint of breach of priviledge by Serjeant Hardress, their

Recorder, and now upon their submission after a week's imprisonment they are discharged, paying their fees and restoring the Recorder to his place.

Now that is a high straine of our priviledge, it being plain that the Recorder is an officer of the corporacion's, and by expresse words in their charter removable at pleasure, and that they may chuse another. Yet it seemes the sense of the house that no possession of a parliament man, how injustly got soever, or how arbitrarily possest, shall be removed during time of priviledge, so that by the judgment in Prettiman's case for our persons and by this of the Mayor of Canterbury for our possessions we seeme now reasonably well secured.

Then we went upon the second article against my Lord Treasurer which concernd the businesse of Mrs Hide, and after long debate to and fro and very confused, neither side well agreeing among themselves what they would have, the debate centred about the calling in of the witnesses against my Lord Treasurer that were at the door, viz. Emorton himself and my Lord Mayor. Much was said for and against calling them in.

[f.15v] At last I ventured to say that I thought this debate was allready adjudged, it having been the whole scope of the debate on Monday upon delivering in of the articles, when it was resolved to heare the proofes of the fact as well as the nature of the offense, as it would plainly appear to every man by reading of the vote made thereupon. And if the president in my Lord Clarendon's case were one way, the president in my Lord Mordant's case was another way. So that I concluded they were to be called in, but I did desire before they were called in, the house would direct the interrogateries that they should be asked, as had been done in other cases, and was very necessarie in this, for I did not desire to let any man into the house only to give him an opportunitie of making an harangue and an oration against my Lord Treasurer, and least of all, such men as we knew allready had profest enmities with him, and between whom there were suits of law depending in all the courts of England and those of (high—*del.*) a value and so nice a nature, as those are now between them.

And again, it was fit to (resolve—*del.*) know to what part of this article they should be heard. Much of it is no crime nor ground of impeachment against my Lord Treasurer if it be proved, so that it is losse of time to examin them. Much of it is a direct controversie between them and there is no reason they should be witnesses in their owne cause. Much of it is quite foreign to this businesse before us, and as [to] the validitie or invaliditie of the marriage it could in no sort be proper to hear it before us, it being now depending in the Arches the proper court. As to what is properly a crime, and may, if it be proved, be a ground for an impeachment, and in which the witnesses were not interested parties. I were very willing to hear them, yet even then some

75

consideracion [f.16] was to be had, how farr they were competent and credible testimonies. I heard but of 3 at the door. Emerton himself, Branly the parson and my Lord Mayor. The first was so deeply concernd (that—*del*.) through out the whole affaire of Mrs Hide as claiming both her person and estate, that I thought he could hardly be admitted a witnesse in any court in this cause. Branly the parson had behaved himself so, as to lye with all men, under a manefest and foule suspicion of perjurie, and by some members witnessed to have been long since of unsound memorie. And as to my Lord Mayor himself, he was hardly to be looked upon as an indifferent person unlesse we should thinke him such from the reason an eminent member of the citie had then given us (that was Sir Samuel Bernardiston) that it was indifferent to my Lord Mayor which way the matter went between my Lord Treasurer and Mr Emerton, for my Lord Mayor had made his bargain on both sides. And another member told us, he had seen a bond from Emerton to pay £1,000 per annum for five yeares to my Lord Mayor's son if this match went forward (this Alderman Love had said in the house) and therefor with these circumstances and consideracions before us, I were of opinion they should be called in.

This after some debate proved the sense of the house and Sir Samuel Bernardiston then was ordered to propose what interrogations he would have the witnesses examined unto.

And he pulled out a paper with about a dozen interrogations and the first was to my Lord Mayor.

How much money doth the King owe you? and many other as impertinent as that, which being severally put to the Question, were all resolved in the negative, that they should not be askd except one which was about sending a man with a servant of my Lord Treasurer to Branly, and taking him by a warrant from Sir Joseph Williamson and examining him before the King. And to this it was ordered my Lord Mayor should be called in, and it was indeed the most proper of all the interrogations offerd by Bernardiston.

[f.16v] Then there arose a debate whether my Lord Mayor should have a chair set for him or not which after a long debate the house divided upon and 141 went out who were for a chaire,

173 Noes being against a chair, and staid in.

My Lord Mayor being brought in, the Speaker never telling him the chaire was set for him, he did not set downe but stood by it, and answered briefly to the interrogation.

That he did send a servaunt with a servaunt of my Lord Treasurer to speake with Branley, that he found him not, that a warrant was granted by (my Lord—*del*.) Secretarie Williamson, to bring him before the King, that he conceived he did it as a Justice of the Peace.

And so he withdrew, after 6 houres attendance and not two minuts staying in the house.

Some debate there was after this (whether—*del.*) upon this warrant, which was drawn very cautiously, but only it was directed to a messenger not to a legall officer and the messenger ordered to take a constable to his assistance and he did so. Whereas in truth it ought to be directed to the constable and he to take to his assistance what was needfull. But such a small slip was pardonable to every Justice of Peace, nor did any thing of that appear to be the act of my Lord Treasurer.

So the Question put was whether there appeard to be from the consideracion of this second article any ground for an impeachment against my Lord Treasurer, which had a very few Yeas

and a great majoritie of Noes,

and then the house adjourned to Monday.

[*CJ*, ix, 327-8; G, iii, 58-64, 81-2]

10

[f.17]   *Monday, 3 May*

This day we went on with the remaining 5 articles against my Lord Treasurer, the third managed by my Lord Cavendish, fourth by Sir Thomas Meeres, fifth by Sir John Coventry, sixth by Lord O'Brian and seventh by Sir Thomas Littleton. But nothing at all proved. And the house resolved upon them all severally, that they found no cause of impeachment, so that charge is alltogether laid aside. After which Sir Joseph Tredinham made a speech of the honour and integritie of my Lord Treasurer, and moved that we should declare it so by a publique vote, but it was not seconded and fell flat in the house. Nor did I thinke it was seasonably moved, it being much that he came off so well, though very just I thinke he should do so, but it was not to be hoped that an impeachment should end in panegyrick.

[*CJ*, ix, 328-9; G, iii, 82-96]

Tuesday, 4 May

Sir Thomas Littleton moved that he had met with a report in severall places as if he had bribed one Salter to be a witnesse against my Lord Treasurer and to prove the words charged in the last article, viz., that a new proclamacion was better than an old statute, and that he had offered Salter £4,000 to testify this, and he desired the justice of the house to vindicate his reputacion, and in order to it, that Salter might be ordered to appear at the barr of the house the next day. Which was ordered.

Then we went upon consideracion of the Navy, and ordered a bill to be brought in for appropriating the revenue arising from the bill of tonnage and poundage past in the twelfth yeare of this King to the use of the Navy. Many moved that they would adjourne this debate for one day and then consider it in a committee of the whole house because the consequence of it was very great, [f.17v] it being apparent that the King can not subsist if we do so, the other great branch of the revenue being the excise being anticipated for 18 months, so that the King will have nothing to live upon but the hearth money, which is but £150,000 per annum, all the other branches of the revenue being of small value, and not coming to £100,000 per annum.

But the house was set upon it, and a bill ordered to be brought in accordingly.

[*CJ*, ix, 329-30; G, iii, 96-102; Finch, 4 May 1675]

Wednesday, 5 May

This day Salter was brought to the barr, and being examined if Sir Thomas Littleton had promised him £4,000 to witnesse against my Lord Treasurer, he said no. He being withdrawn, Sir Joseph Tredinham said, that this man deserved to be punished for reflecting upon the worthy member, for there was a witnesse at the door had heard him, and desired he might be calld in. Which was ordered.

Mead the Quaker being come in, said, that Mr Child and Mr Papillon of the house had come to him, and asked him if he knew any thing that Salter could witnesse against my Lord Treasurer, and he said no. They desired him to send for Salter which he did, and Salter told them as much. Yet they desired Salter to come up to Westminster Hall, where some of the house would speake with him. Which he did, and then those 2 and Sir Thomas Littleton and Mr Powle came to him. Where Salter at their importunitie did set his hand to a paper which was wrote by Sir Thomas Littleton, which he was very sorry for, not knowing what it did containe, but they told him that if he would [f.18] do it, it might be a measure to recall his friend Otto (who is the Hamburgher upon the hearing of whose cause it is pretended the words were spoken) from his banishment and recovering his damages, though they were 4 or 5 thousand pounds. And all this appeared by a letter of Salter to this Mead, and Sir Joseph Tredinham and Mr George Wild testifyed something they had heard Salter say to that purpose.

Mr Powell and Sir Thomas Littleton did not much deny the matter, but said that Salter came freely to them in the hall, and what was wrote, was read to him and then he did willingly signe it.

Heare was upon the whole matter a proceeding by these 4 members, which was not very fit for judges, a searching for evidence urging a man to it, writing downe what he should testify, after he had said he knew nothing of it, which was plain as to Child and Papillon, though not so as to the other two, and in summe, a proceeding not very gentleman like. But heare was nothing could be a ground for a sentence against them in the house, it being no more than a testimonie of a man who by his owne confession, had set his hand to something which was not true. So that, when it had been fully opened, and fairly bespatterd their reputation, I thought it best to befriend them so farr, as to move the house to go to some other businesse and that they would read a bill come downe from the Lords about explanacion of an act for suppressing danger from popish recusants, and so we went off from this matter.

[f.18v] Then a message was sent up to the Lords, in behalfe of Sir John Fagg, a member of our house, against whom an appeale was brought in the house of Lords. The message was in generall termes, to desire their Lordships to be tender of the priviledges of this house.

[*CJ*, ix, 330-1; G, iii, 102-4]

Thursday, 6 May

This day was appointed for considering the accusacions of Dr Burnet against the Duke of Lauderdale, but the debate adjourned till to morrow sevennight.

Then we voted a second addresse to his Majestie, to be made upon the former addresses made to him concerning the Duke of Lauderdale and the French forces, to which we had yet received no answer.

A bill reported by Serjeant Rygby for the securitie of such who claimed under auncient fines, and ordered to be ingrossed.

The afternoon I attended the committee of elections, the case was between Sir William Wentworth and Whatton, of which it is plain that Wentworth had the majoritie of voices, and that Whatton's agent had been guilty of the grossest briberie imaginable. Against Sir William Wentworth it was urged, that he had given £30 to 3 men of the electors, and 20s. apiece to their wives, to which it was answered that the money was to pay the reckoning, they all keeping publique houses, and the 20s to their wives was denied. But for this reason, the committee voted it a void election in both.

[*CJ*, ix, 331; G, iii, 105-6]

[f.19]   11

Fryday, 7 May

This day we received an answer from the King to the addresse concerning the Duke of Lauderdale, which was that the act for raising

22,000 men in Scotland was past (before—*del.*) long before the Duke of Lauderdale was commissioner there, and the second act there was but a consequence of the former.

And as to the words alledged against him. That it appeares by the time that if they were spoken at all, they were spoken before the last act of generall pardon, and therefore not to be punished now, without giving great apprehencion to the people.

A long debate arose concerning this matter, whether this answer were satisfactory or not. Many spoke against it and showed no reason. Few spoke for it. Mr Sacheverill, that we should vote it not satisfactorie, and adjourne the house till we had a satisfactorie answer to it. But that which was insisted upon was to take time to consider of it, and so it is ordered, the debate upon the King's answer should be adjourned to Tuesday next.

A bill (brought in—*del.*) read for preventing of the mischiefs by arrests and the insolence of bayliffes, and committed.

It stands now only upon bonds and sealed billes, but there is no reason but to extend it to actions upon the case for slander, batterie and to shop debts, whereupon the mischief is as great or greater than the other.

On the other side it may be reason to prevent this summarie way of leaving notice and proving it by affidavit, and so going in to judgment in things where the title of a man's inheritance is in question, but it is committed upon the whole debate.

A bill against all pedlers and petty chapmen read the second time and committed.

The best way seemes to me to allow only such as shall be licensed at the quarter sessions.

[*CJ*, ix, 331-3; G, iii, 106-12]

[f.19v]   *Saturday, 8 May (we did not sit it being May day[1])*

Monday, 10 May

This day the house turned into a grand committee to consider of the King's answer to our addresse concerning the recalling all his subjects in the French King's service. The forces there were under three heads:

1. Those who were there before the peace made with Holland, raised by the King's permission and by the King of France his money, levied heare and conducted thither, which are agreed not to exceed the number of 2,300 men.

---

[1] This entry is mistaken, cf. *CJ*, ix, 333-4; G, iii, 112-16.

2. **Those** who have gone thither since that peace made.
3. Those that are now ready to go, or may heareafter go.
Touching the first, the King's answer was he could not recall them with his honour, nor without hazarding the peace that he now enjoyeth with all his neighbours.

To the second, he said nothing at all in his addresse.

To the third, that he would both by proclamacion and all other effectuall meanes, take care for it.

And as to this last part, we all agreed that the King's answer was satisfactorie.

The debate was very large. Many moved for thankes to be given the King for his gracious answer, as the secretarie, Sir Henry Ford, and others. But that would not passe. The generall sense was to vote another addresse for a fuller answer from the King. [f.20] Of this mind, Garaway, Meeres, Sacheverill, Vaughan, Lord Cavendish and very many more. And the debate growing very hot, some moved for adjourning it till to morrow. To that sense spoke Sir Robert Howard, Sir Charles Wheeler, Secretarie Coventry, Mr Sawyer and my selfe. I showed them that in peticions and addresses of this nature (where—*del.*) the matter was wholly in the King's power. Where no positive law was broken, no one man of the Kingdome could say he was personally injured, sooner or later we must acquiesce in the King's pleasure, and then the sooner we did it and the more decently we approached it, still the better. That we might well do so in this, where the answer was a plaine and full compliance in one and that the greatest part of our desire, which was the prohibiting any for the future going thither. That for those which were gone since the peace, it seemed to be rather under deliberacion than denied us. That those forces having been all the last winter in the King of France's pay and done him no service, to take them away now they were just marching into the field seemed a little harsh. That therefore it was probable the King might rather do it by his embassadour who was upon the place, who might do it with the respect that is fit to be observed between great princes, than by his proclamacion. That in all it was but to stay till tomorrow by adjourning this debate which was asked. That it was not fit to deny so small a matter to a prince who had hitherto denied us nothing.[1]

Soon after this the Question was put, not for adjourning this debate which had been the proper Question, but upon the mocion, viz., whether the addresse should be made to the King for recalling all his forces in the French King's service.

The committee divided, the Yeas on the right hand, the Noes on the left. Sir Trevor Williams teller for the Yeas and Sir Gilbert Talbot for the Noes, and the numbers happend to be equall, viz., 135 on each side.

[1] See Dering's full account of his speech, pp. 175-8 below. G, iii, 128 summarises it in a single sentence.

The Noes called to report. The Yeas called to tell again, saying that one member, viz., Mr Cofferer was told twice. Sir Gilbert Talbot refused to tell again, it being the rule when the tellers disagreed, to tell again, but not when they agreed, though others did call to tell again. [f.20v] Upon this, the house fell into some disorder, my Lord Cavendish coming out of his place, and telling Sir Gilbert Talbot he should tell again. Sir John Hanmer saying that was against the orders of the committee, my Lord Cavendish spit at him, which he returned, and my Lord Cavendish thrusting Sir Herbert Price from the table, Price laid hold upon his owne sword, but did not draw it. Severall other disorders were committed, and the whole house upon the brinke of falling into bloud, when presently, the Speaker very seasonably steps into the chaire and cryes 'to their places', which was seconded by most of the house, and with much ado obtained. Some were angry that the Speaker tooke the chair without a question put by the committee, but all that were sober thought it very well done, and happily, it being impossible otherwise to have prevented bloud and intolerable mischiefes. As soon as silence was made, severall healing mocions were made, by Sir Thomas Lee, Sir Robert Carr, Sir Philip Warwick and others, which ended in a forme of words dictated by the Speaker, and assented to by every member standing up in his place as it came to his turne, which was that they would not send or receive any challenge nor otherways remember or resent any offence or displeasure for any thing had past that day, which they promised upon their honour.

Which being done, we adjourned till next day without returning upon the dispute or so much as entering (upon—*del*.) our bookes the said protestacion.

The quarrells which were most apparent to the house were between my Lord Cavendish and Sir John Hanmer, Lord Castelton and Sir Robert Holmes, Sir Robert Thomas and Sir James Smith, the 3 first being Yeas, the other 3 Noes.

[*CJ*, ix, 334; G, iii, 116-30; Finch, 10 May 1675]

[f.21]   12

(*Monday—del*.) *Tuesday*, *11 May*

This day we revived the former debate concerning the French forces, and a very long debate was entertained concerning those only that were in France before the peace made with Holland and which the Dutch did not insist should be recalled, and that the King did say he could not with his honour recall. And the debate then was reduced to whether the word 'All' should stand part of the question, and this debate lasted at least 4 hours upon that word. Garaway, Birch, Sir William Coventry [*interlineated*], Sacheverill, Powle [*interlineated*], Littleton [*interlineated*], Hickman, speaking the word should stand. Vaughan and Meeres that they would have all or none. Mr Secretarie Coventry and Williamson, Sir Charles Wheeler, Sir Henry Ford [*interlineated*] and myself, to leave it out. At last the Question was put and the house divided upon it, and the Yeas who staid in were 172, the Noes who went out, 174. Then much exception was taken to Sir Winston Churchill's vote, who was upon the staires coming downe from the gallerie. Upon examinacion it appeared he was there not before but during the time the Speaker did put the first [*interlineated*] Negative, and before the Noe was pronounced, but he was set aside, being not clearly there before the Negative was put, though it appeared he was at the gallerie door, but could not get roome to come in there, the gallerie door being crowded, and so came running to get place in the house just as the negative was putting. But this being granted them still we had the majoritie by one, so it past in the negative.

Then the Question past without the word 'all'.

Then informacion was given the house, that an appeale was brought against Sir John Fagg in the Lords' house by one Mr Sherley, and that the Lords had entered an order in their booke that no member of either house should have priviledge against writs of error or appeales brought before them [f.21v], which was ordered to be considered the next morning.

[*CJ*, ix, 334-5; G, iii, 130-9]

Wednesday, 12 May

We first proceeded upon the bill for explanacion of the act for the dutie of hearth money, and a very long debate arose about the certificat to be made for the excusing such [as] do not pay to church or more (*sic*).

It was brought in the certificat thereof shall be made by the minister and churchwardens and overseers or any two of them, whereof the minister to be one, but it being asked what should become of those poor people where by death or removall there was no minister, which happened often for 6, 12, 18 months together, as is notorious, and no answer being given to it, the house divided upon the Question whether the minister should be of the quorum, so that no certificat should be made without him.

The Yeas who staid in were 108.
The Noes who went out were 150.
I were a Noe and severall other gentlemen who loved the church very well, and did not thinke that the honour or interest of the church were concerned at all in this matter, and for this matter, as small as it seemes to be, were complaind of to the King as deserting of his interest, Sir Joseph Tredinham and my selfe by name. Which is something (very—

del.) hard measure, but I know no rule to give my vote by but that of my judgment and conscience.

[f.22] Then we went upon the businesse of priviledge between us and the house of Lords in the case of Fagg, and many aggravacions there were made against our member for waiving his priviledge and that not only without the leave of the house, but after he had by his complaint desired the reliefe and protection of the house and ingaged them in it. But the consideracion of the member was put off till another time, but the house made an order at the Speaker's advice, to send for Mr Sherley in custodie, and that no member should waive his priviledge without leave of the house first had ¹and appointed a committee to inspect the Lords' bookes as to Fagg's businesse.¹

[*CJ*, ix, 335-6; G, no report]

Thursday, 13 May, being Ascension day—we did not sit.

Friday, 14 May

The committee appointed to inspect the Lords' bookes gave us an accompt of what related to Sir John Fagg's businesse.

Then the serjeant's man reported that he went with his order to find out Dr Sherley and found him in the inner lobby at the Lords' door. That he told him he had an order to bring him to the Commons' barr. Sherley said he was the King's physician and would not obey the order. The man replied that he would not serve the order in that place but he would follow him home till he could serve it, if he would not rather chuse to go with him willingly and freely. My Lord Mohun being by, asked him about it, and he showed my Lord the order under the Speaker's hand. My Lord Mohun laid hold of it to take it from him, which the man held fast till it was like to be torne to pieces, and then let it go. And after my Lord Mohun had the order in his hand, the serjeant desired him to give it him again, which my Lord Mohun refusing carried in to the Lords' house. In the meane Dr Sherley escaped, and the man was advised by the company to be gone, least he were clapt by the heeles by the Lords.

So he came and gave us this accompt of it.

So now all the debate ran upon this fact of my Lord Mohun's, and the matter being wrote downe, it was aggravated by all the circumstances of it, and at last it was ordered [f.22v] that a message should be sent up immediatly to the Lords to complaine against my Lord Mohun and demand satisfaction for his forceably taking away and detaining the order of the house. Which was sent up by the Earle of Ankram.

¹ . . . . ¹ inserted subsequently.

Then we went upon our priviledge and entred in our bookes that the appeale brought against Sir John Fagg by Dr Sherley, and the proceedings thereupon, were (a breach an—*del.*) a breach of the undoubted right and priviledge of this house.

Then it was informed the house that Mr Onslow and Mr Demahoy were also concerned in writs of error or appeales in the Lords' house and had waived their priviledge and appeard to them in the Lords' house, which was much blamed in them, and it was moved by Sir Nicholas Carew and Mr Garaway that Sir John Fagg should be sent to the Tower. But it being very late and the house very thin it was moved to adjourne, and so we did allthough my Lord Ankram were not returned from the House of Lords.

[*CJ*, ix, 336-7; G, iii, 139-47]

Saturday, 15 May

This day was wholly spent upon our difference with the House of Lords. Began by a report from the Lord Ankram who received for answer from the Lords after 7 hours' attendance that the Lords had considered of our message and complaint against the Lord Mohun and were of the opinion the Lord Mohun had done nothing but his dutie. Then came a message from the Lords to us, to know whether we had given such an order as the Lord Mohun had brought in to the house, signed Edward Seymour. This was aggravated as the highest breach of priviledge imaginable and some would have sent an answer that the message was unparliamentary, unusuall, extraordinarie impertinent. Some would have sent up to the Lords to know if they had sent us such a message. At last the word 'unparliamentarie' was put to the question, and the house divided upon it. 127 Yeas. 151 Noes. So that was left out, and of a soudain agreed the answer should be that the house would consider of the message, but the house would not send back the paper it selfe that was the warrant signed by the Speaker for bringing Dr Sherley to us in custodie,

[f.23]   13

yet we went on afterwards to vote this proceeding unparliamentarie and so to enter it in our bookes: which was thought better than to make it part of our message to the Lords, for that cut off all farther conference, which this entry in our bookes doth not do.

Then we ordered a new warrant to take Sherley in custodie.

Then we commanded Mr Anslow and Mr Demahoy, members of the House, not to proceed any farther in the causes depending in the. House of Lords against them.

To this I spoake, beseeching them to consider what hardship they put upon their members, to deprive them of the sentences and judgments they had obtained for them. That if now they did not appeare in the House of Lords the Lords would either heare it ex parte, or if they would not go so farr, they would at least suspend all execucion of that decree or judgment till it had been heard. So that, instead of a priviledge it was a very great mischiefe we contended for, to ourselves, unlesse we would suppose that parliament men had allwayes unjust causes and such as would not endure the light. That not to be heard was an advantage where justice was against us, but farr otherwise where the law was for us. That I could prompt them with no other expedient but that which offered itselfe naturally in this case, which is, to give leave to Mr Onslow and Mr Demahoy to go on and appeare in the causes depending now against them in the House of Lords. That it being at their desire, they would not complain, but take it as a favour and bountie to them, and it being entered in our bookes to be done by leave of the house, it did not at all weaken, but rather assert and fortify our priviledge which we claimed, that the Lords had not right of themselves to call us to their barr. That I saw no other handle to take it by, to get out of the difficulties we were now in about it, nor could I understand the meaning of the order we had made that no member should appeare at the Lords' barr without leave of this house, to be consistent with a resolucion in us never to give leave though it shall be asked.

Some others, as Sir Charles Wheeler and Sir John Berkenhead and in some measure Sir Thomas Meeres, seemed to second me in it, and to apprehend the inconveniencies we (*deletion*) were bringing ourselves into, but the vote past against us, and added farther that Sir Nicholas Stoughton should be brought in custodie, and all others that should bring any appeale in the house of Lords and appeare at their barr in prosecucion of any member of the house of Commons, as those who did highly violate and infringe the priviledge of the house.

[*CJ*, ix, 337-9; G, iii, 148-56]

[f.23v]   *Monday, 17 May*

We carried up our vote that the appeale brought in the House of Lords against Sir John Fagge, a member of our house, and the proceeding thereupon was a breach of the undoubted right and priviledge of this house, and therefore desired their Lordships no farther proceeding might be had therein. This vote we delivered to their Lordships at a conference.

As soon as we returned from the conference Mr Eyres offered a question in writing that no new bill might be received before our recesse mencioned in his Majestie's speech, except such bills as were allready ordered by the house to be brought in, or such as should come downe from the Lords.

This received a very long debate, highly insisted upon by Sir Thomas Lee, Mr Vaughan, Littleton, Swinfin, Sir William Coventry, Mr Waller, Garaway, Temple and Birch, opposed by Secretarie Coventry, Sir Charles Wheeler, Sir Harry Ford, cousin Daniel Finch, Sir Joseph Tredinham, Mr Sawyer and myselfe. But all in vaine. It was then insisted upon that the words without extraordinarie occasion. And upon those words to be part of the Question we divided, the Yeas who went out were 173, the Noes who staid in were 161. So it past without those words.

And those words were in truth not very proper, for it left all loose. I would rather have had the words without especiall leave of the house, which words were long insisted upon but waved and lost in the debate.

I would have had (*deletion*) the debate adjourned for two dayes, that men might consider, what good billes were fit and ready to be brought in, and likewise what the consequences might be, for certain it is, the vote is new and unusuall and I did challenge any man that was for it, to produce one precedent of it, that is with like circumstances, for private bills have sometime been concluded, and publique bills after our time of recesse had been signified to us by the King, but this was generall, and for we know not how long, the time of our recesse being alltogether unknowne, but this would not prevaile at this time.

[f.24] They that pretend to know anything of their mind, say this was not a fit of jealousie, but of ill nature, for it was not done to prevent a bill for supply of the navy, but because they had intelligence that the King would interpose in the difference between the two houses, and desire them wholly to intend the publique good and such billes as might secure their religion and propertie, and declare at the same time that this was the whole aime of his calling us together this session, and that he did not desire any money or supply for himselfe. Therefore this vote was now clapt in, that the King might not have the thanks of his intended kindnesse to us, but might seeme necessitated to let it alone, rather than inclined, and now the deniall of those bills they have prepared or the soudain proroguing or adjourning us, may be thought an effect of his displeasure upon this disappointment in matter of money.

[*CJ*, ix, 339-40; G, iii, 156-66; Finch, 17 May 1675]

Tuesday, 18, Wednesday, 19, Thursday, 20, Friday, 21 May

These days were spent chiefly about the dispute between us and the Lords in the case of Sir John Fagg, and of Mr Anslow and the dispute about the warrant which my Lord Mohun took from our serjeant in the Lords' lobby.

We had a conference with them, and they had one with us which we voted not satisfactorie, and that we would desire a free conference with them after the holy dayes so we did not send (with—*del.*) up to desire it but took that time for our managers to prepare reasons for the conference.

We also sent up to the Lords for a conference about the subject matter of the last conference, and their answer was, they would send us an answer by [a] messenger of their own.

[f.24v] On Thursday we divided upon a private bill which was ingrost and the Question put for the passing it. It was for a small estate in Sussex which was mortgaged first and after in marriage setled upon the eldest son, and the mortgage money would plainly eat out all the estate, the father being dead, and the heire a minor. So that all other private bills are for taking something from the heir, this bill only was beneficiall to the heire. But the house divided upon it, the Yeas who went out were 68, the Noes who staid in were 71, so the bill was rejected.

[*CJ*, ix, 340-5; G, iii, 166-85]

(*Thursday, Wednesday, each del.*) [*Thursday, 20 May*]

The house divided upon the case of Sir William Wentworth who had clearly the majoritie of votes, but the committee of elections had voted it a void election upon the accompt of briberie laid to Sir William's charge. But there were these circumstances to be considered

1. Heare was nothing paid or promised before the election
2. The money that was said to be given was only to alehouse keepers, which was in truth for meat and drink there spent, and so not given. Nor were the sums excessive, about £40 to four houses, at the two elections, viz., that of my Lord Shaftesburie's writs and the next.
3. This was proved but by one witnesse, and he of ill fame and denied expressly by the man who was said to have been imployed in it, and was before us.
4. The witnesse who testified in this fully proved to have bribed others himselfe for Mr Wharton.

   For which reasons the House did disagree with the committee.
   119 for agreeing.   146 for disagreeing.

So Sir William Wentworth is admitted as well chosen.

This day the second or third addresse to the King was moved to be read. It was desired to stay till tomorrow, the proclamacion for making them being in the presse. Upon the Question whether it should be now read, the house divided. The Yeas went out because it was a new mocion after 12 a clock and therefore against the orders of the house,

[f.25]   14

which was the reason the Speaker gave for the Yeas going out for bring-

ing in a thing which did come in by a former order made for that purpose. Some would have disputed that point, but the Speaker is allways allowed to determine that point, without which the house could not proceede.
The Yeas which went out were 94
The Noes who staid in were 94

So the Speaker determined it by his casting vote, that it should be read. The reason he gave was he had read it over himselfe, and found nothing in it to be excepted against. But no doubt the true reason was popularitie. For after it was voted to be read and read accordingly the house would not proceed upon it, it being long and fit to be read deliberately a second time.

The bill for the fisherie in the Severne and many other rivers sent up to the Lords by Sir John Trevor.

[*CJ*, ix, 342-3; G, iii, 176-8]

Fryday, 21 May

A mocion was made for keeping the 29 of May solemnly and to go [to] church as a house attending the Speaker, which was well approved, and consented to.

Then it was moved by Mr Stockdale and seconded by my Lord Cavendish that Mr Burnet should be desired to preach before us. Which was very unpleasing to the house that a Scotchman and one forbid by the King to come into the court should be pitched upon to preach before the house on the King's birthday. Then Dr Oughtram, Minister of St Margaret's, was moved by Sir Phillip Warwick, Dr Sandcroft by Sir Charles Wheeler, Dr Tillotson by Sir Henry Ford. At last it was resolved that no man should be pitched upon, but to let Dr Oughtram know we intend to be at his church, viz., St Margaret's, Westminster, on that day. Which would be sufficient intimacion to him [f.25v] and then we adjourned till Wednesday in Whitsunweeke, but with a resolucion to call over the house that day which we should meet, and an order that no man should go out of towne without leave.

[*CJ*, ix, 343-5; G, iii, 178-85]

Wednesday, 26 May

This day the house was called over according to order. The first call, we only did marke those who were absents without hearing any excuses for them.

Then we called over a second time those who were absent, of which many did appeare upon this second call, and many were excused by their friends. About 80 were absent, for whom no excuse was made.

And these were to be called over again on Tuesday next and then to be censured. I suppose that time given for them who are neare the towne to appeare, but in the meane time Sir Thomas Littleton moved that we might do something in this matter.

That we were unwilling to send our members to the Tower. That was too harsh, and would never be done by this house. That pecuniarie fines would never be levied. That we have formerly ordered the serjeant of the house to go downe and fetch them up, and that proved ineffectuall, for they would not come and the serjeant lost all his paines and charges.

That we had since that proceeded so farr as to send to the sheriffes of the counties to summon them and to require their attendance at the house, but that also to little purpose. That he could wish we would go one step farther, which was to write to the particular cities and boroughs for which such absent members do serve, to give them notice of the negligence of those whom they trusted in discharge of that trust reposed in them, and if they were knights of shires, then this letter to be addressed to the sheriff of the countie [f.26] with expression that this he thought the gentlest way that could be taken with them, being no kind of punishment but only a little to shame them, and lessen their credit with those who sent them hither.

And this was ordered to be done and 3 or 4 members to draw up such a letter for the Speaker to send and to present the draught of this letter on Tuesday. I do not like this, or any other way of appealing to the people.

[*CJ*, ix, 345; G, iii, 185]

Thursday, 27 May

This day was read the bill for suppressing the growth of poperie, which was very long, and the rest of it in considering of an addresse to the Lords and we sent up Sir Thomas Lee to desire a conference with the Lords.

And we rose before the returne of the messenger which I never knew done before, for it being allwayes in the Lords' power to appoint time and place for conferences if they had agreed to a present conference, and the Commons had then been up, it had certainly been a disrespect to them which they would have had just reason to complain of. But I believe this was not thought upon till the Speaker was out of the chaire, and no inconvenience happened thereby, the Lords appointing the conference to morrow morning.

[*CJ*, ix, 345-6; G, iii, 185-93]

Fryday, 28 May

This day after a private bill read or two, I were ordered to report the bill for repaire of churches, and when I had begun, I were interrupted by Sir Thomas Lee with his report from the Lords concerning the conference. Which being to be at ten of the clock, which it was now, it was necessarie for him to go on with his report and to waive mine. Which was done accordingly.

[f.26v] His report was that the Lords gave this answer to our message. That they had not given a conference to us in the case of Mr Onslow, because it only related to matter of their judicature, in which they ought not to give a conference. But the conference now demanded being upon our priviledges they would allow a conference, upon this proviso, that nothing should be said thereat which did any wayes relate to judicature.

This was highly resented by the house as the most unparliamentarie answer could be given. The Question was first to go up to the conference and not take notice of these restrictive words but to speake our minds freely against their judicature, as indeed it was not possible to speake to our priviledge which we conceive to be broken by them without touching upon that right of judicature which they say they have to overrule in this case of appeales our priviledge. Sir Thomas Meeres, Sir Robert Howard and some others were for this.

And others opposed it because by this we should give a countenance to these limited conferences, and as they had now told us what we should not say, the next time they might enjoine us what we should (no—*del.*) say. And besides, we did know that they had given instructions to their managers to rise and go away as soon as any word should be offered relating to their judicature, which we knew would but enflame things more, though this, which we knew but from some of the Lords, was not an argument to be used in the house.

[f.27]   15

Others were for desiring a conference upon this their answer to us, which they thought could not be denied us, and then we should doubtlesse convince them of the unreasonablenesse and unusuallnesse of such an (cons—*del.*) answer, it being never knowne before that they should in expresse termes insert a restrictive proviso in a conference, and such a proviso as made the whole conference vaine and indeed dumb. It being in plain termes to say they do graunt us a conference, provided we do say nothing of the matter we would confer upon. And beside it is not limiting our managers, but indeed, imposing a sense upon our whole house in what termes we shall expresse ourselves to them.

And this proved the sense of the house. But before they would passe this vote it was urged by Sir Thomas Meeres that we should declare that the Lords had not graunted a conference by this answer but denied it, for if they have graunted a conference, and the time at ten of the clock, it is a breach in us that we do not attend then. Whereupon the house fell upon that debate and resolved that the Lords had not by their answer to our message graunted a conference upon that matter of Mr Onslow as was desired, and by this vote we thought ourselves dispensed with from going up to the Painted Chamber to meet them.

Hitherto, the moderate partie were pretty well satisfied, for no man could thinke the answer of the Lords reasonable or parliamentarie, or indeed other than a meer contradiction to it selfe. But this being over, when we called to send up to the Lords to desire a conference upon their last answer, it was said that this day was appointed to consider of the jurisdiction of the Lords upon appeales in generall and not only where priviledg of parliament was concernd. And they desired to heare what could be offered to that point. Mr Sawyer, who was prepared in that matter, made a long discourse of that, about 3 quarters of an hour, showing how cases of equity had been severall times [f.27v] redressed by acts of parliament, and therefore not then used to be by appeales to the Lords. That the Lords had no footsteps of this jurisdiction before 18 King James, that Queen Elizabeth in 41, I take it, of her reigne, or thereabout, refered the review of the case of Sir Moile Finch which had been judged against him in chancerie to the 12 judges of England, where it was heard and reversed.

That therefore there was no need of a triall in the house of Lords. That it was derogatorie to the King's prerogative, for in writs of error it was graunted by petition to the King upon whose answer to it, the writ of error went out returnable coram domine Rege in parliamento, whereas in these paper peticions they were addressed immediately to the house of Peers, the King being not so much as named.

That by this meanes, the Lords might draw the cognisance of all originall causes to themselves, for let any man put in his bill in chancerie, be it never so unreasonable, never so unjust, in which the chancerie will not relieve him, or perhaps can not by the course and constant practice of the court take cognisance of it, as is the very case between Fagg and Sherley, and thereupon his bill is dismist, and now without more adoe he may appeale to the house of Lords, and they make what sentence they please in the matter.

And so concluded that in his opinion, the Lords had no right to receive any appeales from any courts of equity.

[f.28] This was presently seconded by many others, and after an hour's debate the Question earnestly called for. At last I ventured to stand up and say:

That in all votes of this house which were declaratory of the common law of the land, I could wish we did take a little more time for deliberacion than usually we did, and if in other cases then certainly in this, which was accompanied with as much difficultie and attended with as great and important consequences as any that could come before us. That if I were now to speake to the expedience or inexpedience of having this power of receiving appeales in the Lords, I thinke I could offer something to them which had not yet been touched, but I should chuse rather to speake to the time and seasonablenesse of this debate and move them to an adjournment of it, rather than to come to a present determinacion.

That it has been the wisedome of this house all this session and particularly this very day to think of expedients how we might come to a good understanding with the Lords, that we had at last pitched upon one that probably might have that effect and keep us from splitting upon that rock we are now very neare striking upon. That we have just now voted to desire a conference with them upon their last answer to our message, which, if they graunted us as I did believe, and a free conference upon that, we might probably come to understand one another, and either to give or receive satisfaction. That if we did arrive at that end, it would be thought a very successfull method we had put it in, and no man would then regret that we had not made the breach wider, as this vote would certainly do. And if we failed in that expectacion, we could then resume this debate and come to this vote with more justification from the world and more unanimitie among ourselves.

[f.28v] That of three lawyers who had spoke in it, one had been cleare indeed in the point, but the other two had been doubtfull and desired longer time to thinke of it. That the Lords had been in possession of this right of hearing appeales, as was confest by them who had spoke against it, ever since 18 Jacobi, which was now about 55 years. That though this was not long enough to make a prescripcion, yet it was too much to be blowne away with a breath in an hour's discourse. That the mischiefes we had suffered all this w[h]ile had not been very grievous to the publique, no complaints having been tendred to the house against any of their sentences of this nature. That we could not suffer much by a delay of 3 dayes, which was all I would desire.

(That I did not see the Lords proceed—*del.*)

That it was probable now the house had asserted their right in opposicion to that judicature, they would proceed with more caution rather than with lesse.

That I did not see they proceeded on with obstinacie as it was phrased on the other side by Sir Thomas Meeres, but rather with moderacion, for they had not yet judged either of the causes of Mr Onslow or Sir John Fagg, but had either accidentally or perhaps artificially (and ca—*del.*) let them fall to the ground, and remaine sine die.

That we had not only taken care of ourselves but in some measure also for all the commons of England, there being ordered in one of our messages some prefatorie words, by which we did intimate that though we do at this time dispute with them only their [f.29]   16

judicature in appeales relating to priviledged persons, there being no
other cases before us but those of Sir John Fagg, Mr Onslow and Mr
Demahoy, all members, yet we did not admitt their jurisdiction upon
appeales in generall, so that we were at libertie to resume that discourse whenever we found their proceedings upon appeales grievous to
the nacion.

That upon the whole matter, my mocion was, that leaving Monday
for a conference and Tuesday for a free conference, if there should be
occasion, we would adjourne this debate till Wednesday next.

This was seconded by Secretarie Coventry, Sir William Coventry,
Collonel Birch, Sir Charles Wheeler, Sir Thomas Jones, and Sir
Leoline Jenkins, this last adding one reason, which was that by voting
the Lords had no power of judging appeales, we did take away and
avoid all the judgments they had made for these 55 yeares, which was
of dangerous consequences.

It was opposed by Sir Thomas Lee, because if the lawyers were not
ready to give their opinion in this matter, it was their owne faults, for it
came on by order. By Sir Thomas Meeres, because he would have this
matter being of great consequence determined whiles we were warme,
for all things would grow flat and cold in our memorie, 3 dayes hence.
By Mr Vaughan, who answered Sir Lionell[1] Jenkins that these sentences
the Lords (would—*del.*) had made would stand good, though they were
coram non judice, because of the consent of parties, but that was ex-
ploded by Serjeant Mainard, and Serjeant Jones.

[f.29v] At last the Question was putting (for—*del.*) and the previous
Question demanded when I stood up and said the proper question was
for adjourning the debate, which was acknowledged to be true. But
then Sir Thomas Meeres stood up and said that it was true that was the
proper Question and a fair Question, but then he desired to be graunted
to him that upon that Question, the Yeas were to go forth and the Noes
to stay in. Which the (Que—*del.*) Speaker yielded to be true because
the Question came on by order of the house and therefore it was orderly
it should be determined before we rose. But I thinke that reason will not
hold, for we may order when we will begin a debate but never when
we will end it, and it is as orderly that a debate should be adjourned,
when we are not ready for the Question, as that it shall be ended by a
Question when we are ready for it, and I never saw it done this manner
before. But the Speaker having yielded it, the Question for adjourning
the debate was put.

The Yeas who went forth were 116
The Noes who staid in were 124

---

[1] *sic*, for Leoline.

After which they put the maine Question, which was likewise carried, and then we adjourned.

[*CJ*, ix, 346-7; G, iii, 193-207; Finch, 28 May 1675]

[f.30]   *Saturday, 29 May*[1]

This day we met at the house and staid there a great while before we could make 40 to adjourne. At last that being done we waited on the Speaker to church, where we found about 20 members more, making about 60 in all, and in the church the thinnest congregacion that ever I saw. Dr Oughtram, the minister of St Margaret's, preached before us.

Monday, 31 May

This day I made my report of the amendments to the bill for repairing of churches, which I were chairman of. Some addicions being offered, the house entred into it but adjourned the debate till tomorrow.

Then we went upon the businesse of Mr Demahoy, which had been heard on Fryday last before the Lords.

We ordered the counsell which were against Mr Demahoy to be sent for, and many urged they should be sent for in custodie, but that would not passe, it being plaine, that Mr Demahoy was no partie to the cause in court, nor had any counsell there, but was concernd in the consequence of it as a legatee.

Then we went to the businesse of my Lord Lauderdale, and the Question was for a second addresse to the King upon the former proofes, viz., the words he had spoke and the armie raised in Scotland, to both which the King had given us an answer.

But they did not proceed upon any farther proofes, or the words testified by Burnet, as it was thought they would.

They who spake against a second addresse went alltogether upon the act of grace by which those things alledged against him were unquestionably pardoned, and these were Secretarie Coventry, Sir John Berkenhead, Lord Ogle [inserted in margin], Mr Sayer, Sir Thomas Jones, Sir Charles Wheeler, my Lord Anckram, Mr Demahoy and my selfe.

They who were for it, insisted upon nothing but that the house was ingaged in it by the former addresse, and made a vaine distinction between an act of oblivion and an act of grace, which had no foundacion at all in reason or in law, they being alltogether the same and no difference allowed between them in Westminster Hall, nor ought to be here. [f.30v] They who spoke against my Lord Lauderdale were Sir Kingsmill Lacie, Lord Cavendish, Sir Thomas Lee, Mr Vaughan, Mr Powle and

---

[1] There is no entry for this day in *CJ* or in G.

Sir Robert Howard. Sir Thomas Littleton nor Sacheverill did not speake at all, which was taken notice of and the reason given to me in private, that my Lord Lauderdale was agreed with Sir Thomas Littleton in private about accusing my Lord Treasurer, but that might be false and given out only to divide my Lord Treasurer's partie from him.

At 3 of the clock we came to a vote for a second addresse to his Majestie for removing my Lord Lauderdale.

The house divided, the Yeas who went out were 136

The Noes who staid in were 116.

That which I spoke was chiefly directed to what Mr Vaughan had said

1. His instance of a deputy lieutenant who had raised warr against the King, and had got his pardon. We might yet in Parliament doubtlesse addresse to have him put out of commission.

2. We had broken in upon the great act of indemnitie by removing men in corporacions after faults pardoned by that act.

3. We did no more in this, than the parliament had formerly done. 29 of Henry 6, we find an addresse to the King to remove about 30 people from the King and court meerly because they were displeasing to the people.

1. I said, that was not the case. A pardon of the King's did in great measure leave us the libertie of our owne sentiments and proceedings, but a pardon by act of parliament which was our owne act and done by and on behalfe of all the commons of England, did certainly ty us up, and if a deputy lieutenant had such a pardon I tooke it to stand neither with our honour nor justice to question him again for it, nor indeed so much as to mencion it, it being to all intents and purposes as if the fault had never been committed.

2. The second instance made against the Question. It is true we had broken into the ¹great¹ act of oblivion, but it is as true that that was done by a new act of parliament, a plain confession that [what] was done by act of parliament, must be avoided by an act of equall authoritie or not at all. And so was an argument against a second addresse, but none for it.

[f.31]   17

3. To the third I said it was most directly against the Question, for the case cited was 29 Henry 6, against the Duke of Somerset, Lord Dudley and many others. The King's answer was, that all should be removed ¹at the desire of the Commons¹ except the Lords, and this person being a peere of this Kingdome, we could not possibly make that president a ground of our addresse, to which the answer had been so contrarie to our desires.

¹ . . . . ¹ interlineated.

I also showed the vanitie and emptinesse of the distinction made between acts of oblivion and acts of grace. In which part I were seconded by Mr Sawyer and Sir Thomas Jones.

[*CJ*, ix, 347-8; G, iii, 207-17]

Tuesday, 1 June

This day after 3 private billes of small importance, we called before us Serjeant Pemberton, Sir John Churchill, Serjeant Peck and Mr Porter, who had been counsell in the Lords' house for Sir Nicholas Crispe in an appeale against my Lady Bowyer who was executrix to the Lady Dirleton, who was executrix to the Lord Dirleton, father to the Dutchesse Hamilton, wife to Mr Demahoy a member of the house of Commons. So Mr Demahoy was a legatee. Now the Lady Cranbourne and the Lady Bowyer and Mr Demahoy had had a decree in chancerie against Crispe for some money, from which decree Crispe appealed to the Lords, who had ordered notice to be given to Mr Demahoy to appeare if he pleased. Who thereupon did appeare to the appeale, but after that the house having forbad any of their members to appeare in the house of Lords, he had forbore to proceed. But the other defendants did appeare, and he was really concerned in the successe but not properly a partie to the suit. At least, he did not appear so, nor had any counsell there.

That which was laid to the charge of these counsell, was that they had been counsell at the Lords' barre against a member of our house, and so given up the priviledge of the house.

To which they answered severally but all to the same purpose, [f.31v] That 2 of them were serjeants at law who are sworne not to refuse to be of counsell with those who desire them.

That they had all refused their briefes and fees, because a member of the house of Commons was concerned.

That affidavit had been made against them in the house of Lords for doing so.

That they had been assigned councell for the plaintiffs by the Lords.

That they had a second order from the Lords served upon them to be of councell with the plaintiffs at their perils.

That they never had any notice at all of the order of our house, it being never promulgated, by posting up in the lobby, the first and lowest kind of notice that ever is given of our orders. Much lesse were they served with the order.

That Mr Demahoy had put in his answer before the Lords before they meddled with the cause, which they conceived a waver of his priviledge, and is so understood in all inferior courts.

That the councell on the defendants' side, all declared that they were of councell with my Lady Bowyer and Lord of Salisbury, heire to the Lady Cranborne, who was dead before the triall, and not at all for Mr Demahoy, who was concerned indeed in the consequence of the judgment, but was not properly a partie to the suit, he being only a legatee claiming under my Lady Cranborn as executrix.

That their case was very hard, since the Lords would certainly have sent them to the Tower if they had disobeyed their order, and now they were in danger of the same punishment by us for obeying it. So they protested their innocence, their respects to the house, and submitted themselves to the judgment of the house.

[f.32] This was said by them and they being withdrawne, was urged on their behalfe in the house. But after a long debate, the Question being put for taking them into custodie of the serjeant, and being put severally and first upon Serjeant Pemberton

The Yeas who went out were 154

The Noes who staid in were 146

and then the rest put severally, were all carried.

I thought the whole matter very unreasonable and that they were in no fault at all.

This being over Mr Sawyer moved to send Sir John Fagg to the Tower, whose compliance with the Lords in putting in his answer after he had complained to our house, was the cause of all this misunderstanding between us and the Lords. This was done, without doubt, in revenge for our having sent the 4 lawyers to our serjeant in custodie, and after some debate it was carried in the affirmative.

It was then moved by the other side that Mr Demahoy might also be sent to the Tower, but it not appearing that he had done anything at all since our order against appearing upon appeales; and protesting to us that neither directly nor indirectly he had applyed himselfe to them or owned their power; that all the councell had declared they did not appear for him, and one word which was said of him appeared plainly to be extorted from the councell by the Lords, only that they might use it as a proofe that they had proceeded upon a member of parliament, and it being not in his power to stop the suit, or hinder the other defendants from going on, the house absolved him, but ordered summons to be sent to Sir Nicholas Crisp to answer for his prosecuting an appeale against a member of parliament.

[*CJ*, ix, 348-50; G, iii, 218-30]

[f.32v]   *Wednesday, 2 June*

This day the house called again the defaulters and ordered letters to be sent to the severall counties and boroughs which they serve for.

Then they ordered a conference to be desired of the Lords upon the matter delivered by their Lordships at the last conference, and reasons were drawne up to be used at that conference. And one of those reasons being not proper to the matter in hand, which was to give reasons against a limited and restrained conference, but striking at their Lordships' judicature in generall, I spoke against adding that to the other reasons, but it was voted to passe and then I were nominated to (carry— *del.*) go up to the Lords to desire a conference, and the reason was because I had spoke against it, though that reason was not given. (and— *del.*) I went up accordingly, and their Lordships granted a conference as I desired, and presently in the painted chamber.

The house sent up to the conference.

Then we received a message from the Lords by the Lord Chief Justice North and Lord Chiefe Baron Turner, that the Lords desired a conference with us about matters of high importance where in the dignity of the King and safetie of the government was concerned. To which we agreed.

Then we went upon the 4 lawyers ordered yesterday to be taken into custody, of which one, Sir John Churchill, was taken by our serjeant, and taken from him by the Black Rod.

After a long debate whether they had been in custody and escaped or not, some confession from their mouths to the Speaker at dinner was urged to prove they had been in custody, for the serjeant could not testify any such thing. I was made use of for proofe, and voted that 3 of them, viz., Peck, Pemberton and Churchill, had been in custody, and that they had escaped, and should be brought again tomorrow.

[*CJ*, ix, 350-1; G, iii, 230-8]

[f.33]   18

Thursday, 3 June

This day was appointed to consider how to regulate the increase of the court of chancerie, but nothing done in it.

The bill for Habeas Corpus, being ingrossed, was read the third time and passed.

Then we went up to the conference which was appointed this day at the Lords' desire, and there my Lord Privy Seale, who managed, delivered their Lordships' sense in very high words, calling our proceedings a strange usurpacion, as transcendent invasion upon Magna Charta and the peticion of right and the highest indignitie to the King. That we were no court and had no judicature at all, and they were the highest court and had jurisdiction over all persons and in all causes.

And concluded with a roll which they produced being 1 Henrici quarti, numero 79, as it is cited by them, but I observed in Cotton's abridgment it is num.80.

Upon this, being returned from the conference, we had long debate and were generally well pleased that in their Lordships' discourse there was more of words and noise than reason and argument, and resolved to demand a conference with them in answer to this, and appointing severall members to draw up reasons for this conference against to-morrow we adjourned.

[f.33v] In the afternoon I were sent for to Wallingford house where were my Lord Keeper, Lord Treasurer, Duke of Lauderdale and Bishop of Salisbury, and of our house Sir Charles Wheeler, Mr Cheney and my selfe.

(we—*del.*) That being past, Mr Cheney and I went to the committee which sat till past ten at night about the businesse of Newarke, where they referred the validitie of the pattent back to the house, but voted that if the pattent be good

1. The right of election is in the mayor, aldermen and inhabitants paying scot and lot;
2. and that Mr Savill is well chosen by the said mayor aldermen and inhabitants;
3. And Sir Paul Neale also chosen by the said mayor aldermen and inhabitants.

I were in the negative as to the first and third. The first as conceiving the election well limited by the pattent to the mayor and aldermen alone. And to the third because Sir Paul Neile did never pretend to be chosen by the inhabitants but waived and denied all right of electing in them, and did so, both at the election and at the committee by his councell.

[*CJ*, ix, 352-3; G, iii, 239-47]

[f.34]   *Friday, 4 June*

This day, after a private bill or two, the Speaker informed us that coming through Westminster Hall he had taken notice of Serjeant Pemberton one of the lawyers ordered to be taken by the house into custody, and that he had been so contemptuous as not to put off his hat to him, and that he had commanded his (servant—*del.*) mace bearer and servants to lay hold of him and take him prisoner, which they had done and brought him into the Speaker's chamber.

Then the house ordered the 3 other lawyers to be sent for from the barres where they were pleading, this being the first day of the terme. I moved to deferr it till the afternoon, in regard the courts of justice were now sitting and the place thereby priviledged, and that I thought there was no example yet made, when we had fetched prisoners away while they were attending the courts.

The Speaker took me downe and said it was much otherwise for that a warrant of this house had fetcht a judge off from the bench in Westminster Hall to answer at our barr. I sate downe with it, but I could not then nor yet can heare of any such instance, nor anything like it. It is true that an order from the Lords did fetch Judge Berkley from the bench up to the Lords' house, but that was after he was impeached by the Commons of high treason, and so in no part sutable to the present case.

[f.34v] The house having ordered the serjeant to go downe he went and many members went downe with him, which I thinke they ought not to have done. The serjeant coming to the chancerie challenged Sir John Churchill, Serjeant Peck and Mr Porter for his prisoners. They replied first, they had a protection from the Lords, which they read to the serjeant. He told them, they might plead it at the Commons' barr, for he must carry them thither. They then stood upon the priviledge of the place, that was the King's court, and in his presence and never violated by arrest of any person, and appealed to the Master of the Rolles who was then sitting, the Lord Keeper being by great providence just gone at that moment into the court of Exchequer to sweare Mr Bertie into the place of a Baron. Which was very lucky and fortunate as his friends thought, but the Master of the Rolles refusing to meddle in it, and leaving it to their discretion, they all submitted and were brought to the Speaker's chamber. Where they continued 3 or 4 hours. The question was to send them to the serjeant's house or to the Tower, or to set up beds in the Speaker's chamber for them. They agreed upon the Tower for the securitie of the place from being forced by the authoritie of the Lords and the question being put the Yeas were 152

and the Noes who staid in were 147.

They were sent by water and the Black Rod soon after them but the Lieutenant answered they were committed by the house of Commons, and he could not deliver them.

[f.35]   18 [*sic*]

A strange and to my thinking most improper vote, there having been no warrant to seize them, no service upon them, no notice of any order or rule of the house to imprison them and[1] strange was the escape, which was no more than that the serjeant had not brought them to the barr that morning, whereas there was no order for bringing them thither, nor for them to come of themselves, nor had the serjeant ever told them they should come, or so much as been to look after them.

But this was voted against 3. As to the fourth, Mr Porter, he was past by, for as little reason as the others were ordered to be brought, for aught appeared to me.

Then we tooke into consideracion the behaviour of our serjeant Sir James Norfolke, in this and many other occasions. That he had not kept these men when they came out of the parliament door, that he had

---

[1] written over 'no less'

never taken them, and that he had let them go when he had them, but more particularly, that he and the Black Rod had met so just at Sir John Churchill's chamber, which seemed to be a contrivance between them. And many other misdemeanours were heaped up, so that fairly we did vote him to the Tower, and he hearing it, being then in the house, as fairly tooke his heeles and ran away. We sent the deputy serjeant to arrest him and carry him to the Tower, but he could not find him.

Then a mocion made by Mr Stockdale and seconded by Mr Thynne, that Sir Edward Bainton should be called to the barr for crying to a Question put it again, setting still in his place with his hat on. And this he did 3 times, twice after he was told of it. But it was past by.

[*CJ*, ix, 353-4; G, iii, 247-60]
[ff.35v, 36, 36v blank]

[f.37]   19

Saturday, 5 June

This morning being met, the house not very full, Sir John Mallet offered a report from a committee to a bill. Sir Thomas Lee presently rose and said he observed gentlemen very forward in the reading of billes, but there was something upon us that was more important, which was the securing of our privileges. That he saw a new serjeant attending us, that we had a very good one yesterday who had done us good service, that if he were turned out for that and especially, as it was reported, at the complaint of the Lords for his obeying our orders, we should never have obedience paid to us any more, and therefore moved, that before anything else we should enter upon consideracion thereof and do nothing till our priviledges were secured. This was seconded by others, who added that the doores should be locked. Then Colonel Sandys moved that all our members should be sent for up out of the hall, and then he had something to move us, which he thought for our service. This was ordered, but then presently Secretarie Coventry stood up saying he had something to deliver to us from the King, which was that it was his pleasure we *should immediately adjourne till 4 of the clock in the afternoon, and then attend his Majestie in the Banqueting House and that he had sent the same message to the Lords. Some would have gone upon the businesse of the serjeant, but we generally cried to adjourne. But it being moved by Sir Eliab Harvey and Sir Thomas Littleton to adjourne first the debate about the serjeant, it was consented unto, and so we rose*[1] adjourning till four in the afternoon.

On the afternoon we met and attended the Speaker to Whitehall, on foot, but not adjourning the house because we all thought fit to sit

[1] The section italicised was subsequently underlined by Dering.

after we had heard the King's speech, not knowing what it might import. The King spoake to us of the unhappy differences between us and the Lords. That it was the effect of those councels he had forewarned us at our meeting. That it were worth our while to find out the promoters and contrivers of it, being assured that they were enemies to him and to the church of England, and if we knew the persons, we would abhorre the councells which came from them. That for the present he knew no better way to get out of the difficultie [f.37v] we lay under by the misunderstanding between us, than by frequent and full conferences, which he said would either bring us to a good understanding between ourselves, or give him the opportunitie of interposing as a mediator between us, when all had been said, on either side, which the matter would beare, and that his judgment should allways be impartiall between his two houses. But while he was carefull of our rights, he intended not that his owne should be violated. And commending to us care and moderacion, so left us.

Upon our returne to the house, we entered upon consideracion of the King's speech, and Sir Phillip Musgrave first moved that we should give the King thanks, which was agreed unto, only the old dispute whether it should be thanks for his speech or for the gracious expressions in his speech. And the last was consented to as being much the same thing, and more unanimous. So it past nemine contradicente.

Then Sir Thomas Littleton moved that we might cleare ourselves, the King's speech intimating that contrivers and fomentors of these differences were among us. That if any one knew any such he should name him. If not, that we should passe a vote for vindicating the honour of the house and every particular member of it. This was opposed by some as unnecessarie (but gener—*del.*). And Colonel Sandys and Mr Cheney moved a committee might be named to enquire after the authors of these differences, but this was rejected in great earnest, by Garaway and Meeres and the rest. But the dispute rested whether we should say: It did not appeare to this house or in the judgment of this house, no member thereof was guilty of any such contrivance. At last the house divided, and the

Yeas who went out were 117[1]
The Noes were 104

So the words it doth not appeare, stand in the Question. And so it past.[2]

(*CJ*, ix, 354-5; G, iii, 260-8; Finch, 5 June 1675]

[1] *CJ, op. cit.*, gives 171.
[2] No diary sheets have been preserved for the sittings of 7, 8 and 9 June (cf. *CJ*, ix, 355-7; G iii, 269-89 and Finch, 7-9 June 1675).

4

THE ACCOUNT BOOK OF SIR EDWARD DERING

April 1680 to April 1683

Kent Archives Office, U 275 A3; photocopy in the House of Lords Record Office, Historical Collections, 86/1. Transcripts from this and the succeeding volume of Accounts (item 5) were made by the Rev. Thomas Streatfield for additions to Edward Hasted's *History of Kent* (1778, etc.), and are now preserved in BL Add 33,892, ff. 617 et seqq.

The Account Book of Sir Edward Dering
April 1680 to April 1683

The volume is entitled on the cover in a somewhat later hand 'Sir Edward Dering's Private Accounts from 1680 to 1682'. Some leaves are defective as a result of fungoid decay; many have been torn out. The existing pages have been given a continuous numeration in this text for ease of reference; the intermittent original pagination by Dering is indicated within round brackets.

page

[Autobiography of Sir Edward Dering]

[p.10]   *April 1680*

Intending to enter in this booke all occurrences as they shall dayly
happen, that it may serve for a repertorie to my son if he have occasion
of any informacion heareafter, which were advisable in all familyes, and
I wish I had begun it sooner, I shall in the first place give though very
briefely and succinctly an accompt of my life past, a dreame now of
54 yeares continuance.

   November 12, (1625)[2] Saturday in the evening I were borne at
Surrenden. I were christened December 8 being kept so long (as I have
heard) in expectacion of the Duke of Buckingham coming to be my
godfather, my mother being related to him,[3] but that failed, and the
first misfortune I had was the losse of that prudent and virtuous mother
(1628). The next was that of my Father marrying again which followed
soon after (1629). At 6 I were put to schoole to a barbarous tyrant at
Hethfield (1632). Soon after removed to Mr Farnaby in London (1633).
The yeare following to Mr Craig a private schoole at Throwley (1634)
and in 1637 to Mr Copping at Woodford in Kent, and from thence I

----

   [1] It had been rumoured that Daniel Dering had refused to drink the King's health.
   [2] Those dates placed by Dering in the margin have been incorporated in the text between
round brackets.
   [3] See the genealogical table at the end of this volume.

went to Sidney College in Cambridge (1639) and from thence I removed to Emanuel (1640), where I kept my act publiquely in the schooles (a thing not very usuall for fellow commoners to do) and tooke my degree of Bachelor of arts.

I went with my father to wait upon the King, who was then driven from his parliament, and were with him at the raising of his royall standard at Nottingham (1642). I were with him also before the walls of Coventry, which refused to open their gates to him and which he could not force.[1] I returned to Cambridge, but about the end of '43, Oliver Cromwell coming to reforme the Universitie, I thought best to retire, and by my father's leave went over to Leyden to follow my studies there. Where I too soon had the sad newes that my deare and worthily dear father was dead 22 June (1644) of an imposthume in his head, taking beginning as it was verily thought, from a box on the eare given him many yeares before at Westminster schoole, he having a long time complained of a great paine in one side of his head.

I came over immediatly upon this occasion, and the rather because all my estate was under sequestracion, by the parliament, which upon my peticion to the committee was discharged,[2] and I went presently after (not so much as coming to London during my stay in England) into France viz. in December 1644, where I staid about 18 moneths and came back in 1646. I had hitherto followed my studies very well, my owne sedentary inclinacions and my father's encouragement and example having disposed me to it, but now the cares of the world, the distraction of the times, a broken fortune and great debts, and some disputes at law between my stepmother and myselfe[3] tooke up much of my time which might have been imployed that way, and the warrs being ended by that fatall battle of Naseby, and most men believing things would end in some kind of accomodacion between the King and [*ms. torn*] the overthrow of the monarchie and murther [*ms. torn*] last it proved, and having [p.11] past the small pox, which tooke me just when I were 21 yeares old, I began to thinke of marriage, which sometime after (1648) I happily effected with Mistress Mary Harvey daughter of Daniel Harvey esq., a Turkey merchant of very eminent loyaltie, prudence, integritie and generositie.[4] He had one son, afterwards Sir Daniel Harvey and the King's ambassador at Constantinople, who

---

[1] On 20 Aug. 1642; cf. Gardiner, 1603-1642, x (1891 ed.), 218-19.

[2] Dering's father on 7 Feb. 1644 had petitioned the Commons for the benefit of the declaration of both Kingdoms, consenting to the House taking out of his estate what proportion they pleased but preserving him from ruin (*CJ*, iii, 390). He took the Covenant, was allowed two-thirds of his estate, on security to pay one third to Parliament. On 27 July, as Dering had been 'in actual war against Parliament', a fine was fixed at £1000 (he having an estate of £800 p.a.) but on 20 Aug. this was remitted and the estate discharged. (*CC Comp.* pt. ii, 831-2.)

[3] For letters indicating the somewhat constrained relations between Dering and Unton, Lady Dering, see p. 4, n. 1, above.

[4] The marriage was on 5 April 1648, 'at Little St Bartholomewes in London, Mr. William Hall officiating' (Blake MS. D).

married the daughter of the Lord Montague of Boughton, and 3 daughters, Elisabeth, married to Sir Heneage Finch esq., now Baron of Daventry and Lord Chancellor of England, Mary my wife, and Sarah wife to Robert Lord Bulkeley.[1]

We lived 4 yeare with my wife's mother at Lambeth on free cost, when my brother Finch's children and mine growing numerous on both sides, it was time to part, and I hired a house in St Johns Close near Clarkenwell (1652) where we lived a yeare, but finding London chargeable for housekeeping we removed to Old Comb neare Croydon, a house of my brother Harvey's, where we lived till the death of that most excellent woman my mother Harvey (1655). Then we removed to a house I hired of my cousin Cooke in Pluckley Street. In 1658 my grandmother being now dead, we removed to Church House.

We put off our house and came to take lodgings in London (1659) so to be as private and unobserved as we could in respect of the times. We had not been long in London but some dawne of a better day appeared, and by Fleetwood and Desborowe's forsaking Richard Cromwell the then protector, and by the jealousies between the then governing power and generall Monke in Scotland we began to have some hopes of the returne of the King, and upon Monke's declaring for a free parliament I thought fit to leave my lodging in London, and having most carefully and resolutely refused during all the time of the usurped powers all manner of publique imployments either in the militia, the peace or in their many mock parliaments, knowing them unlawful in the foundacion and either mischievous or at best insignificant in the execucion, and thinking this the first opportunitie ofered since the last King's death of doing service to my country, I went downe into Kent, and declared to stand for knight of shire. Many would have discouraged me, by reason of an order then published by the councell of state that none whose fathers had been in the King's armie or sequestred in that accompt should be chosen, but my answer was, that when we met in parliament either the greater number would be for bringing in the King and then the restraint put on elections by the councell would signify nothing at all, for the parliament when met would [*ms. torn*] the councell, and not the councell the parliament [*ms. torn*] the parliament should not be of the same mind with me [*ms. torn*] restoring the King, I should not value the being turned [*ms. torn*].

[p.12] Accordingly Sir John Tufton and my selfe having the assistance of all the royalists and moderate men in the countie, and Coll. Weldon and Mr Bois of Betshanger being set up against us by those of differing judgments, at the day of election, viz. [*blank*] we had it by so vast a disparitie, they being not one thousand and our partie judged to be 6,000, that it was yielded without polling, and all over in two houres time.

[1] See genealogical table at the end of this volume.

The parliament being set and the King voted home, he entred London 29 May (1660), being also his birthday, and I believe there never was in any nacion upon eny occasion so much joy, both inwardly felt and outwardly exprest, as was in this kingdom from the day of His Majestie's landing at Dover, which was May [25], to his coming to London on the 29th.

The parliament being done and another called in May 1661, I thought of nothing more than setling my selfe quietly at home, to governe my small fortune and many children as well as I could, and all the Kingdome now having the face of lasting peace and increasing happinesse upon it, I agreed with my mother in law for to hire Surrenden House of her, which she had now enjoyed since 1644. Nor indeed had I been earnest to take it till now, having had during the late calamitous times more care to hide myselfe from observation, and by shifting of habitacion to avoid all the dangers of their power and the snaire of their oathes, ingagements and finding of armes, than to appeare in any splendor. And I thanke God I may safely say that though many have deserved better of the King in his exile than I have done, yet I thinke none that staid in England, have offended him lesse than my selfe, having never taken any sort of imployment under them, never taken any covenant, oath, or ingagement, never so much as found any armes, never forsaking, nor more than by silence and avoiding dangerous and talkative companie, concealing my opinion in relacion to the King or the Church. As for not suing my tenants for that part of their rent which they paid in taxes, I thinke under the unresistable and indeed for all my time, viz. from 1648 to 1660, plainly uncontroverted power, that then all men were, it was not [to] be stiled a crime in conscience, nor could be punished at law, though there were no act of oblivion to bury it.

[Two folios have been torn out of the volume at this point.]

[p.13] During our stay heare which was about a weeke (1669) I received news from London that the King had made my selfe, Sir Thomas Strictland [Strickland] and Judge Millward commissioners for the Privy Seale, which did much surprize me, not having made the least application towards it. But as soon as I came to London I found it to be true and the commission was soon after past, which engaged me again to leave my owne home and to take a house in towne. The salarie we had was £5 per diem from the King, among us three, and the fees of the seale, which never came to two hundred pound per annum, so that the whole was about 650 per annum to each of us, and I am sure the difference of expence between living in the country upon one's owne and leaving the country to live in the towne, was as much to me as that came to. However the honour of so great a trust, my desire to serve the King and to give some countenance to my children who now began to grow up, made me very willing to receive that imployment.

Sir Clifford Clifton being dead (1670) who served as burgesse for East Redford in Nottinghamshire, and my Lady being my very good friend, and the interest of that towne being chiefly in the family of Clifton and in my Lord Ogle now Duke of Newcastle, upon their recommendacions, being my selfe totally a stranger, I went downe thither with my son Southwell, and was there unanimously chosen their burgesse,[1] and in the next session which was in November tooke my place in parliament.

April 19 (1673). The King having about Christmasse before put the Treasurie that had been since my Lord Southampton's death, 1667, in commission, into a single hand, viz. my Lord Clifford's, was now pleased to put the Privy Seale also into a single hand, viz. my Lord Anglesey, and accordingly I did this day, the other 2 commissioners being out of towne, deliver up the privy seale to his Majestie in his closet at Whitehall.[2] We had fair promises made us by the King, Lord Treasurer, Lord Arlington, of being considered by the King for the imployment we quitted, there being indeed no manner of fault found with us in that administracion, and accordingly my two brethren had presently each of them a pencion of £400 per annum settled upon them, but no such thing was done for me, nor anything else during my Lord Clifford's time, and I who never knew what it was either to pray or pay for court favours (the two most prevailing topicks in our time) did not so much grieve as wonder at the distinction then made between us, and the disobligacion laid particularly upon me, which I did ascribe in my thoughts particularly to my Lord Clifford, the factotum of that time, and thinking that too dearly bought to a modest man which cost much submission and long importunitie, neglected all farther sollicitacion, resolving to apply my selfe with more care to my private affaires.[3] This moneth I treated two matches, one for my eldest son with Mistress Norton with Sir John Norton her unkle. Her porcion, left by Sir John's elder brother her father, was but £3,000, but the expectacions were great from Sir John who had no children. But Sir John, though full of expressions of kindnesse to her, yet absolutely refusing [*ms. torn*] her anything at present, or secure anything at his [*ms. torn*] I could not settle my estate as I desired upon my son [*ms. torn*] for £3,000, which was all she had or probably enough suit [*ms. torn*] and so I [*ms. torn*].

[p. 14] The other match was between my daughter Mary, and Mr Thomas Knatchbull, second son to Sir Norton (1673). The estate was not much but being a very civill man, well beloved by all that knew him, one that seemed to love my daughter very well, and the hopes of future kindnesse from Sir Norton to him, and my owne friendship with the family, induced me into it, which accordingly was consummate 10 May at Covent Garden church, Dr Patrick officiating. And this

---

[1] The return is dated 8 Nov. 1670 (*Return*, i, 526).
[2] See p. 55 above.
[3] But see the Introduction, p. 13 above.

being done, in a few dayes after I retired to Surrenden, once more thinking my selfe setled there and allwayes being well content so to be.

In August I treated a match for my eldest son with Mistress Culpeper. Her mother (widdow of Sir Richard) had often said she would give her £5,000, and had to Dr Stapeley severall times exprest an inclinacion to marry her to my son. The fortune was not great, but my son was now 23. This was a very considerable family in our owne country, and the young lady of competent beautie and of great repute of prudence, sweetnesse and obedience to her mother, so that I resolved to take £5,000, and a meeting being appointed at Mr Thornhill's, did not doubt but it would soon have been concluded, but instead of £5,000 she offered me £1,000 in present money and £1,000 after her death and some parcells of land in Oxfordshire and lease about Raynam, which alltogether did not in my valuacion come to above £4,000, and in a most broken and confused manner even that. I would have consented to take the £1,000 in money and the rest in land and left the valuacion of that land to any indifferent person, but she was very high and resolute. I would take what she would give and as she would value it, either not being able to give £5,000 or believing my son had an affection for her daughter. They would indeed I thinke have been content with a very moderate settlement upon my son, but I that had as much care of him as of myselfe in his marriage, had no mind to make my selfe whole upon him, of what they failed my just expectacions in, and so being not at all satisfied with my Ladye's manner of treating I parted and soon after broke it quite off, having read a letter from Sir Thomas Culpeper of Hollingborne (as I remember) that my Lady would do no more than she had said at Mr Thornhill's, and I having had but an ill informacion of the lease at Raynam which was indeed the principall part of the porcion. Mistress Culpeper after married Mr Stapeley.[1]

This yeare (1674) I built a house in Great Russell Street in Blomesbury, and in the end of the yeare, viz. February [1675], before it was quite finished, I let it to the Countesse of Middleton for 21 yeares at £70 per annum rent, and £100 fine. I had this yeare a very great deale of trouble with Philpot my principall tenant who was much in my debt and was mightily intangled with Mr Brett, Mr Pullen, John Harrison and others.

[p.15] This summer (1675) I began to build my second house in Great Russell Street in Blomesbury.

September 14, Mr Sandford Treasurer of the Hamburgh companie, Captain Collier, Mr Carleton, Mr Clarke, Mr Holman, Master Jones secretarie and others, 13 in all, of the companie came to Surrenden to me to intreat me to accept of the name of Governor of the Hamburgh companie, I having been unanimously chosen to it by the companie there. I were very much surprized at it, being utterly a stranger to every

---

[1] See letters in *DS Corr.*, A/24 and A/28.

one at Hamburgh, and were very unwilling to ingage in a businesse I understood not, but their importunitie and my good nature prevailed, and I accepted the government but only so as I might have my libertie to leave it, at the end of the yeare, yet upon perusing their charter I found they were bound to chuse a freeman of their owne companie, and when I came to London I refused to act as governor because though now a freeman, I were not so at the time of my election. Whereupon the company heare wrote over to Hamburgh, and there I were upon a new court held for that purpose re-elected governor.

This yeare, 9 January [1676] Mr Cheyney and my selfe were made commissioners of the customs by his Majestie's favour, in the room of Sir William Thompson and Mr William Garaway whom he thought fit to remove. Our pattent beares date 8th of January 1675[/6]. Our salarie was £1,200 per annum.

This yeare (1676) I remember nothing remarkable, more than that I sold to Mr Peter Browne my farme in Tenterden consisting of lands of £36 per annum and about 17 Acres of wood. The price I had for it was £800, being the same I had paid about 20 yeares before when I bought it of Mr Curteis.

There having been a treatie (1677) between myselfe and my Lady Strode about a marriage between my eldest son and Mistress Elisabeth Cholmeley, my Ladye's eldest daughter by her first husband Sir William Cholmley, all things being now agreed the 9th of May was appointed for the wedding, when upon the 6 at night my son coming home from Whitehall was overturned in a hackney coach driving very fast at the corner of Bedford Street turning into Henrietta Street, against the corner post there, and so unfortunatly as he broke his left arme, upon which occasion the match was of necessitie defered for a moneth's time and at last upon Saturday the 9th of June was happily consummate at Chepsted. God give them many and happy yeares together.

On the 3rd of July they came home to Surrenden [*ms. torn*] for all that moneth and the next I had the company [*ms. torn*] most of my relacions and most of the gentlemen of [*ms. torn*] country who in kindnesse to me and my son came to [*ms. torn*].

[p.16] This yeare (1678) I began to build my house in Gerard Street and covered it though it was not finished till Michaelmas 1679.

July 24. My wife and I went to Epsom welles and dranke the water there for a weeke. I thinke it a very good and wholsome water. With some it bringeth the pain of the piles but I thinke neither that nor Northpall waters good to be drunke in towne, they being without doubt bought and sold either counterfeit, or at best mixt.

12 November. I received his Majestie's letter to the Duke of Ormond Lord Lieutenant of Ireland to passe a revercion of the auditor's place in Ireland after Mr Ware's death, who is in possession, and my owne who have the next revercion, unto my son Charles, which I sent out to

Sir John Temple and by his Grace's present consent to it it was soon dispatched and past under the Great Seale there.

Fryday, January 23 [1679]. The parliament which began 8th May 1661 and had been by divers sessions, adjournments and prorogacions, continued to this time, was by his Majestie in councell ordered to be dissolved and a proclamacion accordingly issued out and writs sent out immediatly for calling another upon the 6th of March next.

14 February. I together with Captain Deeds were chosen burgesses for Hith.

24 February. Sir Vere Fane and my son [Edward] Dering were chosen knights of the countie of Kent, Sir William Twisden who stood missing it.

March 26 (1679). His Majestie was pleased by his great seale to make the Earle of Essex, Mr Laurence Hyde, Sir John Ernely Chancellor of the Exchequer, myself, and Mr Sidney Godolphin, commissioners to execute the office of the Treasurer, which was now vacant by the Earl of Danbye's having resigned his staffe the day before. I were never more surprised at anything than the newes that I were to be one, having not made the least applicacion either to the King or any person in the court for it, nor ever having entertained a thought of it, being well enough contented with the employment I had in the customes, of lesse honour indeed, but lesse envy, less danger, lesse expence, and the profit not very different. However I resolved the King should dispose of me as he pleased.

Afterwards I came to know, that I were named one, purely and solely upon the recommendacion and good character given of me to the King by Mr Sidney Godolphin, one very high in the King's favour and most deservedly so for his great loyaltie integritie and abilitie. To me he was an absolute stranger. I knew his face, he being a member of parliament, but I do not remember that I had ever spoke one word to him upon any occasion whatsoever before this was done, and it was to me a wonderfull thing and of which I believe there are few instances in our court (or indeed in any) that one gentleman should preferr another to so considerable a place as this without any consideracion of friendship alliance or interest, without importunitie, without applicacion, indeed without the knowledg of the person himselfe or of any friend or relacion of his.

[p.17] The first thing we did considerable (1679) was to reduce the commissioners of the customes from 7, the commissioners of excise from ten, the commissioners of appeales from nine: all to five in each commission, by which the King saveth about 6,000 per annum, and his businesse better done. Then we tooke occasion frequently to expresse our resolucions against graunting revercions and against graunting any offices under us for any other terme but during the King's pleasure. By both which we much lessened our owne power and advantages if we had designed any for our selves, but they were both certainly good rules for his Majestie's service.

3 June. I married my daughter Anne to Wortley Whorwood esq., of Denton Court in Kent.[1]

8 August. The parliament having been lately dissolved and writs issued out for new elections, I was chosen again burgess for Hith. I had 20 voices being all that were present. Captain Hales had 15 and Sir William Honywood had five.

1 September. We removed from Great Russell Street to our new house which I had built in Gerard Street behind Leicester garden.

10 September. My son, after 3 days polling, was chosen knight of the shire of Kent. Sir William Twisden stood and lost it. The poll for Twisden 1,452, for Dering 2,106. But of the particulars of this and his last election see my daybook wherein the whole progresse is set downe.

But since of the last five legall elections for our countie our family hath succeeded in four, viz. in 1640, my father and Sir John Colepeper, in 1660 the healing parliament which brought in the King, Sir John Tufton and myselfe, in 1661 Sir Thomas Peyton and Sir John Tufton, in the last and this present parliament Sir Vere Fane and my son both times, I thinke it is now time to set downe in quiet and leave other gentlemen to take their turnes. Few having in our countie had the honour to be chosen twice knight of the shire, and no young man that I know of, during his father's life but only my son.

As to the many mock parliaments and illegall elections during the rebellion and usurpacion, as I never attempted to stand myselfe, nor would ever appeare to give any countenance to them or any vote in them, so I reckon them all as nothing or worse than nothing.

17 October. This day the parliament met according to the writ and was immediately prorogued to 26 January, and upon the 26 of January again to the 15 April 1680.

2 December: My son Daniel went from home to port in order to go to sea, his Majestie having been pleased to make him lieutenant to captain [*ms. torn*] commander of the Bristoll, a third rate frigate. Fortune [*ms. torn*].

[p.18] February (1679[/80]). Mr Dene received out of the Exchequer £1,590 for my son Whorwood,[1] being 1,500 which I paid him as part of my daughter's porcion, and at his desire lent it to the King in the Exchequer on an order on the tax. £1,550 thereof Mr Dene tooke and lent Mr Temple and past me on their bond, and the £40 was left with me and I paid it my son in Aprill following.

18 March. My cousin Clotworthy Skeffington married my cousin Hungerford, daughter of Sir Edward Hungerford, her porcion £5,000 when the bridegroom cometh to age, and £10,000 at her father's death.

[1] Wortley Wherewood; see the pedigree at the end of the volume.

10 March. My son Southwell began his journey for Brandenburgh whether his Majestie sends him his envoye extraordinaire. I sent Charles[1] with him, taking this opportunitie to let him see this part of Europe under so good a guide. God send them a happy voyage and a safe returne.

20 [March]. My daughter Southwell, her children and family came to lodge with me.

[p.22 (60)]   *Saturday, 22 May 1680*

This day I lent £1,800 into the [Ex]chequer, taking a tally upon the customes for repayment. Many do blame me and few perhaps will imitate me, because of the casualtie of the King's life, with which the customes do determine. But

1. if the customes be not granted by parliament after the King's death, the monarchie it selfe is at an end, there being nothing to maintain it.
2. The loane is but for a yeare, and in all probabilitie the King may live many.
3. I were willing to encourage others by my example to lend the King money at 6 per cent (and 1 for defraying charges) whereas he now hardly borroweth any under ten.

The necessitie of the occasion more than anything else induced me to it, £1,000 being expressly lent towards carrying on the new ships, viz. the first rate ship now in the [p.23] stocks at Chattham, and a second rate ship at Harwich which is very forward and wants but about £3,000 to finish her, and the whole fund allotted by the parliament for building 30 ships being exhausted, and six ships being yet unbuilt, by reason the King was persuaded to exceed the rates agreed upon by the parliament, either we must leave them with shame and losse, they being all began [to be] laid which will be alltogether spoiled, if not carried on, or we must take up the money as we can, which will be very difficult to do. However, this little summe was a helpe at present. I hope better supplyes will be found out before this is quite spent, Sir Anthony Deane and the commissioners of the Navy having told us, that £1,000 would keep them on a month.

The other £800 I lent expressly toward payment of tickets, which is a very good and charitable worke, for there being at least ten thousand pounds due in the ticket office, and generally to poor seamen, and these being to be paid in course, and the Treasurie not being able to supply for that use more than £500 a weeke, it would be 5 moneths at least before they could be paid, and their necessities pressing them they must either starve or sell their tickets for halfe their due, and this to so generall a dissatisfaction to the seamen, that it would extremely discourage them.

1 Dering's second surviving son, then aged 23.

from serving the King again, since they may have much better payment from merchants and not a few of them are tempted thereby to serve the Dutch and even the French and so in a little time from our usefull friends, may become our dangerous enemies. And it hath allwayes been complained of as a most mischievous thing the paying the seamen by tickets. This could not indeed at this time be avoided, by reason of the vast charge laid upon us at our coming in to the Navy, which is not yet cleared of, but I thought it good service for me to offer my poor mite towards it, and on that consideracion I lent this £800, which together with the £1,000 for the new ships, are the money I received from Sir Eliab Harvey, being money I had lent my brother Harvey, and Sir Eliab leaving it for me at Sir Robert Clayton. I this day tooke it thence and paid it into the Exchequer.

[p.24]   *Wednesday, 9 June 1680*

The King came to the Treasurie chamber, where we offered him as our advice, to give notice to Dashwood and the other farmers of the excise, that he would resume that farme at the end of 12 moneths, as by his covenant with them he might do. Which his Majestie resolved to follow. Lord Chancellor, Lord President, Earl of Essex and the two Secretaries of State, present at the debate.

Tuesday, 15 June 1680

The commissioners of the Treasurie went up to the mint, to enquire of Mr Slingsby whether the money were there which was wanting to satisfy the King, being about £4,900, and the merchants importers of bullion, to whom is due about £5,000, and not receiving satisfactory answers, we resolved to go forward with suspending him.

[p.26]   *Wednesday, 4 August 1680*

At 9 at night the commissioners of the Treasurie adjourned their publique meetings to the Monday after Michaelmas day.

[p.32]   *Thursday, 9 September 1680*

I met with the Hamburgh companie at Founders Hall. Mr Tite elected deputie having not yet accepted the place, and without the Governor or deputy no generall committee can be held, but an assembly may.

Wednesday, 15 September 1680

The King came to the Treasurie chamber where beside the commissioners of the Treasurie were the Lord Chancellor, President and Secretaries, and severall of the Privy Councell of Ireland. The matter in debate was Sir James Shaen's proposall to pay the £288,000 per annum for the Irish revenue which he now hath in farme at £240,000 per annum, so as the King would refuse the £200,000 now offered him by the Lord Lieutenant and Councell of Ireland by a bill transmitted for that purpose and to be past in parliament there. Sir James Shaen could show no good reasons why this act should prejudice him in his farme, since it would be laid by a land tax, and not upon trade, and payable in 4 years so that it seemed the King might have this without hurt to Sir James Shaen, and consequently have the benefit of his raising his rent also.

But it appearing that Sir James was behind with his rent at the value he now hath it,

That Sir James would have involved and swallowed up £60,000, which he oweth the King, by making this new bargain.

That in all likelyhood in the world we should differ with Sir James in the provisos and powers he would demand in his new lease, which he did not expresse what they were, but that he was to have all the King could give, and if we should first refuse this offer of the parliament and then differ with Sir James Shaen about the termes, the King would then have lost them both. We thought not fit to conclude anything but parted with order to Sir James to put his proposalls in writing and distinctly and for my owne part, I believe his project will come to nothing.

[p.34]   *Thursday, 14 October 1680*

I tooke in the £1,000 I had formerly lent in the Exchequer upon the disbanding act, the money being paid in there, and I lent it again to the King upon the revenue of the wine licences. I lend it at six per cent, which is not usuall, but I thinke not fit to take more while I am in the King's service. I have a tally for it in William Briggs his name bearing date [*blank*].

p.35]   *Thursday, 21 October 1680*

The parliament summoned as I take it to meet in October last, and then prorogued to January the 26, after that and many other prorogacions did begin to sit, and Mr William Williams chosen Speaker.

But all this parliament being spent in disputes and proposalls in discourse which came to nothing at last, the chiefe ground whereof seemed to be the earnestness of the house to passe the bill against the Duke of Yorke's succeeding to the crowne if the King should dy without children, he being taken and thought universally to be a papist. Which bill also past in the house of Commons but was rejected by the Lords.

And many messages from the King and many addresses from the house to the King about it and about Tangier. And I being obliged to attend dayly at the Treasurie and consequently coming late, and tired out commonly when I came hence, I tooke no notes at all though there were many things very remarquable, especially about breaches of priviledge, sending for men in custody upon slender profes of breach of priviledge, impeachment before the Lords of Lords and Commons and judges, understanding the statute of 25 E.3: in the point of declaring treasons not those exprest, and many other great points.

[p.36]   *January 1681*

Memorandum. The parliament businesse and the Treasurie businesse tooke me up so much I were commonly so tired when I came home, that I had no leisure to write anything, for those four months October, November, December and January.

The 10th of January the parliament was prorogued and by proclamacion dissolved on the 18th, and another summoned at Oxford for 21 March.

February 1681

The Earle of Sunderland turned out from being Secretarie of State and the Earle of Conway put in his place by the King, the latter end of January. His Majestie was pleased by his signe manuall to authorize Mr Laurence Hyde, cousin Daniel Finch and myselfe, to treat with whom we thought fit, for the improvement of his revenue in Ireland, and the reducing the civill list and enlarging the armie there, so as the garrison of Tangier might be both supplied and paid from thence, which would be a great ease to the King heare. We have met 3 times heare at my house about it, using for informacion chiefly the experience of Mr Roberts, and at this third meeting, taking in also Sir James Shaen the principall of the present farmers of the Irish revenue.

[p.38]   *Monday, 21 March 1681*

Monday being the day appointed by the King for the meeting of the

honour of those who have undertaken it, but the
honour of the whole house is engaged in it. &
therefore we ought to know upon what good
grounds we go.

All my Ld Treasurers friends were for having
the proofes produced to the house & so it was
carried.

— that night we met at wallingford house with my
Ld Treasurer. and found ye answers he could give
to every particular. we are to my thoughts
very satisfactory.

Tuesday. 27th

this day we proceeded upon the first article
objected agst my Ld Treasurer. it was that
of mr mentwords treasure of ye excise
a long debate of it.
and at last we came to a vote that we saw
no ground from that article to impeach my lord

In ye afternoon was at ye committee of election
the case between sr Lionell Jenkins & mr Hales
wch had depended above two years. before
the committee. the house having forborne
wheare it because most of the time of that
sitting sr Lionell had been abroad at Collen.
and so could not be summoned

mr Hales objected. 1 want of notice of ye time
of election. keeping out some wth offerd their votes
and were refused. & building two house for the
house & putting two poor children apprentices
all yt was clearly ansowed by sr Lionell Jenkin
and his election adiudged good

1 Sir Edward Dering's parliamentary diary for Spring 1675, fo. 12
(entries for 26 and 27 April 1675)

Within the painting, upper right:
Sir Edward Dering
Ob. 1684. Æt.
FATHER OF CAT
LADY PERCIVAL
DIED. A.D. 16

2 Sir Edward Dering, from the painting by Sir Godfrey Kneller

3 Lady Dering, from the painting by Thomas Hawker

4 Holograph draft speech by Sir Edward Dering concerning the Popish Plot
(see pp. 184–5 below)

parliament at Oxford, I set out from London, Mr Watson and my son going downe with me, and arrived at Oxford.

[*CJ*, ix, 705]

Wednesday, 23 March 1681

I tooke the oathes and test as required by the laws for all members of parliament.

[*CJ*, ix, 705-6]

[*Thursday*], *24 March 1681*

Past in the same manner by the severall members and in naming of the grand committee and other formes.

[*CJ*, ix, 706-8; G, viii, 292-9]

Friday, 25 March 1681

The house began upon businesse. One of the principall matters were the relacion made by Sir William Waller concerning a writing in the nature of a declaracion in which he most venomously bespattered King James, the last King and the present, with many foule and [*ms. torn*] aspercions upon them all. [p.39] And concluded with inciting all men to take up armes against the King. This the house thought so reflecting that they only suffered Sir William Waller to read it out of his paper, but did not let it be read by the clerke at the Table, for then it ought to be entred in their Journall, which they thought indecent toward the King, but the examinacion of the said Fitzharris taken before Sir Robert Clayton and Sir George Treby was read first by Sir George Treby, then by the clerke and ordered then to be printed.

The house also being informed that the Earle of Danby now a prisoner in the Tower and committed upon an impeachment of parliament, had peticioned the Lords to be bayled, they presently sent up the Lord Cavendish to put the Lords in mind that the Commons had in a former parliament by their Speaker demanded judgment at the Lords' house upon their impeachment against the Earle of Danby of high treason. And they do now desire their Lordships to appoint a day to give judgment against the said Earle of Danby upon the said impeachment.

They ordered also that Mr Edward Fitzharris be impeached before the Lords of high treason.

And that Mr Secretary Jenkins do go up and impeach him. Mr Secretarie Jenkins sate still not at all opposing this mocion, nor desiring to be excused from it, though it lasted some time between jeast and earnest.

But as soon as it was voted and fully setled, he stood up, and said Mr Speaker I understand this matter very well. This is a reflexion upon the King my master, and this had not been put upon me but for the character I beare. I know the value of my life and libertie as well as another, but do what you will, I will not go.

This sate the house in a flame, and To the barr, to the barr, was the generall cry. Those who were most favourable to him could not in the least justify or excuse the words, for there was in truth no reason to say it was a reflexion upon the King to send the Secretarie up to the Lords, nor did ever any man refuse to go, when the house [*ms. torn*] by vote commanded him to go. [After—*del.*] All [*ms. torn*] done was to get him time to explain himself [*ms. torn*] did so as to make it rather worse than better [*ms. torn*] he said he was sorry he had given of[fence] to the ho[use] [*ms. torn*] obey their commands [*ms. torn*].

[*CJ*, ix, 708-10; G, viii, 299-309]

[p.40]   *Saturday, 26 March 1681, a.m.*

The house ordered an humble addresse to be made to the King that we may sit in the theatre for in truth the house where we did set, being the convocation house, was too little, neither could those who did set, heare what was said, which some ascribed to the great imbossments of plaister hanging downe from the roofe which broke the plain and even superficies thereof, and being also extremely hot, and the aire of the great quadrangle of the schooles being extraordinarie cold when we came out, would certainly have proved very prejudicial to our health.

The house had also a conference with the Lords, upon the miscarriage last parliament of the bill for repeale of the 35 of the Queen [Elizabeth][1] which bill had past both houses, but was never tendred to the King for his assent, which it ought doubtlesse to have been. We proposed a committee of both houses to examine how it came to be omitted, which the Lords took time to report to their house.

The house entred upon the debate for the securitie of the King's person and of the protestant religion.

Sir Robert Clayton first stood up and said we were heare to serve our countrys that sent us, and that we ought to have regard to their desires, who best knew their owne interest, that the city of London who sent him thither, had given him instructions, to proceed with the bill tendred last parliament for the exclusion of the Duke of Yorke, and he saw no other way to secure us from poperie but by bringing in another bill for that purpose. He was seconded by my Lord Russell, and thirded by

[1] The Protestant Dissenters bill, cf. *CJ*, ix, 681.

Mr Ralph Mountague. Mr (Secretarie—*del.*) Henry Coventry moved we might go into a committee of the whole house to consider of this matter.

But that not being graunted, and it being often moved that whosoever could propose any expedient which might secure our religion beside excluding the Duke should do it—and after a long pause [*ms. torn*] Earnely moved that the Duke might hold the [*ms. torn*] of King [*ms. torn*] the princess of Orange be by act of parliament [p.41] declared Regent, and in case of her death, the Lady Anne her sister to be Regent.

This was much inlarged and insisted upon by Sir Thomas Littleton, as a safe thing to the people, since all the power would be in the Regent —that it had been commonly practised abroad in other Kingdomes, that it would make no innovacion or considerable alteracion in our lawes, but be easily reconciled to practise, since all writs and commissions must be issued in the King's name.

That this was no kindnesse at all to the Duke, who would have no power at all, but only the name of a King and must be allwayes at 500 mile distance from any part of England, and therefore he did believe the Duke would thinke this worse than an exclusion.

Sir William Jones replyed sharply upon this, that since it was worse for the Duke than the exclusion as the gentleman that proposed it did confesse, what purpose to spend any time upon it since they who had refused the bill would certainly refuse this also.

That no man could give any reasons to persuade them to passe this bill, which might not equally or better prevaile with them to passe the bill for exclusion.

That if it were the same with the exclusion, why do they deny that and offer this, if it be not the same, let them shew the difference.

But the truth is, that is a solid security, this is only a snare, for leaving the Duke the title of King which they owne to do, and leaving him also the right, for they say nothing of any exclusive words which may be in the act, but indeed plainly reject them, why then there is nothing at all to barr him, for barred he can not be but by act of parliament, and when he is King both de jure and de facto too, what pretence can there be to restrain him in anything, and if you would resist him by force, how can that be since all commissions are to be in his name. So in conclusion all that submit to him will [*ms. torn*] be slaves and all that oppose him will be reb[els].

[p.42] And this gentleman knows very well that it is the common opinion in law, that when the crowne once descends upon the head of the right heire, all impeachments, outlawrys, attainders, crimes and forfeitures are all gone and vanished. And a regencie put upon him as a minor or a lunatique will easily be avoided by a prince of full age and ripe understanding, and between the lawyers' interpretacions and distinctions in his favour, and the divines preaching up in every church 'give unto Caesar the things which are Caesar's', all the restrictions put upon him will be but weake cords and easily broken by him.

And therefore there was nothing could deserve to be thought a securitie but the totall excluding and incapacitating the Duke, and vesting the crowne in such hands after the death of the King, as by law it should come to, if the Duke were then actually dead.

This opinion was followed and seconded by

Sir Francis Winnington	Mr Leveson Gower
Mr Trenchard	Mr Boscawen
Mr Vaughan	Coll Birch

and severall others, nor was opposed by any one that I remember except Coll. Legg who frankly said he owed all he had to the Duke and would not forsake him. That for the thing itselfe, he did not like it, that he thought it was not lawfull to disinherit the Duke, that wheresoever it had been done, it had proved very unhappy to the Kingdome in generall and in particular to the family who thereupon did succeed. That for the expedient propounded of the regencie, it was as bad as the other (that is the exclusion) and he liked neither of them.

All which was well enough received from him, as one whose obligacion to the Duke were very great.

And upon the Question for a bill of exclucion, it past in the affirm-[ative] with about twenty negatives.

[*CJ*, ix, 710-11; G, viii, 309-32]

[p.43]   *Saturday, 26 March 1681, p.m.*

The house rose not till 4 of the clock, yet ordered to meet again at five in the afternoon.

The occasion was this, the impeachment against Mr Fitzharris being carried up this morning by Secretary Jenkins. The Lords had resolved that he should be tried at common law, and that they would not proceed upon the impeachment of high treason sent up by us. Resolved, it is the undoubted right of the Commons to impeach before the Lords in parliament any peer or commoner for treason or any other crime or misdemeanour, and that the Lords' refusall to proceed in parliament upon such impeachment is a deniall of justice and violacion of the constitucion of parliament.

Resolved, that their refusall to proceed against Fitzharris is a deniall of justice, a violacion of the constitucion of parliament and an obstruction to the farther discoverie of the popish plot and of great danger to his Majestie's person and to the protestant religion.

Resolved, that for any inferior courts to proceed against Edward Fitzharris, or any other person lying under an impeachment in parliament, for the same crimes for which he or they stand impeached, is a high breach of priviledge of parliament.

Ordered, a bill be brought in for the better uniting of all his Majestie's protestant subjects.

Ordered, that a bill be brought in for banishing the most considerable papists of England out of his Majestie's dominions by their names.

[*CJ*, ix, 711-12; G, viii, 332-8]

[p.73(118)]   *Good Friday, 1 April 1681*

This day I returned from Oxford to London. The parliament which met there upon the 21st of March, being dissolved by his Majestie the 28th and that so soudainly, that only his Majestie was in his robes, but not any one of the Lords. Nor was the sword of state there.

Tuesday, 5 April 1681

This day I have been married just three and thirtie yeares. Great changes have been in this time in the publique affaires. When I married, the King was alive and great hopes of an accomodacion between his enemies and him, from the outward expressions of respect shewn him by Cromwell and the armie, from the inclinacions of the parliament partie and of the Scots and the treatie at the Isle of Wight. But all those vanished in the beginning of winter, and by the end of January that yeare, viz. 1648[/9], he was wickedly murthered by them. Soon after the most perverse part of the parliament got the power in their hands, in conjunction with Cromwell, and this held till about 1655, and then the protector Cromwell turned them out and held the power absolutly himselfe, making warr and peace, calling and dissolving parliament when and in what manner he pleased, and raising money and cutting off heads as he would. This he held about 4 yeare and his son Richard one yeare after him. And those confusions and changes of government coming fast upon us, it pleased God to move the hearts of the nacion to bring in the King and to make Generall Monke the great instrument in it.

This was in 1660, and then for 12 yeare more, we lived in peace plentie and happinesse above all nacions of the world.

But this blessing was too great to be continued long to those who deserved it so ill as we, and then the nacion began to thinke that the court enclined to favour poperie and France, grounding their suspicion upon

1. The declaracion coming out about this time for laying aside all the penall lawes in matters of religion.

2. The second warr made with the Dutch in conjunction with France, there being no sufficient visible cause to provoke us to it.
3. The departing from the Triple League, which seemed so honourable and so advantageous to England.
4. The connivance at the Jesuits and priests, who did abundantly swarme in the Kingdome, and even about the Court.
5. The conference between the King and his sister, Madam, the Dutchess of Orleanse, at Dover, the cause of meeting and the matter there debated and resolved on being kept very secret.
6. The imploying of severall known or suspected papists in great places of trust, especially Lord Clifford made High Treasurer.
7. Lastly to these and much more than all these together was the Duke of Yorke's being first suspected and afterwards universally believed to be a papist, which gave no unreasonable foundacion to feare that the King having no children, when the Duke should come to the crowne the protestant religion would be at least opprest, if not extirpated.

[*ms. torn*] the falling of allmost all gentlemen's rents since [*ms. torn*] Dutch warr (whatsoever the occasion of that [*ms. torn*] put very many men out of humour.

[p.74]   *Friday, 8 April 1681*

Yet notwithstanding all this, the nacion continued very quiet untill in 1678, about September, a popish plot in which many of the nobilitie, and gentry, of that religion, and abundance of Jesuits and priests were said and sworne to be ingaged, and with them Mr Coleman the Dutchesse of Yorke's secretarie as a principal correspondent, with the French King's confessor and the pope's nuncio at Bruxells, to imbroile the nacion and by force of armes to bring in the popish religion, was discovered, by Doctor Oates, confirmed afterwards by Captain Bedlow. The burning of London charged upon the papists by Dr Tong. And Sir Edmundbury Godfrey a sober justice of peace who had taken Oates his examinacion upon oath, in October 1678, most barbarously murthered, by (them—*del.*) six persons of that religion. This began to open more mouths against people professing a religion so inconsistent with all honestie and moralitie, and all that favoured it, and the parliament which had then sate about 17 yeares falling into the same sentiments, lawes were proposed for the better and more speedy conviction of papists, for excluding them from the house of Lords, for putting a new test upon all persons who should be admitted into offices, by declaring against transubstantiation first. Afterwards, invocacion of saints, and the sacrifice of the masse was added. Then followed ease indulgence and toleracion to dissenting protestants, a law for banishing all papists by name, and other things of this nature in the present and succeeding parliaments, it making the greatest part of their businesse, to provide against poperie and the growth of the power of the French King who at this time began to appeare very formidable. And some of these lawes came to be enacted, others were lost by the frequent prorogacions and dissolucions which we have lately seen. And since Christmass 1680 to this day, which is but a yeare and quarter, we have seen fower parliaments dissolved. And the three last plainly upon the single point of having a bill to exclude the Duke of Yorke from succeeding to the crowne, which the Commons have 3 times insisted upon, but the Lords once rejected, and the other times we were dissolved before it came up to them. In the meane time the King of France increaseth dayly at sea and on land, all his neighbours make their termes with him as they can [ms. torn] but ourselves [are in] no condicion to oppose him. The papists [ms. torn] shortly to their religion uppermost. From [ms. torn]

[p.76(121)] *Friday, 20 May 1681*

This day my Lord Finch (for that is now my cousin Daniel's title, his Majestie having lately created my Lord Chancellor Earle of Nottingham) went to Windsor, having agreed so to do with my Lord Hyde, where we three had the libertie of discoursing privately with his Majestie an houer and halfe none else present but Mr Edward Roberts.

Our businesse was to make proposals to the King for the improving and better managing of his revenues of Ireland, in pursuance of his Majestie's commands given to us three by his Majestie under his signe manuall about January last, and which we had now brought into a system fit for his Majestie's knowledge. His Majestie seemd very satisfied in it as a thing much to his advantage and orders a day to be scttled [ms. damaged] as Lord Conway returned to have it [ms. torn] the Tre[asury]

[p.77(122)] *Wednesday, 1 June 1681*

The Commissioners of the Treasurie were summoned to attend the King at Windsor about the businesse of Ireland, where the Lord Chancellor, Lord Chamberlain, Earl of Hallifax, the 2 Secretaries and Mr Seymour likewise were. The King first read the proposall which was brought to the Treasurie by my Lord of Arran, with some explicacions made of it, but this seeming not very considerable, and in truth coming below the present rent of £240,000 per annum, was soon rejected. Then the King brought out of his pocket, a second proposall which he said he thought was better, which being read, and some things liked well, some disliked and many that seemed obscure, nothing was resolved but that his Majestie would speake with the proposer, and direct him to attend some one or more of them there, the proposer not being willing as yet to appeare before the whole body of the councell or of the Treasurie.

Wednesday, 8 June 1681

The King came to the Treasurie chamber at Whitehall. Present, Lord Chancellor, Lord President, Lord Chamberlain, 2 Secretaries and Mr Seymour, where the explanacions to the Irish proposall which had been made to my Lord Hyde and myselfe by the proposer (the King having directed him to attend us two), were read and most of them well liked of. The result was, the King was pleased to order a warrant should be sent to Mr Sollicitor Generall to prepare a draught according to those proposalls, that care should be taken the trustees should be such persons as the King might rely upon, as well as acceptable to the contractors.

That the King would reserve the modelling the army in Ireland to himselfe. That the trustees should be renewable at the King's pleasure which was [*ms. damaged*] by myself but well approved by all. That my Lord Ranelagh should be recompenced and [*ms. damaged*] the contractors charge not at the King's.

[p.80]   ## Sunday, 14 August 1681

This day I went to Windsor upon report made to the King on Wednesday before by the Earle of Winchelsey in these words as I am informd: Collonel Dering[1] is the man that opposeth us in our elections and in our addresses in every thing we indeavour for your Majestie's service, and he saith he doth it not out of his owne inclinacions but by the command of his father, who hath threatened to disinherit him if he do it not, and hath promised him if he do persist in it, as long as there is a penny in the Treasurie, he shall not want.

This hath so much improbability in it, and [*ms. torn*] much mischiefe also, that I could not [*ms. torn*] [p.81(126)] notice of it, and most of my friends were of opinion I should do so to the King himselfe, and my Lord Hyde having introduced me to the King I had the opportunity of speaking to him, and denying the thing as utterly false, and yet not adventuring to excuse my son from all indiscreet speeches. The King seemed not to give much credit to the words but said, where he had obliged a family as he did mine in me, he might expect some returns of gratitude and respect, which I acknowledged to be most reasonable, and I should endeavour that all mine

---

[1] Edward Dering, the second baronet's eldest son.

should do so. The King said if your son can not by his principle serve me, at least I am sure he may (still—*del.*) sit still and be quiet without such particular opposicion and that was all he did expect from him. I said it was too little, and in the circumstances I were in, I should expect a great deale more from him than so, and I did not doubt but he would find him very faithful to him. That the ground of this anger in the countrey, was his standing for knight of the shire, and their jealousie that his interest was still great enough to support him against all theirs. That I did not know whether it were so or not, but could wish there were some way of better understanding in the country. That however I had no hand in it, neither ingaging him to it nor assisting him in it. That if his Majestie pleased to put these words into examinacion, I did not doubt but the truth would appeare to be very much otherwise than had been represented to him. But the King saying the words were not much to be taken hold upon, I added that this being the time of our recesse at the Treasurie, I were going into the countrey, that I would enquire into the matter and give his Majestie a true accompt at my returne, which his Majestie bid me do, and so dismist me.

But certain it is that calumnies, slanders and cutthroat whispers never were so common and rank at court as they are now. I am sure I have met with more within these two moneths of myselfe, my eldest son, son Southwell, Daniel and some other friends than I ever met with in fifty and five yeares before.

[p.88]   *October 1681*

In the first place and at the beginning and entrance of the present I can not but seriously reflect upon the last halfe yeare, which seemes to me to have been though not unhappy in any considerable particular, yet in the whole to have been perplexd with greater cares and anxieties of mind and made uneasie and wearisome by severall occurrances more than former halfe yeares have been. Of which I shall note some with the success and issue thereof, not mencioning the cases incident to my place as commissioner of the Treasurie, being a trouble I am well enough paid for, and a trouble I am not yet desirous to be freed from.

The first hath been the new Irish farme together with the better modelling and managing of the revenue of that Kingdome, so as that his Majestie may be totally freed from the charge of maintaining of Tangier and his garrison there, that charge being as we conceive possible to be furnished from Ireland. This upon the first proposall of it having been by his Majestie recommended particularly to my Lord Hyde and myselfe, hath given us a great deal of trouble, many and tedious meetings and discourses with Sir James Shaen and Mr Roberts, severall times at Councell table. The thing hath the face of a great

K

service to the King, but it meets with great opposicions from the judgment of some, and the interest of others, some not liking the persons of the old farmers supposed to be interested in the proposall, many complaining that it is kept a secret, though more exposed than any contract for a farme hath yet ever been. It is now drawn in writing fit to be offerd to the King at his returne, and what will be the fate of it I know not. In [the] meane time I have had next to my Lord Hyde a great share of the trouble of it, and also of the envy and ill will [*ms. damaged*].

[p.94] The eighth trouble[1] and the last which I shall reckon but not the last nor least in my esteem is the concerne of my eldest son as to reputacion with the King and all that love him, and my place also in his Majestie's favour and my imployment which I hold under him, both directly and eagerly strooke at by persons who would recommend themselves by finding fault with others, having no vertues of their owne.

The originall seemes to be my son's having three times been chosen Knight of the shire for that countie,[2] a thing unusuall and I thinke unpresidented. This no doubt hath given some cause of envy to others who thinke themselves as capable and worthy of it. And it being apprehended that my son would stand again this fourth time, great endeavours have been used and contrivances and sollicitacions to prevent him from succeeding in it. And if it be true as it is reported, my Lord of Winchelsea, Lord Lieutenant of the countie, by himselfe and his son, hath made a little [more?] use of his authoritie, than was usuall in that point.

[p.95(140)] But since they saw the great body of the freeholders of the countie, as well as very many of the gentry stood firme for to have their old knights, it was now endeavourd to bespatter him all they could, reporting that he was an enemie to the church, and had drunke a health to the confusion of lawn sleeves. This he absolutely denyes, yet this tale is sufficient to set all the clergy in the countie against him, and most industriously do they labour against him.

A second report is that he spake very scornfully of a limited monarchie, saying it was a —[3] in a chamber pot. A nasty piece of senselesse folly certainly, which he denyeth absolutely, and appeales to the gentlemen that were at table with him, when it is reported to have been said. But this is avouched (as it is commonly reported) by Sir John Tufton as said to himselfe at Rochester, and by his credit finds credit up and downe and exceeding much to my son's prejudice, as it ought in reason to be, with those who believe it.

1 Dering described his other troubles as being: (2) his son's debts; (3) his lawsuit as executor of Thomas Lenthall; (4) obtaining his son Daniel employment at sea; (5) his attack of the stone; (6) his failure to lease lands at Northwood; (7) the illness of his daughter Elizabeth.

2 Edward Dering was returned to represent Kent on 24 Feb. 1679, 8 Sept. 1679, and 21 Feb. 1681.

3 Thus in the text.

A third report was that he had said he would raise men, of which the truth I take to be, that just when the plot broke out in 1678, all men being affrighted with the danger then hanging over the King's person, and the correspondence then supposd to be managed between Coleman and the other papists and the French, did expect no lesse than in pursuance of that designe the King's person would be attempted, and if that did succeed, a French armie would land in that consternacion and confusion which must unavoidably attend it, and he and many other gentlemen said they would not be murthered by the French like sheep and have their throats cut in their beds but would get their neighbours [*ms. torn*] defend themselves as long as they could.

[p.96] A fourth objection much insisted upon, is, that all the fanaticks of the countie are for him. To which he answers they are so, and there is not one of those who are against him but would be glad to have them for him selfe also.

That for himselfe he is no fanatick, nor ever was or pretended so to be. Never was at one conventicle, never forsooke the Church of England in any one thing. That he is for monarchie and for the government of the church both as they are established by law. And if he thinke there is more present danger to church and state from the papists than from dissenting protestants, he thinkes it is an opinion that wants not not [*sic*] strong reasons for its defence.

A fifth report made use of to lessen his interest with some is, that he is turning courtier and hath made his peace at Whitehall. This though no great fault in itselfe, yet is managed in some places to his disadvantage, and this is said to be the dexteritie of Sir John Bankes.

A sixth report and that most concernes me, is what was reported by my Lord Lieutenant the Earle of Winchelsea to the Earle of Conway, Secretary of State, and at the same day, (being the day when he presented the Kentish addresse to his Majestie at Windsor) to the King himselfe, viz. The principall person who obstructs your Majestie's service and hinders us in our addresses, all we endeavour to serve you in, is Collonell Dering, and he saith he doth it not by his owne inclinacion but by command from his father, who threatenes to disinherit him if he do not do it, and hath promised him if he persist in it, he shall not want money as long as there is any in the Treasurie. My Lord Winchelsea had two gentlemen with him, Walters [*ms. torn*] I conceive were Sir Robert [*ms. torn*] Taylor [*ms. torn*].

[p.97] But of this matter I have touched in this booke in August last,[1] and as this seemes aimed not at my son but directly at myselfe, I had reason to justify myselfe to the King which I hope I have done, though no man knowes what effect such poysonous toungues may have, especially upon such a person as I am, who have a great place, have but few friends, and very seldome come personally to the King, con-

[1] See pp. 128-9 above.

tenting myselfe to do my duty as well as I can in that trust he hath imployd me in, relying upon the King's goodness and my owne integritie for my preservacion. And in truth I ought not to wonder that many of the court, and some of my owne countrey, do maligne and stomach it, that I should hold so good a place in court, and my son have so considerable an interest in the countrie. Not considering that the true interest of the King and of the Kingdome is the same, and their prosperitie inseparable one from the other.

Yet after all I have reason to doubt my son hath taken more libertie in words than could well consist with the dutifull respect owing to his King. But the worst that I know of hath been words, not deeds, that they have been rather irreverent than malicious, and many times rather spoken as divertisement to the companie than anything serious, much less mischiefous, and which if he had not set himselfe up as a marke for envy by standing again for knight of the shire, might have past with as little notice from him, as they have done from others. However, I thinke he would do better not to stand at this time, by giving place to envy which may possibly proceed so farr as to do him, or me more likely, some mischiefe, whereas his standing can do himselfe no good if he do carry it, and if he should misse it it would abate something of the credit he hath had, in carrying it so often.

[p.99]   *Wednesday, 12 October 1681*

The King returned from Newmarket to Whitehall.

Thursday, 13 October 1681

This day the commissioners of the Treasurie did begin their sitting after their vacacion recesse.

Saturday, Monday, 15, 17 October 1681

The commissioners of the Treasurie sate at the Lords of the Councell appointed by the King, upon the new contract for Ireland.

Tuesday, 1 November 1681

I dined at the Archbishop of Canterbury's at Lambeth.

Wednesday, 2 November 1681

I dined at an invitacion made by the Hamburgh Company for Bevill

Skelton esquire whom his Majestie hath nominated his envoye to the Prince of Luneburgh, and then to settle his residence at Hamburgh, in the room of Sir Peter Wych, who is now his resident there and is recalled.

Saturday, 12 November 1681

This day I reckon myselfe just 56 years old, and if any one shall say they have known a wiser at six and twenty, I shall not contradict them.

5

THE ACCOUNT BOOK OF
SIR EDWARD DERING

April 1683 to 9 June 1684

Kent Archives Office, U 275 A4; photocopy in the
House of Lords Record Office, Historical Collections, 86/2

The volume is entitled on the cover in a somewhat later hand 'Sir Edward Dering's Account Book, 1683-'. As in the case of the preceding Account Book there is some fungoid decay and certain leaves have been torn out. The existing pages have been given a continuous numeration in this text for ease of reference; original pagination by Dering is indicated within round brackets.

page
157-9   blank
160(171)-   Account of the estate of Thomas Lenthall, 20 April 1683
   161
162-3   blank
164(175)   Receipts and payments for the Lenthall estate, 11 April 1683, 26 Nov. 1683
165   Mr. Scrimpshire's accounts, 25 March-30 Nov. 1683
166-8   blank
169(180)-   Diary, April to Sept. 1683, including the entries printed
   193   below, pp. 138-47; with other entries concerning the purchase of land in Leicester Gardens; the leasing of houses in Gerard St.; family visits, etc.
194   blank
195-201   Diary, Oct. to Dec. 1683; including the entries printed below, pp. 147-8; with other entries concerning the departure of Dering's son, John, to France; the purchase of land in Little Chart; a visit to Parsons Green, etc.
202   blank
203(214)-   Diary, Jan. to 23 March 1684; including the entries
   210   printed below, pp. 148-9; with other entries concerning payments to the trustees of Michael Scrimpshire's creditors; Dr. Clegget's sermon on King Charles's Day, 30 Jan.; the frost of February; purchases of books; deaths of Sir Thomas Peyton and others, etc.
211-12   blank
213-20   Diary, March to 9 June 1684; including the entries printed below, pp. 149-50; the education of Dering's son Robert; Dering's own health; the return of his son Daniel from abroad, etc.
[89 pp. blank]
At the end of the volume:
310-11   Receipts, Christmas 1683 to Jan. 1684
312-13   blank
314   Memorandum concerning Henry Dering
315   Expenses concerning Henry Dering's debts, 1683-4
316   blank
317   Index of pigeon-holes (printed below, pp. 150-1)
318-20   blank

[p.170(181)]   *April 1683*

Soon after these in time[1], but much before them in concerne to me followed [i.e., died] my Lord Chancellor, my neare relacion by birth,

---
[1] on 18 December, 1682.

much nearer by marriage, and nearer yet by a tender and uninterrupted friendship of 34 yeares' continuance, cultivated and improved all that time by constant and familiar conversacion, and by a perpetuall succession of all good offices and instances of kindnesse. He was certainly a man of great abilities in his profession, confest by all men, the greatest orator of this nation, a man of most exemplarie pietie, most profuse charity, unmoveable justice and integritie, and most affectionate and faithfull to the King and the church, and in short, a person that [possessed] all the vertues man is capable of, and none of the vices.

The King, the church, the law, the poor, his relacions and friends, and among them I and mine, have an irreparable losse in him. He did visibly decline this winter, but especially from the death of his brother Sir John Finch, and receiving from him an accompt, that he found himselfe declining apace and saw he should not overcome that sicknesse, my Lord sent him back word, that his life was bound up with his, and that he should not long survive him. I think he mencioned the time of six weekes, and so it proved, for Sir John Finch dyed the 18 November and my Lord the 18th of December both at my Lord Chancellor's house in Great Queen Street. He was though sometimes troubled with the gout yet in no great excesse of paine, but weake in his feet and knees, but otherwise no man more happy in a great estate, the highest imployment, the favour of his prince, the love of the people, and above all men living happy in his children all growen or growing up to his full content in every respect, and yet withall this the most willing man to dy that ever was, having without doubt a comfortable assurance of those joyes in heaven in respect whereof all things in this world even the most charming and pleasant are but drosse. We cannot certainly say what he dyed of, but lay it upon the gout, which seemed to have got in to his stomach. That which was most visible was a swelling and soarnesse in his throat, which made both food and physick very ingratefull to him.

He wanted but 4 dayes of being 61 yeares old.
Et cum supremos Lachesis perneverit annos
Non aliter cineres mando jacere meos[1]

[p.171]   *Monday, 2 April 1683*

This day the King came to the Treasurie, attended there besides the commissioners of the Treasurie, by the Lord Keeper, Lord President, Lord Privy Seale, Lord Lieutenant of Ireland, Lord Chamberlain, and the two secretaries.

The Question was whether the excise of ale and beare, the farming

---

[1] Martial, *Epigrams*, bk. i, lxxxviii.

whereof expireth at Midsumer day next, should after that time be farmed again, or managed by commissioners.[1]

The reasons for farming it were

1. That this way the King would be at a certaintie
2. That the King might borrow money upon it.

Against farming it were

1. That more would in all probabilitie be made of it this way, since the King would have the whole produce to himselfe.
2. That no man would farme such a revenue, but with hopes of getting at least £20,000 per annum for their paines and hazard, all which would be now come into the King's owne purse.
3. That if you do farme it, you must take such men as can lay downe a vast summe of money, which are but few, whereas the other way you have the choice out of the whole Kingdome.
4. That if you farme it, you must do it for 3 yeare. None will take it for lesse, but if you manage it, and alter your mind at a yeare's end, you may then farme it.
5. That if you take it now into the King's hands, you may keep it so for one yeare. If it prove well, you may at the yeare's end put the hearth dutie which will then come out of farme into the same hands, and thereby save a great part of the charge of management of both duties. If it then prove ill, you may then farme them both either together or asunder.
6. As for taking up money, it may be as well done when it is in management as when it shall be in farme.
7. The King hath never yet known the true value of this revenue, nor ever shall do while it is in farme, nor are we satisfied with the accompts we have yet from the farmers, but if it be in commission, there will be a certaintie then to the utmost farthing what is made of it, the commissioners having no interest at all to conceale anything therein.
8. As for what is said, that men will not worke for the King with the same care as they will for themselves, it is answered that honest men will certainly do it, as much where they are trusted as for themselves. Besides in truth they do worke for themselves, since they are to have good salaries, and to hold them only during the King's pleasure, which will soon be determined if they behave themselves ill.

[p.172(183)] The King himselfe was very positive for a management and in respect to his opinion, or for the reasons before mencioned especially the 5th and 7th, not only all the commissioners of the Treasurie, but all the other Lords except one, were for a management, not a farme. That being resolved the next thing was to fix upon the commissioners to be intrusted with it.

[1] cf. *CTB*, 1681-5, 756, 761, 782.

Thursday, 5 April 1683

This day they were setled, viz.

1. Sir Denny Ashburnham)	5. Mr Felix Calvert
2. Major Huntingdon)	6. Major Friend
3. Mr Francis Parry)	7. Mr Nathaniel Hornby
4. Mr Davenant	

The 4 first were allready in possession as being the present commissioners of the excise, during the present farme.

The 2 next are two of the present farmers, and are men of great abilitie and experience in this matter, well acquainted with the present method, and with all the inferior officers now imploy'd, and besid have a great share in the money now owing to the present farmers, which will be of use to the King, to accommodate any difficultie may happen in that matter, as to the time or manner of their repayment. And these six were unanimously named by the commissioners of the Treasurie. The 7th man, viz. Mr Horneby, is an eminent banquier, and a man of great credit and fair reputacion. He was named by the King himselfe.

These being call'd all into the Treasurie Chamber, were told by my Lord Rochester, that the King had made choice of them to be the managers of his excise, wishing them to apply themselves heartily to it, and to discharge it with as much care and fidelitie and diligence as any one of them would do for themselves if it were their owne particular concerne. That if it happen to miscarry in their hands, the King would lay it at their door, and will sooner think himselfe mistaken in the men he imployeth than in the measure he hath taken, and the reasons which he hath so well weighd and considerd, and which have induced him rather to a management than a farm.

[p.173(184)]   ### Friday, 13 April 1683

We had a hearing at the Treasurie Chamber, the King present and the great Lords of the Councell. The matter was a complaint made by Collonell Strode to the King against the judgment of the commissioners of the Treasurie in his case, as he was farmer of the 4 and ½ per cent customes in Barbados and the Leeward Islands.[1] 2 things he chiefly insisted upon

1. To have £400 per annum allowance for the 3 last yeares of his farme to him and his 2 partners Spencer and Sir Charles Wheeler each, for which the main reason was that my Lord of Danby had allowd it so for the first 4 yeares, and intended it for the rest.

   To which it was answered

1. My Lord of Danbyes intencions were not binding to us.

[1] cf. *CTB*, 1681-5, 795, and other references indexed *sub* Strode, *op. cit.*, 1928.

2. That the privy seale drawn by Lord Danbyes order and past in 15 March 1678, which was after a long dependence, and even after the last 3 yeares of the farme were expired, did make plain provicion for £400 per annum for the first 4 yeares, but left the last 3 yeares to such allowances as should be made by the Treasurie.

3. There was nothing the same reason for such large allowances to be made in the last 3 yeares, which were in the first fouer.

4. Whereas we had referd the matter to severall merchants of great note and judgment, their opinion was that 3 per cent was sufficient allowance for agencie or management and we had allowd them that, and in respect of their qualitie had allowd them as much more, as did about double the summe.

5. That whereas they complaind that they were made accomptable by my Lord of Danby, that was no hardship to them but a favour and we believe they would not now be content to waive being accomptants, and to answer their rent as farmers.

The second point was, that Mr Blathwait the auditor had applyed some tallyes Collonell Strode had delivered in to the discharge of the Barbados accompt, which he desired might be applyed to the accompt of the Leeward Islands, he being solely concerned in the farme of the Leeward Islands but joind with Spencer and Wheeler in the Barbados farme, and this he much prest, his councell saying they were his owne tallyes because he had them in his possession, and therfore he might apply them as he would.

[p.174(185)] To this it was answerd

1. That the talleyes were not his owne or at his disposall because he had them in his hand, but they were doubtlesse left in his hands by his partners, who had equall interest therein.

2. That his partners, Sir Charles Wheeler particularly, did oppose his desire, insisting that the tallies ought to be applyed to the discharge of the rent of the Barbados farm.

3. That it is certain, the tallyes were struck plainly and singly upon the Barbados farmers and not upon the Leeward Islands farme.

4. That it is true my Lord of Danby did give a subsequent order, that they might be satisfied as well out of rent of the Leeward Islands farme as out of the Barbados.

5. But that it is very doubtfull whether a Lord Treasurer after talleys are struck can apply them otherwise, at least without the consent of the persons interested. (He may—*del.*) And in this case, there is not a positive command it should be so, but a permission that they might be so satisfied, if the Barbados rent fall short. Which in this case it doth not. And at most, this can but give an equall proporcionable part, and the rent of the Barbados farme being about ten times the other, or more, I thinke the Barbados farme £7,000, and the Leeward Islands but £500, the most it could be straind to, was to place a

tenth or 14th part on the Leewards Island farme. That Collonell Strode had had severall hearings before the Treasurie, and being dissatisfied at their judgment had now begun a suit in the Exchequer to be relieved against their judgment, which alone could conclude him.

The Lords were of opinion to leave him to take his remedy at law, which his Majestie was pleased also to resolve upon.

[p.178]   *Friday, 12 May 1683*

This day one Mr Ezekiel Lampen came to me bringing with him one Warburton a kind of attorney or sollicitor, and Mr Hastings the Under-sheriff of Middlesex.[1]

Mr Lampen said he came to desire my appearance to an action. I told him I knew of nothing I owed him. He said it was concerning his tallies as he was an assignee of the banquiers. I told him I were not concernd particularly in that and should give him no particular answer.

Mr Hastings shewd me the writ which he held in his hand but did not read it, nor serve it, saying he only came to know whether I would give him an appearance or not. I told him I would give him no answer whether I would or would not. Mr Lampen or one of the three I know not which, askd me if I would appoint them to come again some other day. I told them I had nothing more to say to them of that matter in this place. So away they went.

Coming to the Treasurie Chamber I found they had been with Mr Chancellor of the Exchequer and Sir Stephen Fox who both answerd them much after the same manner.

My Lord Rochester they had not been with nor Mr Godolphin, I suppose not knowing where to find the last, and not thinking fit to serve a writ upon the other as being a peer.

This (men—*del.*) man Lampen is certainly ill advised as to his manner of proceeding.

For this writ was out of the Kingsbench, whereas out of doubt the Lord Treasurer, and consequently they who supply his place and are in the same office power and trust, have priviledge of being sued only in the Court of Exchequer, as every the meanest attorney or officer of every court in Westminster Hall hath, so that they would undoubtedly have miscarried, and we may wonder what weake councell they are advised by, that could fall into so grosse a mistake as to sue the Chancellor himselfe of the Exchequer by writ out of another court of law. But this mistake they will quickly be aware of, therefore we must consider and be informed by councell.

[p.179] 1. In case one that hath priviledge of one court, be served with a

---

[1] cf. Lampen's case against the Excise, *CTB*, 1681-5, 613.

writ out of another court, and he told the sheriff so, yet the sheriffe will not believe but deny either the fact or the law to be so, and the partie still refuse to appear or to give baile, and thereupon by the sheriff be carried to prison. First whether he may resist the sheriff.

2. Whether if he be carried to prison, which way he can come out again but by Habeas Corpus, and then what remedie or damages.

3. If a man do give baile or signe the bond to the sheriffe or so much as promise him he will appeare to the action whether he may after that plead his priviledge, or whether his apparence to the action as then laid have not concluded him from all objection to the meane processe.

4. In this particular case, whether if some of us shall stand upon our priviledge, some others of us should give baile to appeare and my Lord Chancellor or Keeper should refuse to graunt a letter of summons to my Lord Rochester (the only way against a peere), what would be the consequence of it.

If we should all appeare and plead and before judgment given one of us five should dy or be removed and the commission changed, what would be the consequence.

The truth is that the commissioners of the Treasurie are not to blame in this matter allthough the banquier and their assigns, are now about 5 quarters behind of their interest, since we have made no stop at all in their payments, nor intend to do farther than the want of money doth inforce it, for we do allott £1,000 per weeke one weeke with another, which is about 2 thirds of what their interest doth come to in the yeare, that is to say about £4 per cent which is no ill payment, as money doth now go. Neither is the rest cut off or taken from them but only the payment forestood, till some better opportunitie shall inable the King to pay it. Nor they yet more in arreare than very many others and those of qualitie in town and in the King's immediat service now are.

[p.184]   *Wednesday, 11 July 1683*

The Hamburgh companie having been exceedingly obliged to his Majestie for his favour to them (in—*del.*) upon all their applicacions, and very lately for his most gracious order in councell and a proclamacion thereupon concerning interlopers especially foreigners, they were desirous to expresse their gratitude in the best manner they could, and therefore intend to set up a marble statue for him in the midst of the Royall Exchange in London. And this day he was pleasd to see the modell of it, as it is prepard by Mr Gibbons a most famous artist in carving and eminent also for working in marble.[1]

The pedestall is to be 5 foot high, being to rise with 3 marble steps.

[1] The only statue of Charles II surviving from the second Royal Exchange (built in 1671) is that by John Bushnell. It is now preserved in the Central Criminal Court, the Old Bailey (N. Pevsner, *London*, i (1957), 168).

Upon the 4 facies of the marble pedestall the front is to have the inscription, the other 3 the armes of England, Scotland and Ireland. The figure to be 6 foot 10 inches.

All which the King was pleasd to approve of.

He then told me familiarly speaking to me that he had a project, by which he could get £50,000 presently, and askd me if that were not a very good thing. He went on telling me that he was offerd £50,000 by my Lord Russell's friends for his pardon, not that they did owne my Lord Russell to be guiltie of the treason laid to his charge, but, said the King, it is the price of bloud and he would not hearken to it.

I said, I did believe his Majestie when he did shew mercie would do it for mercie sake, and not for any other consideracion.

[p.186]   *Saturday, 28 July 1683*

This day my son[1] Dering had the favour to kisse first the King's hand and then the Duke's. The King received him with all the sweetnesse and benignitie in the world and which will I believe fix him in the good intentions he hath of being a faithfull and loyall subject to him. The occasion of my son's addressing himselfe at this time, was to expresse to his Majestie his detestation of the late treasonable conspiracie against the life of the King and of the Duke, and for raising a warr within the Kingdome which must have overturnd the government wholly if it had succeeded, and involved the whole nacion in bloud and confusion, and the Lord Russell, Captain Walcot, Rouse and Hone having been allready tried condemned and executed for this plot, and many others being imprisond upon it, it was judged convenient and reasonable, my son should declare to his Majestie his detestacion of this plot, and of all principles tending to it, which many other gentlemen had done. And I pray God keep all mine from having a hand in such bloudy contrivances, whatever fair pretences they can be cloathed with, for they are certainly the instigacions of the Devill, the disgrace of our protestant religion, the ruine of the whole nacion if they succeed, and of the conspirators at least in their lives, fortunes, families and soules also if they do not. Neither do I remember of any conspiracie in story of this nature that ever hath succeeded, there being allwayes, too few to carry it through and too many to keep it secret.

[p.187] My son, feare thou the Lord and the King and meddle not with them that are given to change.

This day also the marriage was celebrated at St. James his house, by the Bishop of London between Prince George brother to Christian 5th now King of Denmarke, and son to Fredrick the [blank][2] and the

---

[1] Edward, whose loyalty to the Court interest was, and continued, doubtful (see pp. 130-2).
[2] King Frederick III (1648-70).

Lady Anne daughter to his royall highnesse James Duke of Yorke. The match seemeth to be to the generall satisfaction of the nacion he being a protestant, of which religion hardly was now to be found another in all Europe for a husband for her, and the King and (Duke—*del.*) having no children, and the Duke never a son, and his eldest daughter the Princesse of Orange having yet no children, the succession of the crowne is apparently and nearly concernd in her marriage. And as to his being a younger brother and having no dominions of his owne, the reason given by Henry the 7th upon his match of his eldest daughter with Scotland, is unanswerable and holdeth still true; that the marriage of the heiresse of the crowne with any foreign prince who had a great estate of his owne, would make England a province and dependent of that other crowne, whereas otherwise it will draw a lesser principalitie to itselfe. And if ever he come to inherit these crownes, they are enough without other addicion to support the grandeur of one of the first monarchies of Europe. For the present he is sufficiently provided for, by his owne fortune, to which the Duke of Yorke addeth a settlement of £10,000 per annum as a porcion with his daughter, and the King giveth also a porcion of ten thousand per annum more.

[p.188]   *Tuesday, 31 July 1683*

These things past at the Treasurie

1. A docquet for the East India companie, enabling them to seise vessells going to and coming from the limits of their charter.

   And to set up a court of judicature there consisting of one civill lawyer and two merchants, to judge and determine.

   And to execute martiall law there, in cases of insurrection or invacion.

   And to have all other powers and priviledges in London which any other companie have.

   We made some scruple at signing it, till Mr Attorney gave it us under his hand it was law.[1]

2. We signed a docquet for determining Mr Conyer's imployment in the ordnance, and disposing it to Mr Bridges.[2]

3. We wrote a letter to the justices of Carmarthen upon a suggestion sent up to the commissioners of the Excise by one of their officers there, that he did believe, the justices meant to judge or were inclind so to do, against gaging in the worts, which would be a prejudice to the King's revenue.[3]

4. Mr Le Gouch made a proposall of lending us £10,000 upon condicion of renewing a debt of £5,000 which he had upon the perpetuall interest as the banquiers and their assignes have.[4]

---

[1] cf. *CSPD*, July-Sept. 1683, 183.   [2] cf. *op. cit.*, 200, 281.
[3] *CTB*, 1681-5, 887.   [4] cf. *op. cit*, 912-3.

5. Whereas the quarters debt to the banquiers is £20,000 and we have constantly paid them £13,000, which is one thousand pound per weeke, in this present quarter we designe them but £6,500.

[p.195]   *Monday, 1 October 1683*

This day I presented to his Majestie an humble addresse [to—*del.*] from the companie of Merchant Adventurers of England, in detestation of the late horrid designe against the life of his Majestie and of the Duke of Yorke, which his Majestie was pleasd to receive very graciously from us. The reason of my delivering it in person is because I am governor of that companie as I have been for about 8 yeare last past, though new elected every yeare at Hamburgh upon Midsumer day.

[p.199]   *Sunday, 23 December 1683*

This day we met at the Treasurie and adjourned unto the 7th of January. The King was present and my Lord Lieutenant of Ireland the Duke of Ormond. The matter in debate was a draught of a commission for setling the defective titles in Ireland by new letters pattents to be graunted for that purpose.[1] The draught had been before us about 12 moneths since, and then I had made severall objections to the particular clauses in the commission, and one to the whole, viz. that the King had the forfeited lands there only as a royall trustee to the uses of the acts of settlement and explanacion, and therefore the lands could not be diverted to any other use, unlesse by act of parliament. These objections were by the Treasurie sent out to my Lord Deputy there, to be by him communicated to the King's Attorney Generall and Sollicitor there, and on Saturday last we received their answer which this day we communicated to the King.
[p.200] The opinion of the Attorney Generall and Sollicitor there, being as to the maine point that the lands are disposable by the King, as he please (as to the particular objections they do yield to comply with most of them.) The opinion was to go forward with the commission.

I then humbly moved the King, in respect of the importance of the matter, that he would please to communicate the thing unto his privy councell in England or Ireland or both of them, since matters of farr lesse moment were usually debated there, or if he would not do that, he would do what he did very often in other matters, and most frequently in matters relating to Ireland, that is, command my Lord Keeper, Lord President and such others of the Lords of the privy councell as he

---

[1] cf. *CTB*, 1681-5, 918-9, 927, 936-7, 999, 1017, 1030; the Commission was set up in Feb. 1684, cf. *op. cit.*, 1046-8.

would nominate to attend him at the Treasurie Chamber, and have it debated before them.

Or at least if he would do neither of these he would command the objections and the answers to be sent to his Attorney Generall heare and his Sollicitor and have their opinion how farre it might be fit to proceed hearein, for I were of opinion the objections were not answerd, and that his Majestie was but a trustee and the lands (could—*del.*) forfeited by those acts, could be disposed to no other uses than the uses of the acts. [p.201] The King said he was no lawyer, and his councell, those who must needs understand the acts, were of opinion he might dispose of them.

I replyed there was no need of being a lawyer to maintain my opinion, for it was enough to read the act, where it was as cleare set downe as words could expresse it.

It was said (these—*del.*) the time limited by the acts to the commission was expired.

I said it was true, the powers given to those particular men were expired long since, but the trust in the King continueth still, that upon many parts of the act, as the putting of claimes judging nocencie and innocencie, stating '49 arreares, there are negative clauses in the acts, but none such upon the trust in the King, which might and ought still to be executed, and it was to me a contradiction in the Attorney Generall and Sollicitor there to hold that those parts of the act can not now be executed, and yet at the same time to move for a commission to dispose of the remaining undisposed forfeited lands, as if the King had a power in him to (graunt—*del.*) make commissions to apply and graunt out the lands to such persons as had no title unto them, and yet could not graunt a commission to set out the lands to such as had a right.

It was ordered that all the papers, draught, objections, and answers should be sent to the Attorney and Sollicitor Generall heare, with order that they prepare such a new draught as may stand with the King's service.

[p.203(214)]   *Thursday, 17 January 1684*

This day the King was pleasd to come to the Treasurie chamber about the commission for remedy of defective titles in Ireland, Mr Sollicitor Generall of England having delivered his opinion in writing that as to the lands vested in the King by the acts of settlement and explanacion, the King had them only as a trustee to the uses of the act and consequently they were not disposable to other uses while those uses were unsatisfied. (But the A—*del.*) And I were of the same mind but the Attorney and Sollicitor Generall of (England—*del.*) Ireland, having delivered their opinions that they are disposable and Mr Attorney of

England having agreed with them, the King was pleasd to order it to passe and nominated the judges and some others to be commissioners for that purpose.

[p.215]   *Monday, 14 April 1684*

This day Mr Sidney Godolphin one of the King's Privy Councell, and one of the commissioners of the Treasurie, had the seales delivered to him, and by that forme is constituted Secretary of State in the roome of Sir Leoline Jenkins who resigned up his place, which his ill health persuaded him to do. Mr Godolphin is a gentleman eminently endued with all the qualities necessarie to this great trust. Being of a quick apprehencion, solid judgment, excellent temper, free from ambicion and covetousnesse, those whirlwinds which overturne the chariots of so many ministers of State, of incorruptible integritie and exemplary modestie, and of a sinceritie not usually found in this age, and beside all this very much master of the moderne languages, and exceeding well verst in the present state of Europe, and I pray heaven with all my heart he may successfully discharge it and long enjoy it.

It is generally thought, this removall of Mr Godolphin will certainly in a little time dissolve the commission of the Treasurie and put it into one single hand of a Lord Treasurer, and the Earle of Rochester is in all men's thoughts designd for it.[1] But he doth alltogether disowne it, and to me truly seemeth not to desire it. However it be for that, certain it is, that the removing of Godolphin, is taking out a corner stone, which if it do not ruine and dissolve, doth at least much weaken the building.[2] But I have learnd

permittas ipsis expendere numinibus quid
conveniat nobis rebusque sit utile nostris
nam pro iucundis aptissima quaeque dabunt dii
charior est illis homo quam sibi etc.[3]

[p.217]   *Sunday, 11 May 1684*

Sunday at Windsor the King was pleasd to put an end to the present commission of the Admiraltie, which was executed by 8 commissioners, viz. the Earle of Nottingham, Mr Henry Savile vice Chamberlain, Sir Edward Hales, Sir Humphry Winch, Sir Thomas Meres, Sir John Chicheley, Reare Admirall Herbert and the Lord Vaughan, of which

---

[1] The Earl of Rochester joined Dering, Ernle and Fox in a reconstituted Commission on 24 April 1684 (Sainty, 18).
[2] A transcript of the entry to this point is preserved in BL Add 28,053, f. 300.
[3] Juvenal, *Satires*, x, 347 ff., with some slight variations.

the 7 first had £1,000 per annum salarie. The last was to have no salarie till one of the 7 died or removes.

This resolucion seemed to be soudainly taken, but in truth there was reported to be so ill agreement among them, that some expedient was absolutly necessarie either to reconcile them or dissolve them. The King declareth he will govern this matter of the Admiraltie himselfe, and that he will therein advise with the Duke of Yorke. I suppose the King will himselfe signe all commissions and instructions as he doth at present in the armie, since the death of the Duke of Albemarle, and so be himselfe both generall and admirall.[1]

[p.317]   *Index, Michaelmas day, 1683*

36 pidgeon holes[2]

1. Treasurie papers
2. Treasurie papers
3. [blank]
4. Custome house papers
5. Custome house
6. Ireland
7. Ireland
8. Excise
9. [blank]
10. hearth money, ordnance
11. first fruits, navy, Admiraltie
12. Dr. Barebone
13. Hyth
14. Memoranda aliorum
15. oeconomica
16. Rolfes accompts
17. Mr. Collins papers
18. Building papers
19. Billes paid, 1680-1681
20. Billes paid, 1682-1683
21. Annuall acquittances rent, poor rates, chimney
22. Severall papers not sorted
23. [blank]
24. particulars of land, Irish farme
25. Mr. Pashley
26. [blank]
27. [blank]

16 pidgeon holes

1. Billes and acquitt. 1683
2. Letters not answered
3. Letters
4. pens, wax etc
5. billes, 1683, unpaid
6. Treasurie papers
7. Treasurie papers
8. Custome house
9. bookes
10. oeconomica
11. Varia, not sorted
12. Ireland
13. memoranda aliorum
14. varia
15. particular peticions, etc.
16. [blank]

[1] From 19 May 1684 King Charles II himself executed the office of lord high admiral.
[2] The entries in each column were subsequently deleted by Dering.

28. Letters
29. Letters from Bickbiron
30. Hamburgh companie
31. [blank]
32. [blank]
33. poetica, medica
34. varia not poetica, medica.
35. [blank]
36. [blank]

6

MISCELLANEOUS
PAPERS OF
SIR EDWARD DERING

1644 to 1683

British Library (Stowe MSS. and Additional MSS.); Blake Collections; House of Lords Record Office (Historical Collections); Kent Archives Office; Public Record Office.

Miscellaneous Papers of Sir Edward Dering

1644 to 1683

1. *Letter from Dering to his father,*[1]
29 February 1644

Colendissime Pater

   Quod in me est feci, neque tamen abeundi veniam impetrare possum, nemini (aiunt) transfretandum, nisi qui prius foedus Scoticum praestitit; neque ea quidem lege, quantum video, filio tuo. Omnes quos mihi alloquendi copia datur, Galliam Hollandiae multum praeferunt (tum—*del.*) argumentis ductis linguae Gallicanae praestantia, cui addunt quod ibi minoris quam Lugduni Batavorum degere possumus, (in Gall—*del.*) praesertim si quis artem tripudiandi equitandi etc. neglexerit: in Gallia urbem Aurelianensem, Caenensem, Angiers, et Academiam Monpelier praecupie laudant. Me quod attinet utrumque pariter affecto, locumque quem tu aptissimum, eundem credam et ego incondissimum. Tuum erit imperare auscultare

Obsequentissimi filii
Eduardi Dering

Februarii 29

Amantissima Matri obsequium nostrum praestes, rogo, fratribus et sororibus amorem.

If I should go over into France my Unkle Percivall can helpe me over at Rye.
I will endeavour a pass this weeke. If you would be pleased to write either to the Speaker or some Parliament man, it may be, it might be done.
Sir T. Wroth told me the Speaker (from whom alone a pass must be got) will give none but to those that will take the oath of allegeaunce, supremacy and the covenant: and besides maketh some scruple of me more than an other.
Endorsed, 1643 1⁰ Martii—Ned

BL Add 26,785, f. 68

2. *Dering's First Household Book, 1648-1652*

This volume in Dering's autograph comprises: [unnumbered] 'Chronologia Apocalyptica', 2ff.; 'A Note of what money I have laid out in

---

[1] This text has been printed in Larking, pp. 78-9.

household stuffe and other incident charges upon the occasion we removd, 29 of Aprill 1652', 1f.; 'Incident charges upon going to housekeeping', etc., March [1652], 4ff.; followed by
ff. 12-22 Receipts, 1648-1652
ff. 22v.-37v. blank
ff. 38-74v. Expenses, 1648-1652.[1]

BL Add 22,466

3. *Dering's Second Household Book, 1652-1685*

Perhaps 10ff. are lacking at the start of the volume.
On unnumbered folios: marriages in the family, 1642-1681.

pp. 17-23   Births and Christenings, 3 May 1558-29 April 1685 [the first entries were made *c.* 1652 and the list was maintained for 1652-85, the final entries being in another hand].

pp. 27-32   Funerals and Obits.

pp. 35-42   A Note of several lands sold by the Derings [reign of Stephen to 1656].

pp. 51-73   Lands bought by the Derings [3 Edw. IV to 1684].

pp. 75-116   A Note of the principal conveyances concerning the estate.

pp. 83-102 and 117-134 have been cut out of the volume.[2]

pp. 135-7   Notes of debts paid by Dering.

pp. 138-40   missing.

pp. 141-49   Account in general heads of expenses and receipts since Dering's marriage, omitting debts paid and taxes and fractions, 1648-1668.

pp. 151-174   missing.

pp. 175-78   Condition of estates, 1654.

pp. 179-80[?-2]   missing, one page stub noted 'cut out by myselfe.'

pp. 184-201   Notes of various debts [the pagination here is erroneous].

pp. 204-5   Note of woods sold, 1645-71.

pp. 210-17   Hopground accounts, 1653-1666.

p. 220   Yearly charge of housekeeping 1652-69.

pp. 221-8   missing.

pp. 230-45   Accounts of moneys due or received from relatives, 1657-62.

pp. 247-8   missing.

pp. 249-251   'Memoranda Familiaria' (portions and apprenticeships).

pp. 254-6   Deaths in the family.

pp. 268-76   Dering's itinerary, 1644-1664.

[1] Certain extracts were printed by E. F. Rimbald, *Notes and Queries,* no. 11 (1850), 161-2.
[2] It seems likely that missing pages had not been used by Dering and were cut out as blank paper.

Blake MS D

4. *Letter from Dering to James Brockman*[1]
7 February 1655

Dearest Brother

You concerne your selfe so much in me and my relacions heare, that I can not be silent, though I have nothing more to write than the receipt of yours of the 19th instant, and that we are all in health: my cousin Bell is now with me whom I have acquainted with your care of the constant and timely payment of his annuitie. (He is—*del.*) You have ten dayes after the quarterday, in which time I hope to be returned out of Kent and in a capacitie of rendring you that small service, so that you need not thinke of that till your convenience and opportunitye invite you to it.

My brother Bulkeley went yesterday toward Wales, but without his Lady and to make a soudain returne: you need not change my god-daughter's lot, my brother Finch I am sure will willingly owne the name fortune hath given him. The assizes are next weeke at Southwarke, where being ingaged to attend our high Sheriffe, I shall then, if not before, give him accompt of your fox dogs. I am forced still to deferr a punctuall accompt of my journey into Kent till next weeke, if you now thinke me to put on an unnecessary reservednesse, I am confident at our meeting you will excuse me. In the mean time assure your selfe, your last two letters have made such an impression upon me that I looke with very much displeasure upon all things that seeme either to divert or deferr our meeting, and long for your company with as much zeale and passion as the most desirable object, for such are you, can produce in the most affectionate heart, which is that of

Your most humble servant
and faithfull brother
Edward Dering

Combe,
Shrove Tuesday
1654

BL Add 42,586, f.35

[1] eldest surviving son and heir of Sir William Brockman, of Beachborough, in Newington-next-Hythe, co. Kent.

5. *Dering's Diary and Commonplace Book, 1656-1662*

This volume was sold as lot 2901 at the auction held by Messrs. Sotheby and Co. on 26 June 1974.[1] The MS. consists of 176 pp., with other pp. blank.[2] The catalogue listed, *inter alia*, the following contents: accounts of the funerals of Dr William Harvey and Oliver Cromwell;[3] diary of a journey through Huntingdonshire and Northamptonshire, July-August 1657; entries concerning his work in 1660 as a Lord of Romney Marsh, Deputy Lieutenant, commissioner for raising money and disbanding the army and commissioner for the militia in Kent; notes of his attendance at the committee of religion, 16 July 1660, and of the King's speech; a description of the French ambassador with whom he dined, 30 June 1658; commonplace entries concerning medical recipes, etc., a note of the drawers in his study; and five verses, including a variant reading of John Donne's prayer 'Wilt thou forgive that Sinne Where I begunne', here entitled 'To God Æternal'.

6. *The Militia Acts, 1662-3*

Holograph summary by Dering of the Act for ordering the forces in the several counties of this Kingdom, 1662, 14 Cha. II, c. 3, and of the Additional Act for the better ordering the forces in the several counties of this Kingdom, 1663, 15 Cha. II, c. 4. *Appended*, draft letter to an unnamed person that E. Winchelsea had appointed a general meeting of all deputy lieutenants at Rochester 'the 27th instant' and that the recipient is asked to attend a preliminary meeting at Ashford.

HLRO Hist Coll 85/3

7. *Notes on the Muscovy trade, post 1662*

Holographs extracts by Dering from the Act for the incorporation of the fellowship and society of English merchants for the discovery of new trades, 1566, 8 Eliz. I, c. 1 (private) and from the letters patent of Philip and Mary [of 26 Feb. 1555[4]] for the formation of a company of merchants trading to Muscovy. *Appended*, copies of orders (i) from the Lord Treasurer that there should be no trade with Russia except by warrant from the Governor or Treasurer of the company, 24 May 1661; (ii) for John Chaplin, the company's officer, to execute this order,

---

[1] The sale was to Messrs Maggs Bros. Ltd, 50 Berkeley Square, London.

[2] The following description is taken from the auction catalogue, 26 June 1974, p. 54.

[3] The page of entries for 17-23 November 1658, including that for Cromwell's funeral, is reproduced in the catalogue, p. 55.

[4] cf. *CPR, 1554-5*, 55-9.

24 Feb. 1662, with a subsequent nomination of Benjamin Edwards to succeed Chaplin.

HLRO Hist Coll 85/7

8. *Evidence before the Court of Claims, 6-10 June 1663*

Dering's autograph minutes of proceedings before the Court of Claims. An edition of these minutes together with those contained in nos. 17-19 below will appear in an appendix to the forthcoming publication of the Irish Manuscripts Commission on the Courts of Claims in Ireland, 1662-3 and 1666-9, which is being edited by Dr J. G. Simms.

KAO U350/o 14, ff.24-7

[f.41] 9. *Instructions concerning the forfeitures in the Kingdom of Ireland,*[1] [post *1665*]

Imprimis: You are to have recourse to the records of his Majestie's Surveyour Generall's office in Ireland and demand a certificate of the number of acres of the whole forfeited or reputed forfeited stock of lands in Ireland by the downe survey.

2. You are to demand the like certificate for the value of all the forfeited houses in the corporate townes according to the act and councell's valuacion.

3. You are to repaire to his Majestie's Auditor Generall's office and demand thence a certificate of the annuall value of all forfeited tithes and impropracions in Ireland.

Memorandum, the resolucion of the above questions informes the state of all the forfeitures in Ireland by the late warr there.

These particulars being knowne, you are in the next place to observe these following directions

1. How much of the said stock appeares by the records of the Surveyor Generall's office, to be set forth to the souldiers both before and since 1649, in which you are particularly to distinguish between lands set forth for English arreares, and for service in Ireland.

2. You are to extract out of the records of the said office, what was the whole debt, due to the souldiers, and what part thereof is satisfied and what in arreare.

3. Out of the book returned from the committee at Grocers' Hall, now in the custody of the sub committee to the court of claimes, you are to extract the whole of the adventurers' debt, in which you are to distinguish between the money advanced on the act of 17 and 18 Caroli,[2] and those afterwards advanced on ordinances of parliament.

---

1 The heading and text are holograph.

2 17 & 18 Cha. II, c. 2, *Irish Statutes*, iii (1786), 2-137. The act was passed on 23 Dec. 1665.

4. You are to examine by the records of the subcommissioner's office what part of the said debt is satisfied and what is deficient.
5. You are to distinguish what part of the said debt was by the act of 17 [or 18] Caroli to be satisfied in English measure and what in Irish.
6. You are to examine by the Surveyor Generall's office how much of the forfeited stock was set aside for a support to the government in times of usurpacion.
7. How much thereof appeares by the records of the said office to be given forth to the transplanted Irish in Connaught and Clare.
8. You are by the aforesaid records to examine what was given as donative by the usurper.
9. You are by the same records to informe yourselves what surplus was within the Surveyor and Auditors securitie which was not on the 7th May 1659 set out to either.
10. What number of acres are of the surplus land by reducing the estimate survey to the Downe or mathematicall survey.
11. To enquire by records of the Surveyor Generall and Auditor's office what disposicion was made of all the tithes and impropriacions in the whole Kingdome in the time of usurpacion.

[f.41v]
12. To informe yourselves by the aforesaid records how many of the Irish have proved their constant and good affection to the English interest, and how many of the said Irish were on the said proofes restored to their ancient estate.
13. Lastly in the above enquiries after the common stock, you are to make a particular enquiry what protestant proprietors you find and how many acres the said protestant proprietors are.

Memorandum, the resolucion of the above questions will fully informe the whole forfeited stock, and the dispositions made thereof in the time of usurpacion, before the passing of his Majesties gratious declaracion of the 30th November 1660.

[f.42] The last generall head of instructions are such as referr to the present commissioners for executing the act of explanacion[1] which may be as followeth

1. You are to make diligent enquiry how many acres of the aforesaid common stock not disposd of to souldiers or adventurers were remaining when the commissioners first entred on the explanatory act.
2. What was the number of acres set forth on the ordinances of parliament, English arreares, surplus land or usurped donatives at that time.
3. How many acres the thirds to be retrenched by the souldier adventurers or protestant Connaught purchasers did amount unto.

[1] 17 & 18 Cha. II, c. 2 (*Irish Statutes*).

4. You are to enquire how many acres of the aforesaid stock would suffice to answer two thirds of all souldiers adventurers who were totally deficient.

5. How much would satisfy the adventurers who were totally deficient.

6. To enquire by the Surveyor Generall's office what number of acres the thirds of persons not retrenched by page [blank] of the explanatory act do amount unto.

7. How much of the said stock hath been confirmd to lettrees by the clause p. 107.

8. How many acres claimed and how many confirmed to the claymants by value worth and purchase by the said explanatory act.

9. What quantity of lands decreed by the said commission to persons pretending title in 1641 when no such title appears by records.

10. What disposicion hath been made of the said stock on pretence of preemptcion and mortgages and what mortgages appeare forged in the records of his Majestie's court of (claims—*del.*) common pleas in Ireland, what have been since concealed by order of the said court, and who were pretenders to the said mortgages.

11. To examine whether the adventurers who advanced their money before the 15th June 1641 are not satisfied by Irish measure.

12. To examine the claimes and to observe what souldiers and adventurers have retrenched the same lands, and received double satisfaction for one debt.

13. What rule was prescribed by the commissioners for preserving the common stock.

14. What fees are taken by the commissioners or their officers from the people and what of the said fees were allowed by act of parliament and what added *by the said act*[1] and councell.

15. What method or rules were prescribed by the said commissioners for the gouvernment of their proceedings in the adjudication of claims depending before them.

16. What donations or gifts were given by the act of explanacion or otherwise, and to whom and what the value of the said donatives appeared to be by the said act and councells valuacion.

[f.42v]

17. What abatement of quit rent you find made to any person since the passing the act of explanacion.

18. Whether the subjects were not necessitated to pay more than one acridge for one and the same lands.

HLRO Hist Coll 85/1

---

[1] The words italicised were underlined by Dering.

10. *Draft Letter from Dering to Lord Arlington,*
20 January 1666

Dublin

May it please your Lordship

My son Southwell having from Portsmouth acquainted me with the many favours he hath received from your Lordship, not only in reference to the honourable imployment now intrusted to him, but during the whole time of his attendance in Court,[1] I hope your Lordship will not be displeased, to find the obligacion more extensive than you thought it, and that all his relacions, of which I accompt myselfe the nearest and most concerned, do joine in their most humble acknowledgments of your Lordship's favour, and begg the continuance of your directions to him abroad and your protection at home as the only meanes of making his indeavours in both places acceptable to his Majestie and happy to himselfe.

I must inlarge this trouble to your Lordship upon the occasion of his Majestie's letter of 25th December, in which he is pleased by the mediacion of my Lord Lieutenant and of your Lordship, to graunt to Colonell Cook and myselfe, the profits of some lands concealed from his Majestie untill they shall be disposed of. My Lord we are very sensible of so great and so unexpected a favour, and dare assure your Lordship both in behalfe of Colonell Cooke and of myselfe that a very gentle and moderate use shall be made of it, it being but reason, that we should rather loose the whole benefit intended us, than give any occasion of complaint to a nacion, for whose satisfaction his Majestie himselfe hath quitted all the advantages, which both against the victors and the vanquished, the law would unquestionably have devolved upon him.

My Lord it may seeme very unsuitable to the modestie I have allwayes profest, to begg new favours of you with the same breath that I acknowledge the former, yet I can not dissemble my desire of one that I shall esteem equall with any that I have received, it is that your Lordship will be pleased to lay some commands upon me in reference to your owne particular service heare. No man lives that will receive them with more satisfaction, nor observe them with more obedience and respect, than will your Lordship's most obliged and most humble servant.[2]

Edward Dering

BL Stowe 744, f. 67

[1] Southwell had been knighted on 21 December 1665 and was serving as deputy vice-admiral of the provinces of Munster; in November 1665 he had been appointed envoy to the Court of Portugal (*DNB*).

[2] In reply to this letter Arlington on 6 Feb. 1666 expressed his appreciation of Dering's friendship and would be 'glad to deserve any new occasion, the effects of it which Robin Leigh tells me hee hath already found in my concernes there' (BL Stowe 744, f. 99). In March Arlington was asking Dering to help Col. Fitzpatrick in his claims (*ibid.*, f. 105).

11. *Draft Letter from Dering to Lord Arlington,*
29 November 1666

Dublin

May it please your Lordship:
The concerne of my Lord Nettervill which your Lordship is pleased to mencion in your favour of the 6th instant, is allready, together with some others of the like nature, laid by the Commissioners before my Lord Lieutenant and Councell, from whom I doubt not but it will receive a favourable dispatch, and then it will be in our power to give his Lordship a preference in his reprisalls before most others, which in obedience to your Lordship's commands, I shall have a constant and particular care of.¹ And the business of reprisalls, as to the applicacion of them to particular persons, being very much in our owne power, I shall be very glad to receive any directions from your Lordship therein, and shall evidence by my obedience, that no name in the world hath a greater power over me than your Lordship's. I shall not trouble your Lordship with any accompt of what passeth before us, of which if any thing be considerable it is communicated to your Lordship from better hands, I shall only presume to say, that a great part of our worke is now over, the generall and spreading interests of the act being settled, and as we hope, to good satisfaction, and most also of the particular provisos adjudged, what remaineth being chiefly the distribucion of reprisalls as farr as they will goe, and the settling some part of the interest of the [16]49 officers: and the transplanted Irish into Connaught (if it be thought fit that we shall proceed upon them). All which we reckon may be finished by the beginning of Aprill next, and we then have the permission to returne, and at his Majestie's feet give an accompt of the trust he hath committed to us. But as it is certaine we shall leave our good deeds behind us in Ireland, and meet our faults, if any we are guilty of, at Whitehall at our returne, so it may not be imprudent in me, by this early addresse to bespeake your Lordship's favour and good opinion, which yet I should not presume to do, if I had not an assurance within my selfe, that I have done nothing that can render me unworthy of your Lordship's protection, and some hopes that your Lordship will be pleased to looke favourably upon the inclinations I have to shew myselfe by particular duty and obedience

Your Lordship's most faithfull and most
humble servant

BL Stowe 744, f. 139

Edward Dering

¹ Nicholas, third Viscount Netterville of Dowth had been 'contrary to the general expectation, declared "Nocent" by the Commissioners . . ., on 23 March 1662/3, and, though he afterwards obtained some reparation from the King, could never recover more than about a fifth of his estate of Dowth, for which he passed patent 18 June 1666' (*CP*, ix, 473). Arlington pressed Netterville's claims on Dering in his letter to him of 3 Nov. 1666 (together with those of an infant, John Arthur), cf. BL Stowe 744, f. 136.

12. *Letter from Dering to Sir Heneage Finch,*
26 January 1667

From Dublin; mainly concerning Dering's claim to a reversionary appointment as Auditor in Ireland. Calendared in *CSPI, 1666-9*, 282-3.

PRO S.P. Ireland, 322,35

13. *Letter from Dering to Viscount Conway*
and Killulta, 11 February 1667

From Dublin; concerning Dering's claim to a reversionary appointment as Auditor in Ireland. Calendared in *CSPI, 1666-9*, 295-6.

PRO S.P. Ireland, 322,48

14. *Draft letter from Dering to Lord Arlington,*
11 February, 1667

May it please your Lordship,
by severall letters from my Lord Conway[1] and my brother Finch, I am informed how highly I am obliged to your Lordship for your favourable assistance in my pretencions to the auditor's place of this Kingdome, this declaracion of your Lordship's favour and countenance to me, I set a higher value upon than the imployment I pretended to, and which will make me never repent the having ingaged in this attempt what soever the successe thereof shall be. It is with much satisfaction to myselfe and much gratitude to your Lordship that I confesse I have nothing more to aske of your Lordship in this businesse, in which you have allready been pleased to exceed or provide all my desires, for as I did not imbarque in it, without good assurance that my desires were acceptable to my Lord Lieutenant, and that many persons did believe I might be serviceable to his Majestie in it, so if his Grace by any prior engagement or late consideracion find any inconvenience in it, I should and shall allwayes submit my concernes to his pleasure, without which I neither hope nor desire any interest in this Kingdome. Only if your Lordship should so think fit, I should be glad that no graunt or letter from his Majestie might be sent, at least not sudainly, in the favour of any competitor, that so my Lord Lieutenant may have some farther time to consider how he will dispose of it, and as I believe he will consider nothing in it so much as his Majestie's service, so I am sure I shall submit to his pleasure without further trouble or importunity.[2] I only aske your Lordship's

---

[1] cf. BL Stowe 744, ff. 144, 148.
[2] The King directed that Dering be granted the reversion of the office of Auditor-General of Ireland on 11 Nov. 1667 (*CSPI, 1666-9*, 483).

pardon for saying that as the demonstrations of your Lordship's favour and candour in this businesse, will make me never seeke any other support in the court than your Lordship's favour, so there is no person living that shall more faithfully and entirely design all the actions of their life to your Lordship's service, than shall [incomplete]

BL Stowe 744, f. 150

15. *Letter from Dering to Viscount Conway and Killulta, 19 October 1667*

From Dublin, mainly concerning sitting of the Court of Claims 'in neating and clearing the stock of reprisals', which they hope to do in three weeks. They will then proceed to distribution, and may finish by 4 Jan. 1668, the date on which their commission expires. Calendared in *CSPI, 1666-9*, 472.

PRO S.P. Ireland, 323, 141

16. *Commission for executing the Act of Settlement in Ireland (timetable of work)*[1] [n.d. ?1667]

[f.52] By his Majestie's commissioners for putting in execucion the acts of settlement and explanacion

To the end that all persons concerned in the said settlement may the better know when to attend their occasions before his Majesties commissioners, it is thought fit to publish that they intend to proceed as followeth:

January [1668][2]

8, Wednesday, for reports from the sub commissioners of such particular reprizalls as have been allready referred to them by the court, and which should have been reported upon the 18th of December. And Wednesdays and Saturdays during the said moneth of January, for the like reports.

9, for bringing in the whole neat stock of reprisable lands as well retrench as incumbered.

10, for the causes appointed for the third of January.

13, Monday, for mocions.

14, for such who have contracted for the preempcion of any mortgages, to bring in their acquittances from Mr Bence of the payment of the money contracted for.

16, Thursday, for canting the remaining part of the 49 mortgages according to a list thereof published in print.

[1] Dering did not insert any heading; the notes are holograph.
[2] The entries are set out in two columns.

24, Fryday, for taking out all certificats for preempcions allready adjudged.

28, Tuesday, for bringing in (all—*del.*) the subdivisions of the 49 costs.

31, Fryday, for all persons who have had any judgment of this court as adventurers souldiers or protestant purchasers to take out their certificats

February [1668]

3, Monday, for carrying into the Exchequer all the remaining enrollments of certificats.

5, Wednesday, for dividing and allotting to all (reprisable—*del.*) deficient adventurers souldiers and protestant purchasers so much of the remaining stock as shall be due to them for their reprisalls.

(21 and the 28th of February for such persons—*del.*)

(17,—*del.*)

7 and 14, being Frydays for taking out all certificats for preempcions to be adjudged upon the 16th of January.

The 21 and 28th of February being Frydays, for all people to take out their certificats at their perill.

(After which time we shall be humble suitors to his Majestie—*del.*)

HLRO Hist Coll 85/1

17. *Evidence before the Court of Claims, 3-6 June 1668*

Dering's holograph minutes of proceedings, cf. p. 159 above.

KAO U350/0 14 ff. 1-23

18. *Evidence before the Court of Claims, 6 June 1668*

Dering's holograph minutes of proceedings, cf. p. 159 above.

HLRO Hist Coll 85/12

19. *Evidence before the Court of Claims, 31 August 1668*

Dering's holograph minutes of proceedings, cf. p. 159 above.

KAO U1107/14/6

20. *Correspondence of Dering and Sir Robert Southwell,
1669-1683*

148 letters from Dering to Southwell are included in the 4 volumes which were calendared in 1972 by the National Register of Archives (see *The*

Dering-Southwell Correspondence, NRA). The letters were then in the possession of Richard Neall Esq., of Derings, West Ashling, Chichester, but were acquired in 1972 by the Kent Archives Office. Miss Sonia Anderson in her Introduction to the Calendar describes the volumes as containing 'original letters from the Derings of Surrenden Dering to the Southwells of Kinsale and Kings Weston (former Phillipps MS. 14925), and miscellaneous 19th century papers relating to Dering family history and genealogy.' The period covered by the Calendar is 1664 to 1727, with 8 subsequent items to 1960. Dering's letters were written between 1669 and 1683; the principal references to parliamentary and political matters are noted in the Introduction above, pp. 12-23.

KAO U 1713/C 1-4

21. *Abstract of Privy Seals, October 1669-October 1670*

Dering's register recording the delivery of the Privy Seal to him and Mr Justice Millward on 4 Oct. 1669, their agreement 'to meet constantly Mondayes and Thursdayes every week for dispatch of the businesse of the Privy Seale', and entries of 388 docquets for the following twelve months. *Cf.* the calendar of the volume in HMC, *MSS. of J. Eliot Hodgkin* (1897), 8-16.

BL Add 38,862

22. *Parliamentary Diary, 15 November 1670 to 3 November 1673 with other entries*

The diary is entered on ff. 20-129 of a register which also contains the following holograph entries by Dering:

(i) Partial index to the Parliamentary diary, ff. 135v, 136.
(ii) Abstract of Sir Thomas Browne's 'Pseudodoxia epidemica', dated 28 Aug. 1648, ff. 5-14v.
(iii) Abstract of an educational treatise entitled 'L'Examen des esprits', ff. 15, 15v.[1]
(iv) 'Litis Pontificiæ cum R[e] P[ublica] Veneta ex Italico Patris Pauli Compendium Latinum.' An abstract of the history of the disputes between Pope Paul V and the Republic of Venice in 1605-1607, by Fra Paolo [otherwise Pietro Sarpi], 1624, ff. 17-19.
(v) List of famous modern battles in England, France and Italy down to 1515; arranged under the months, ff. 129v-135.

[1] This item is omitted from the *Catalogue of Additions to the Manuscripts in the British Museum 1854-1860* (1875), at p. 646.

The diary was published *in extenso* by Professor B.D.Henning, *The Parliamentary Diary of Sir Edward Dering, 1670-1673* (Yale University Press, 1940).

BL Add 22,467

23. *Speech by Dering concerning the General Pardon Bill,*
[f.70]   *28 March 1673*[1]

If this bill now before us were of the nature of other billes that we could committ it and amend it, I should be as forward as others are to shew where it might be inlarged and made more beneficiall to the people than now it is, but since we must either receive it as it come from his Majestie or refuse it alltogether, I am neither so vaine as to believe I have nothing to be forgiven (myself—*del.*), nor so ill natured as to refuse his Majestie's grace and indulgence to my selfe, because he doth at the same time extend it to some others that want it much more than I do, and (yet— *del.*) if there be any one in this house that thinkes he is safe enough without this pardon, let him remember we do not sit heare for our selves but for all the Commons of England, and if any man do believe in the countie which he serves for, or in the corporacion which he represents, there is no man that will be the better for this pardon, that member shall have my free leave to give his negative to this bill. But, Sir, the penall lawes of this Kingdome are now so many in number and so intricate in their nature that I believe the wisest man in England doth hardly comprehend them, nor the most wary and cautious man in the Kingdome doth not (ob—*del.*) nor cannot observe them, and I thinke I can instance in one single law, and that no very old one neither, against which alone if all the forfeitures since the act of oblivion should be exacted, (collected—*del.*) it would cost the Kingdome more than all the money we have given the King this session. It may look a little too much to say this, but I thinke there is no extravagance in the expression, not so much as an hyperbole. I meane, Sir, the statute of Queen Elisabeth concerning labourers and wages, and if every man were to pay £5 for every servaunt he have taken this ten yeare without a certificate, and for every time he hath paid any labourer more than the statute wages, I believe (it would—*del.*) there are few persons heare that would not pay more upon that statute than they will pay upon the subsidy bill lately past us. And (therefore—*del.*) I think we shall [f.70v] receive but an ill wellcome from our countries when they shall be troubled and molested upon this or any other penall statute, and shall know they might have been at ease and at peace if their representatives heare had

---

[1] The bill was received from the Lords on 28 March 1673, read the same day by the Commons and passed (*CJ*, ix, 280) being enacted as 25 Chas. II, c. 5; no speech by Dering is given by Grey (ii, 169-71). The text of the speech is holograph.

been pleased to have received for them that grace and indulgence which his Majestie so freely offered to them.

I do see, Sir, that the bill hath in it some names that are very ingratefull to this house, and will for ever be so whiles we remember the affront they have done to us all in their insolence they committed upon one of the number, but truly, Sir, I am not of opinion that for this reason we should reject the whole or put out one of our owne eyes that so we may put out both those of other men. I do not thinke they have escaped justice even for all this. A pardon indeed it is, but a restitucion in integrum, as pardons use to be, it is not. (It is not his Majestie's desire nor indeed is it in his power to—*del.*) Sir, this pardon can not restore these unhappy men to that reputacion and fair opinion in the world which they had before. It will rather perpetuate their infamy, and no man will ever see the names of Sir Thomas Sands and Mr O'Brion in this act of grace but they will at the same time remember that their names are also in another act by which they are convicted of a crime so barbarous and unworthy, as till they (were found guilty—*del.*) did of it, I did not for my part believe that it could ever have fallen into the heart of any English gentleman to have attempted it, and though the pardon do take (off the danger of their arrest—*del.*) ease of their punishment, yet (it—*del.*) leaving them still the shame of the fact (which—*del.*) I believe they will rather (persuade them to—*del.*) wander for ever in foraigne parts then to returne hither, where they can never hope for the friendship and hardly for the conversacion of good men. And I am so far from thinking their impunity will encourage others to attempt the like fact, that I believe not only all other men, but even they themselves do rather wish they had never been borne than ever to have needed such a pardon, and therefore I beseech without apprehending any ill consequences at all (will—*del.*) to passe this bill and receive it with all humble and due submissiveness from his Majestie for his sovereign will.

[f.71v.] *Endorsed*, Second Act of Oblivion

HLRO Hist Coll 85/1

24. *Recovery of tithes bill, 27 October 1673*

[Text in Dering's hand of a bill 'for the better and more effectual repairing of parochiall churches and chappells within this Kingdome and for the more easie and speedie recovering of small tithes . . .',[1] ff.

---

[1] Bills to recover tithes had been introduced and made some progress in 1668, 1669, 1670 and Spring 1673. The present bill was read 1a on 27 Oct. 1673 (*CJ*, ix, 282), 2a on 3 Nov. (when Dering himself moved the reading) (*op. cit.*, 286 and p. 14 above), but parliament was prorogued on 4 Nov. Similar bills were introduced in each subsequent session of Parliament to 1677, but did not reach enactment.

numbered 1, 3 and 4. The omission of time limits, etc., indicates that this is a first or second reading copy. Document 26 below is an amended and filled up text, presumably prepared for a later committee. For the text of Dering's draft see document 26 below; in addition, the following clauses appear in Dering's draft, but are omitted from document 26.]

[i] Provided allwayes and be it enacted that no rate or assessment to be made by vertue of this act shall in any one yeare exceed the summe of [blank] in the pound of the yearly value of any lands or tenements chargeable by this act nor the summe of [blank] in the pound for any goods or stock unlesse by a speciall order to be made in that behalfe at the generall quarter sessions for that countie citie towne corporate place or divicion, such greater and higher rate be particularly provided for and allowed. [f.3]

[ii] Provided allwayes and be it enacted by the authoritie aforesaid, that where the modus decimandi or the manner or custome of tithing shall be denied by any person complaind of unto two justices of peace as aforesaid, in that case it shall and may be lawfull for the person complaining to prosecute and make out his right in any of his Majestie's ecclesiasticall courts having cognisance of the same, and if judgment shall there be given for the plaintive or for the defendant then the judge of the said court his deputy or surrogate shall under his seale of office certify the same unto the justices of peace for that countie citie towne corporate or divicion at the next generall quarter sessions to be held for the same, who thereupon shall proceed to award such treble (or other greater— *del.*) or lesser damages and costs as to them shall seem reasonable, the same to be levied by distresse and sale of the goods of the person against whom judgment had been given in the ecclesiasticall court as aforesaid. [f.4]

KAO U1107/14/2

25. *Petition from the clergy in support of the recovery of tithes bill* [*n.d., ? Nov. 1673*][1]

To the Honourable the House of Commons
As concerning the Bill for repaire of Churches and the better recovering of Small Tythes,

The Poore Clergy Humbly Sheweth

That the more easy and speedy recovery of Small Tythes or the Value of them [by] warrant of distresse under the hand and Seale of the Justice of the Peace when adjudged is the full import of this Bill

Objec[tion], The Bill if admitted to passe distroyes Episcopall Authority and Ecclesiasticall Jurisdiction

---

[1] This petition is not in Dering's hand, but may be the original; it is unsigned. See document 26, following.

Answered, This if admitted doe not distroy Ecclesiasticall Jurisdiction but establish[es] itt.

For Tythes are the undoubted and determyned property of the Clergy. That which is graunted to the Justice if the Bill be Admitted is not to passe sentence for what is determined (by—*del.*) but too impower them to Assist in the execucion of A former Sentence for the Enjoying their propriety.

And whatsoever is in Controversy is referred to the Courts Ecclesiastical as Judges of what is not decided.

KAO U1107/14/3

26. *Recovery of tithes bill*, [post 3 November 1673]

[Text prepared within the House of a bill following Dering's text in document 24 above, but with variations as indicated. This text may have been prepared for or by the committee to which Dering was appointed on 20 April 1675]

[f.1] For The better and more Effectuall Repaireing of Parochiall Churches and Chappells within this Kingdome and for the more easy and Speedy Recovering of Small Tythes where the same are due and payable Bee It Enacted by the Kings most Excellent Majestye by and with the advice and Consent of the Lords Spirituall and Temporall and of the Commons in this present Parlyament Assembled and by Authority of the same That The Churchwardens of every Parish and Chappellry within this Kingdome of England and Dominion of Wales together with the Overseers for the Poore of Such Parish or Chappellry or the major part of them upon Publique Notice first to bee given by the Churchwardens in the said Church or Chappell shall from tyme to tyme make rates or Assessments by Taxation of every Inhabitant within the said Parish or Chappellry for and towards the Repaireing of every Such Parish Church or Chappell respectively and for provideing Bread and Wine to bee used att the Administration of the Blessed Sacrament of the Lords Supper and for repaireing the Walls and inclosures of the Church yards and Burying places thereunto belonging and for paying of Wages to the Clerkes and Sextons, and for doeing all Such things as the said Churchwardens by vertue of their said Office are required to doe All which rates and Assessments shall be equally and indifferently proportioned by a pound rate or other usuall way of rateing upon all Lands and Tenements houses tythes impropriate Colemines Saleable underwoods goods and Stock usually rated or ratable in the said Parish to the releife of the Poore And the said rate or Assessment being agreed upon by the said Churchwardens Overseers for the Poore or the major part of them, being fairely written shalle by the said Churchwardens bee presented unto two Justices of the Peace of the County City place or division in which the said Parish or Chappellrie shall bee, and shall by them if they see no just cause to the Contrary bee allowed and Confirmed under their hands And Bee it Enacted by the Authority aforesaid that all such rates and Assessments [f.2] made and Confirmed as aforesaid shall and may bee Levyed by the present or subsequent Churchwardens by Warrant under the hands and Seales of two Justices of the Peace by distress and sale of the goods and chattells of all Such persons who shall refuse or neglect to pay the Summe or Summes assessed upon them by the Space of Six days after the same shall bee so Assessed and demaunded by the said Churchwardens Rendring the Overplus ariseing by such distresse and sale unto the respective owners; And Bee it further Enacted by the Authority aforesaid that every Churchwarden att the Expiracion of his yeare upon some day within the space of Thirty dayes[1] after the Eleccion of the new Churchwardens and upon Publique notice first thereof to bee given in the Church shall present to the Inhabitants of the Parish a faire Accompt in Writeing in a Booke to bee kept for that purpose of all monyes by him receaved upon any such rates or Assessments as aforesaid and how the same have bin expended and what money doth remaine behinde and unpayd, and if any money shall remaine in his hands shall pay the same unto the Churchwardens elected for the yeare following And the said Accompts shall afterwards bee also presented unto two Justices of Peace whereof also Publique notice shall be given as aforesaid, and the said two Justices of the Peace unless just cause shalbe showed before them to the contrary, shall allow the said Accompts under their hand and the said Churchwardens shall thenceforth bee acquitted of and from any other or farther Enquiry touching or concerning the same:

And Bee it farther Enacted by the Authority aforesaid, that if any Churchwarden shall refuse or neglect to make such Assessment where the same shalbe necessary for the Ends aforesaid or to give such Accompt or to pay over the money remaineing in his hands to the succeeding Churchwardens, then it shall and may bee lawfull for any one Justice of the Peace upon complaint to him thereof made, to summon the said Churchwarden, and upon his Appearance if hee finde cause to binde such Churchwarden over to the next generall quarter Sessions to bee held for that County, City place or divicion, and the said Justices of Peace att their said generall Quarter [f.3] Sessions shall and may proceed to heare and determine the matter, and if they see cause shall and may committ the offender to Prison without Baile or mainprise, untill he shall give up a true Accompt and satisfye and pay over as aforesaid all such money as shall appeare to bee remaineing in his hands:

Provided alwayes and bee it Enacted that any person findeing himselfe aggreived by any rate or Assessment to bee made by vertue of this Act

---

[1] The text to this point follows almost exactly the wording of the bill in Dering's hand, document no. 24 above, f. 1; Dering's f. 2 is now lost.

may appeale unto the next generall Quarter Sessions to bee held for the peace of that County City Towne Corporate place or divicion where such Parish or Chappellrie shall lye and such Order as shall there be made shall be finall and conclusive to all parties:

Provided also and bee it Enacted that this Act nor any thing therein contained shall give power to make any rate or Assessment for or towards the Reparacion of any Cathedrall or Collegiate Churches, nor of any Chappell or Chancell which have formerly by prescription or custome beene repaired by the Parsons Vicars Impropriators[1] or other private persons, nor for or towards the reparation or rebuilding of any Parochiall Church or Chappell which is now wholly ruined or demolished or which hath not bin used for the Publique worshipp of God within the space of tenn yeares last past, neither shall it extend to charge any vicar for or in respect of his small Tythes [2]nor any Parson or Impropriator for or in respect of any glebe lands tithes whatsoever for which hee is bound to mainteyne and repaire any chancell in or belonging to the said Church or Chappell[2]

Provided also and bee it Enacted that if any Action of Trespass or other suite shall be brought against any Churchwarden or other person for takeing any distress or makeing any sale by vertue of this Act, or against any Justice of Peace for makeing such warrant the same shalbe heard and determined in the same County wherein the said distress was taken and not elsewhere, and if Judgement shall goe for the defendant or the Plaintiffe shall be nonsuited, the defendant shall recover double costs:[3]

[2]Provided alwayes and bee it Enacted that where any Parish or Chappellrie haveing no Church or Chappell to mainteyne is lawfully united to any other Parish Church the said parish or Chappell so united And all the Inhabitants rateable therein shall pay all such Taxes towards the mainteynance and repaire of the Church to which the same is united proporcionably with the Parishioners of that Parish in which the Church stands and to [f.4] which by such union they ought to resort to heare divine Service:[2]

And Bee it further Enacted by the Authority aforesaid that all persons shall truely and effectually set out and pay all and singuler their Tythes commonly called small Tythes with all their offerings oblacions and obvencions due to the Parsons or Vicars of their Severall Parishes within this Kingdome and Dominion of Wales according to the Customes and Prescripcions commonly used within the said Parishes respectively, And if any Person shall hereafter substract or withdrawe or any wayes faile in the true payment of such small Tythes offerings oblacion or obvencions as aforesaid, then the person or persons to whome the same

---

[1] Document no. 24 above, f. 3 resumes at this point.
[2] . . . [2] These sections are lacking in doc. 24.
[3] At this point document no. 24 adds proviso (i).

shall be due his and their Executors or Administrators shall and may make his or their Complaint unto two of his Majestie's Justices of the Peace within that County City Towne corporate place or divicion not being any wayes Interested in the said Tythes or other things in Question, which said two Justices of the Peace are hereby Authorized and required to Summon by reasonable warneing every such person and persons against whome any Complaint shall be made as aforesaid, and after his or their appeareance or upon default of their appearance, the said Summons being proved before them upon Oath, the said Justices of Peace shall proceed to heare and determine the said Complaint, and upon the proofes and evidences and testimonyes produced before them shall in writeing under their hands and seales adjudge the case and give also such reasonable Costs and dammages to either party as to them shall seeme just:

And Bee it farther Enacted that if any Person or persons shall refuse or neglect to pay and satisfye any such summe of money as upon such Complaint and proceedings shall by any two Justices of Peace bee adjudged as aforesaid, in every such Case the person and persons to whome any Such Summe of money shall upon Such Judgement bee due and payable shall and may by Warrant from the said Justices or either of them to the Constable or Churchwardens of the said Parish or one of them to bee directed distreyne all and every the goods and chattells of the Partyes so refuseing, or neglecting, and after detaineing of the same by the space of six dayes shall and may make sale of the same, and retaine to themselves soe much of the money ariseing by the said sale as may satisfie the [f.5] said Summe so adjudged to him or them, together with reasonable Costs and charges for keepeing the said distress, rendring the Overplus unto the Owner:[1]

Provided alwayes and bee it Enacted that it shall and may be lawfull for all Justices of the Peace in the Examinacion of all matters referred to them by this Act to Administer Oathes where the same shall bee necessary for their Informacion and for the better discovery of the Truth:

Provided also and bee it Enacted that this Act nor any thing therein conteyned shall extend to any Tythes offerings Oblacions or Obvencions within the City of London or Libertyes thereof nor unto any other City or Towne C [*ms. torn*] where the same are particularly settled by any Act of Parlyament in that Case made and provided:

Provided also and bee it Enacted that no Person who hath made his Complaint to any Justices of Peace for any Tythes Offerings Oblacions or obvencions and had Judgement thereupon by vertue of this Act, shall or may for the same matter or thing have any farther or other remedie in any of his Majestie's Courts Ecclesiasticall or Temporall within this Kingdome:

---

[1] Dering's text in document 24 above here adds proviso (ii), but then ends.

Provided alwayes and bee it Enacted that noe Complaint for or concerning any small Tythes Offerings Obvencions or oblacions shall be
heard and determined by any Justices of Peace by vertue of this Act,
unless the Complaint shall be made within the space of one yeare after
the tyme that the same did become due and payable Anything in this
Act Conteyned to the Contrary Notwithstanding

KAO U1107/14/1

27. *Speech by Dering in committee of the whole house on the King's
answer to the address for recalling such of his subjects as were in arms in
the French King's service; and for hindering any more from going over
into that service, 10 May, 1675*[1]

[f.39]

After so long a debate upon this Question and so much said for and
against the satisfactorinesse of this message, I stand up to (move—*del.*)
propose to you what no man else hath moved, and in which peradven-
ture no man will think fit to second me. However, being assured that I
bring as good intentions to the publique service as any man else doth I
presume humbly to offer you my opinion that you should go off this
debate without putting any Question at all and without determining it
one way or other.

The arguments on both sides have been very considerable and much
hath been said to prove this message satisfactorie and as much on the
contrarie, yet under submission no man hath yet convinced me, that
there is any necessitie of any publique declaracion of our thoughts upon
it. This way of replying and rejoining to the King is not in my opinion
necessarie at all, and as I take it has not been very usuall. They who
thinke it satisfactorie, do acquiesce in it, and thanke the King in their
hearts for his compliance in it. They who do not thinke it such, will not
thinke themselves precluded (by—*del.*) from endeavouring by all fair
and parliamentarie meanes to arrive at that end, which they have
aimed at in their addresse. But out of doubt sooner or later we must
acquiesce in the King's pleasure. I speake of things of this nature which
are wholly in his Majestie's power, which are not against any funda-
mentall law of the land, and in which no man in particular can say he is
injured, for such I take this matter to be. For in matters of a higher
nature, such as we thinke shake the foundacions of our lawes and
liberties, and that was the case of the late declaracion, in matters of
religion, we then were as with good reason we might be, something
more earnest and pressing till the danger was removed.

[1] cf. p. 81 where Dering describes his speech more briefly.

And then I am sure the sooner and the more decently we do it still the better.

If I had any suit to beg of the King, as truly I have done, I would not upon the first refusall tell him I were dissatisfied with it or that I would print and publish my hard case to all the world. I would lay the reasonablenesse of the thing before him. I would mencion the service I had done him or desired to do him, and would then humbly leave it to his farther consideracion, and I should thinke this a more likely way to succeed.

[f.39v] Princes *are as jealous of their honour as subjects are of their libertie. It hath allwayes been so and we cannot reasonably expect it should be otherwise, and our*[1] applicacions with them must be such as do shew that we do consider as well the dignity of the person to whom [*sic*], as the weight of the matter which we do present to them.

But Sir, if this will not claym with you, and that of necessitie we must come to a decisive vote, give me leave to say that the inconveniences of declaring this message unsatisfactorie, are in my opinion much greater than those of voting it satisfactorie. I say there is (lesse—*del.*) more of reason and (more of—*del.*) lesse danger to vote it satisfactorie than the contrarie, more of reason, because in truth the message is satisfactorie so far as it goeth. That is, it is satisfactory to the first part of it. As to the forces that were in France before the peace made with the Dutch, and that the Dutch themselves did not insist to have recalled, even then when the King by advice of this house did treat a peace with them, then when they were at the lowest, and the King of France had possession of the very heart of their country, the Spaniards weakly assisting and the Germans only deliberating what part to take. If even at this time they had so much sense of the honour of souveraigne princes as not to presse his Majestie to it, shall we now insist upon it, when the Dutch have recovered all their owne, both strength and vigour, and are able to put the French upon the defensive, and have now many more of the King's subjects than there are on their side. I thinke the case is much altered, and I hope it shall never be said that his Majestie's subjects have lesse care of his honour, than the Dutch had even when they were his enemies. [f.40] Secondly Sir, I take the message to be very satisfactorie in the last part of it, and the greatest, which is the prohibiting of any future supplyes to the French from here, (our desir—*del.*) which was indeed the maine thing we desired: our prayer was that he would send out his proclamacion, to hinder such from going, and his answer to it he would [*deletion*] use both proclamacion and all other effectuall meanes to that end. I know not what more can be added to it. If the message be not satisfactorie in this particular, I know not how it can be made so.

It is true, there is a blot, which will not faile to be hit, that is there is

[1] The words in italics are those which are underlined in a different ink in the text, probably by Dering.

no direct answer to those forces which are gone over allready since the peace made with the Dutch. I wish for my owne part that it had been more expresse to it, but all that occurred to me is that the message doth tell us his Majestie's mind in what he is resolved, and that the rest is yet under deliberacion, and possibly his Majestie may rather chuse to do that part, by his embassadour there than by proclamacion. What ever they are, if they have been there a whole winter under the King of France his pay and done nothing, it may seeme a little soudain to take them away now in the spring just as the time is come in which he should use them. I do not say still but that I wish them heare, or indeed any where rather than in France, but I do see a difficultie in it and am willing to leave it to his Majestie's prudence and goodnesse to extricate himselfe out of it, as soon and as well as he can, for where his Majestie's honour and our peace are concerned, as his Majestie saith they are, in keeping good termes with the King of France, I thinke we may as well go too fast as too slow, and I would not for my part, by advising that which the King saith would hazard the peace of the Kingdome, be ingaged over hastily in maintaining a warr and justifying the consequences of it.

[f.40v] But after all, to vote it dissatisfactory, is by no meanes to be done. I think truly, Sir, there is not such a vote upon your bookes since the King came in, and *let not this be the day to be marked with that black character.*[1]

Take heed, Sir, how you lessen the King's honour with the people least you raise a spirit you can not lay when you will. Take heed of every little sparke, that may sometimes raise a great flame, since we know not how great a flame it may kindle.

Take heed of treading in their steps which have not long since sate in these walls. And as we abhorr the ends to which they tended, let us be very jealous of all the wayes they tooke to those ends.

For my part, I confesse truly, there are many things I should think fit to be done now, if they had not been done by the long parliament, and this of publishing a dissatisfaction between him and us, was one of their first and most dangerous acts, and therefore I would avoid it.

Yet if it could be kept only within this nacion, the mischiefe were not alltogether so great. But it cannot be. Whatsoever passeth this house of that publique nature, is as well knowne at Paris and Brusselles as it is heare. Not a foreign minister heare, but giveth constant advice of it to his superior, and measures are taken accordingly. *And let us not deceive ourselves, the honour (and happi—*del.) *of the King is our honour, and the reputacion of the King abroad is our defence and securitie (abroad—*del.*) at home.*[1]

Since therefore the voting of the King's message dissatisfactorie can

---

[1] The words in italics were underlined as noted on p. 176, fn. 1.

produce no good fruit, since we are not by that meanes anything nearer to the end we aime at, since it will certainly lessen the reputacion of the King's power abroad, and may shake (some—*del*.) our peace at home, I desire we may not vote it dissatisfactorie but laying aside this debate, may proceed upon something else in which we may all chearfully and unanimously concerne for the honour of the King, and the good of those who sent us hither.

HLRO Hist Coll 85/1

[f.47]   28. *Proposals concerning keeping the House full*[1]
[post *27 May, 1675*]

The justice and reasonablenesse of indeavouring to keepe the house of Commons full during its session, is so evident in itselfe, and so confest by all, that it is needlesse to bring any arguments to persuade it. But the difficultie lyeth in finding meanes proper to that end.

Calling of the house, though with a great penaltie on the defaulters, will not do it, since that will at most but fill the house for that day, as appears by the late experiment, when upon the day of the call the house upon divicion was about 300: and the day before and after not above 180: so that it is plain a third part of the members that are in London do not attend the house.

And the call of the house allwayes spending a whole day, if these calles should be very frequent, as for example once a fortnight, they would seeme tedious and troublesome and the house in a little time grow weary of them.

Punishing the defalters by naming them in a bill hath been rejected by the house, and being indeed something too severe to set that marke upon them to all posterity for deserters of their trust, at least before they are heard at the barr, and after they are heard, no man but either will justify his absence to the house or at least obtain their pardon by promise of future diligence and assiduitie, and because after once recorded there, how just soever we should upon enquiry find the excuse, it would not be in our power, to mitigate the fine nor to salve the infamy.

Therefore it seemes necessarie to find out some such penaltie as may be wholly in the power of the house, may not be too rigid or severe, which like sanguinary laws are allwaies the least executed, and may be continually impending over their heads, though not allwayes fall upon them.

In order to which it is proposed, but with all submission to better judgments, that the (number—*del*.) names of parliament men, being in

---

[1] cf. the diary entry concerning the call of the House on 26 May, 1675, pp. 86-90. above.

all about 508, be written in ten severall rolles of paper or parchemin, viz. about 50 in a roll: joining the several [incomplete]
[f.47v] [endorsed] Concerning keeping the House full
HLRO Hist Coll 85/1

[f.50]   29. *Resolutions concerning Committments,*
                    9 June 1675

Text as in *CJ*, ix, 357, but the fourth resolution, concerning the Message to the Lords, is not entered.
HLRO Hist Coll 85/1

[f.48] 30. *Memorandum concerning the proposed incorporation of the fishing trade¹ [n.d., ?1675]*

1. If his Majestie shall thinke fit to make any corporacion for the fishery, that the same may be limited to the white herring fishing and codd, and the companie so called.
2. That the towne of Yarmouth be heard and those concerned in the Newfoundland fisherie (be heard—*del.*) before the pattent.
Memorandum, there is no restriction for number of people interested, nor of value of stock to be employed, nor of what nacions it shall consist. On the other side they may not only inlarge it too much, so they may also restraine it over much, to a few people, and those if they will all foreigners.
    To fish in all seas and estuaries for white herring and codfish. The clause that all fish taken by them or those imployed by them shall be free from all duties both at exportacion and importacion, which is contrarie to the (Act of tonnage and poundage
                    (Booke of rates
                    (Account for fisherie
                    (Irish Act
                    (Greenland Act
                    (Navigacion
                    (The whole balance of trade
HLRO Hist Coll 85/1

        31. *A note of such publique acts as were before the House of Commons or another place [1675]*

1. An act to prevent imprisonmente of the subject in foreigne parts to Ireland or the plantacions

¹ cf. the papers concerning incorporation calendared in *CSPD*, 1675-6, 76-7, and *ibid.*, 1676-7, 574.

2. An act for graunting Habeas Corpus to such who are imprisoned
3. An act to limit the power of committment by the King's immediate warrant or by the councell table
4. An act to make it high treason to levy money otherwise than by authoritie of parliament
5. An act for the judges to hold their places quam diu bene se gesserint and to ascertain their salaries
6. An act for repaire of churches and better recoverie of small tithes
7. An act for the ease of sheriffes in passing their accompts
8. An act for a test to distinguish between protestants and papists and for more easy convicting of papists.
9. An act for preventing burning of heath in the northern counties
10. An act for preventing robberies in Northumberland and Cumberland
11. An act for preventing vexacious suits at law
12. An act to enable all persons to give lands to parsonages and vicaridges not worth £100 per annum
13. An act for better repairing of highwayes, and review of statutes concerning that matter
14. An act for restraining excommunicacions for small matters and to take away the writ de heretico comburendo: (This was not tendered)
15. An act for preserving the fishing in the Severne
16. An act for enforcing the attendance of parliament men.
17. An act for regulating elections of parliament men, and preventing the undue returne made by Sheriffes.
18. An act for excusing smithes forges and some small cottages from hearth money
19. An act for excusing the recognizances of alehouse keepers from paying to the lawbill
20. An act to prevent exportacion of wooll
21. An act to regulate the abuses of the Alnage
22. An act to restraine the power of pressing men for land or sea
23. An act for a test upon all members of either house of Parliament
24. An act for regulating the triall of peeres sent downe from the Lords

HLRO Hist Coll 85/14

[f.72]   32. *Parliamentary Diary, March 1677*[1]

1. This day, the house being upon the comittment of one Mr Harington

---

[1] Dering does not date this paper more precisely, but item 5 relates to proceedings on 22 March 1677 and item 6 possibly to 22 March or to 2 April. March 22, 23 and 24 are not reported in G, cf. *CJ*, ix, 403-5. The committal of Barington is not noted in *CJ*, but the third reading of the Earl of Manchester's estate bill (item 6) is noted in *CJ*, ix, 404.

to the Tower by verball warrant, as it was said from his Majestie, and many speaking against the unreasonablenesse and illegalitie of keeping any man close prisoner, the Speaker produced a presedent made by this house of Commons upon George Withers, who was taken out of Newgate and sent prisoner to the Tower by order of the house, with an expresse clause, that he should be kept close prisoner, and debarred the use of pen and paper, and so lay about a year before he was delivered.[1]

Birch said that this was an abominable president, and wished it were rased out of the bookes, and Mr Garaway said it was a president he was ashamed of, which was a freedom I had not heard taken before to censure any vote of the house, yet it past unrebuked.

2. If the question be for agreeing with a committee, the Noes go out.
3. If the question be for adjournment, after one of the clocke, that being the regular question, it must be first put, and in that case the Noes are to go out.
4. Mr Secretary, having moved for committing a bill, Mr Sawyer said he seconded that mocion, and gave no reasons for it. Afterwards there grew a great debate for and against committing the bill, and Mr Sawyer standing up to speake, Sir Thomas Lee objected that he had spoken before, and this was debated whether he should speake or not, but the Speaker declared that he might speake, for barely seconding a mocion without giving any reason for it, was not to be called speaking to a matter, but if he had given any reasons for what he spoke, or but said, he seconded that mocion for the reasons given by him that spoke last, it had barred him of speaking again.
5. Whosoever taketh any man downe to the orders of the house must be heard as long as he speaketh to the orders, but he ought not by that meanes to let him selfe in to the matter of the discourse, nor so much as to make any mocion.
[f.72v] 6. A bill coming downe from the Lords to enable the Earle of Manchester to pay debts by selling some land, being read the third time in our house, some objection was made unto it, and thereupon we considered what to do with it, for to put the question upon it then, were to reject it. To recomitt it, it was agreed we could not do it, being ingrossed. To order a farther reading of it after it had been read 3 times we could not. At last we resolved to let it ly upon the table for 3 or 4 dayes, that gentlemen might satisfy themselves in it. And so we did without putting any question at that time upon it. Which is the first example of that kind I remember.
7. A bill for Mr. Bedle to sell land, being ventured upon in the house[2] and read halfe way, the Speaker informed us that his breviat was not

---

[1] *CJ*, viii, 394.
[2] The Bedell estate bill was received from the Lords on 22 March (*CJ*, ix, 404) and was read 2*a* on 2 April (*op. cit.*, 412).

above three lines, so that he could not possibly undertake to open it to us. Whereupon the house left it off reading it, and went to other matter.

f.73v] [Endorsed] House of Commons.

HLRO Hist Coll 85/1

[f.69]   33. *Minutes of proceedings of Commissioners of Customs, 9 November 1677*

A merchant importes goods to Bristoll, and then sends the goods (to Bristoll—*del.*) to London without making oath that these were the goods exported. From London they are shipt beyond sea. The exporter demands the halfe subsidy. The commissioners deny it, because there is no oath made by the importer. The merchant now offers the importer's oath ex post facto. The commissioners do allow it, for there is not time limited for taking the merchant's oath, neither indeed is there any time limited for debenture, which is an inconvenience ought to be remedied.

2d. Quare. Tobacco brought in and paid for. Part of it made into snuffe: Quare (*written over* oath) whether the halfe subsidy be due. The merchant offers oath that

This is made of the tobacco which paid custome.

That it is made all of leafe, and not of stalkes.

That there is no mixture at all in it.

Mr Nicholas, Mr Brener, Mr Dawson, Mr Burton, called in, declared their opinion that it ought not to draw back

1. Because the propertie is altered, it being not tobacco now, but a manufacture upon it.
2. That linnen cut out into shirts and exported doth not draw back, because it is altered.
3. That if it draw back and have a debenture it must have it by the name of tobacco, which it is really not so.
4. That if (tobacco—*del.*) snuffe were imported, it should not pay as tobacco, but as valerien.
5. That it doth not occurr them, that ever it was yet allowed.
6. That it might concerne the King's customes very much. One said, neare £20,000 per annum.

This is the case of one Mr Scot.

And hemp made into ropes, shall not draw back.

[f.69v] Mr Elliston insists to have his guns and sailes and he sendeth into Ireland to (*deletion*) furnish a ship which he buildeth there, and that Irish ships are by the act free as English.

But the commissioners do thinke they ought to pay custom for masts and plankes which come, for his Majestie's own ships do pay custome.

Mr Elliston desirs that he may pay the custome without prejudice, or with a salvo jure, which his councell do advise him to do, that so he may recover again, if the custome shall be due.

The commissioners will not receive the money so, but he must pay it as others do, yet they seem to confesse that though it be paid, yet if it be taken unduly, the merchant may recover it again.

[*Endorsed*] Concerning snuffe, concerning goods exported without oath of the merchant.

HLRO Hist Coll 85/1

[f.55]   34. *Speech by Dering on motion for removing the Duke of York. n.d. (4 November 1678)*[1]

Many gentlemen have on this occasion exprest their zeale for the protestant religion and severall texts of scripture have been cited. On this occasion, give me leave, sir, to put you in mind of one more and that is, a tree is known by its fruits, and to that proofe I referr my selfe.

We are not heare speaking to God Allmighty, he needs it not, he knoweth our hearts, but we are speaking to the world to testify our zeale and concerne for our religion and our government, and we are speaking to the nation which telleth us loudly, they are both in danger.

Many gentlemen say they agree fully in the end, but they differ in the means, which is a reasonable thing. It hath often been so, and it may be so now. I (agree—*del.*) allow it, but he that agrees with me in the end and differs only in the meanes, under favour, he ought then to (propose —*del.*) offer some other meanes to that end as good or better than that which I propose, for if he agree in the end, and yet dislike all meanes to that end, he is beholding more to my good nature if I believe him, than to any argument of his owne, than to my reason.

I know as much as any man the quality of the person we are now discovering of, and the high and extraordinary endowment he is *master of,*[2] (but his—*del.*) but the nature of the crown and the danger of that [illegible] too much *and I shall say that which perhaps is a fault, that is, if we were reduced to that fatall dilemma that either our religion must be destroyed or* this prince, I know not yet *what I should do. I think* I should do nothing at all, but leave it *to God to do his* pleasure, and for my selfe have no hand in either *but, Sir, as that is not yet* the case, and I hope never will be, so neither *are the remedies propounded* anything of that nature. What is then heare that toucheth a hair of his head, or striketh at his succession to the crowne? All we desire is that he would please for the satisfaction of the nation in this time of danger and jealousie, and for disbanding all those papists who must and will be near him, and therefore near the King, he

---

[1] The speech is not noted in G.

[2] Words in italics were underlined by Dering.

would please, for some time to retire into some part which he will chuse at some reasonable distance from London.

Sir, (he—*del.*) if the house that will not go so far as the King himselfe, who best knows what the danger is, hath directed and chalked out (what—*del.*) for his preservacion and the people's satisfaction, what will they say of you or what indeed can they say lesse than either we want religion or we want resolucion.

[ff.55v, 56, blank]

[f.56v] I commend the zeale of that gentleman who spake last, but because he is warme, I would not have them think every man else is cold. I never saw the house more unanimous; whatsoever is proposed, passeth without opposicion. Hitherto it is true, much hath not been said, for in wise men great anger and just indignation do not vent themselves with soudain and vehement exclamacions. The head is taken up not what to say but what to do. We have hitherto been considering of the nature and symptomes of the disease. Now that is past and we have declared our opinion—of the (treason and—*del.*) of the danger and of the causes of it, we come now and but now to the remedies.

HLRO Hist Coll 85/1

[f.57] 35. *Dering's draft speech concerning the Popish Plot,*
n.d. ?prepared for 16 November 1678

We have now sate allmost a moneth and it seemes to me not farr advanced in anything usefull to the publique. The first day we met, we were informed by his Majestie of this plot, and we have sate constantly upon it, day after day, forenoon and afternoon, Sundays and all, and we are not yet come to any one resolucion more than in the single particular of my Lord Arundel of Wardor[1] that tends to the preventing the dangers in complain[ing] of (*blank*) some Addresses. (*blank*) if bill sent up to the Lords.[2]

Tuesday last we received from him who best knows and is most concerned so to do, his Majestie. The condicion we are in[3] (*sentence unfinished*).

We have voted some time since [1 Nov.], and that unanimously, none dissenting, that there is a damnable and hellish plot, those I thinke are the words, against his Majestie's person and government[4] and our religion[4] and we have desired the Lords concurrence with us in such meanes as we should propose for our securitie. [5]And we had it.[5] His

---

[1] The House resolved to impeach Lord Arundel on 1 Nov. (*CJ*, ix, 531).

[2] The whole of this paragraph is deleted. Dering made three successive attempts to draft an opening for his speech.

[3] This paragraph is deleted.   [4] . . . [4] Interlineated.

[5] . . . [5] Interlineated.

Majestie also was graciously pleased on Saturday last [9 Nov.] to quicken us to it and to promise his concurrence.[1] Monday was [2]solemnlie[2] appointed for it, and I believe the papists (expected— *del.* it) apprehended that day with some terror and apprehencion, and all good and loyall subjects with longing desire and impatient expectations.

(Monday—*del.*) That day is past and 3 dayes more and nothing done in it, not so much as another day appointed for it, and it is visible that the papists do lift up their heads [2]and make that argument that we do not believe what we say[2] and the protestants hang downe there upon.

Are we colder than we were? I hope not.

Are we safer than we were? I thinke not.

Sir, the eyes of the people are upon us and as we must measure our (danger—*del.*) proporcion our care (remedies—*del.*) (by—*del.*) to our danger, so the people who can not see all particulars so distinctly as we do, will judge of the danger, by the remedies you shall propose and by the care you shall take. If they see you do nothing, or slowly do it, they will thinke there either was no danger, or it is farr of.

[ff.57v, 58 blank]

[f.58v] I do imagine that what silenceth those men that use to be very forward in these matters is a desire to see what the Lords will do with the bill before them:[3] and upon that ground I have acquiesced hitherto, and if yet one day more may contribute to the passing that bill, I thinke it very well bestowed, and therefore shall not presse you to go on immediately at this time, but consider, Sir, whether the delaying the proceeding to other meanes be really a way to passe that bill; or whether an argument may not be drawne from there to the contrarie, and since all depends upon the concurrence of both houses whether a seeming unwitting[4] coldnesse in us, may not beget a reall one in other places. I am sure, then if the meanes and remedies we (pro—*del.*) shall propose be solid and effectuall, and the zeale we promote them with be reall and unanimous, I doubt not but they may not only have a passage themselves, but also give encouragement to those who do most appeare in justification of that bill, and so be rather a help to the passing than a hindrance, and therefore I beseech you not to arise without appointing some day and that a very short one too, (Fryd—*del.*) tomorrow, if you please, to consider of meanes.

Do that which you should have done on Monday last, and that is to

---

[1] *CJ*, ix, 536.

[2] . . . [2] Interlineated.

[3] On 28 Oct. the Lords had received from the Commons the bill 'for the more effectual preserving the King's person and government by disabling papists from sitting in either house of parliament'; they were still considering it in committee on 14 and 15 Nov. (*LJ*, xiii, 305, 358-9).

[4] This word interlineated.

consider of effectuall meanes to preserve his Majestie's person, our government, and the protestant religion.¹

HLRO Hist Coll 85/1

[f.59]   36. *Dering's draft speech concerning the Popish Plot,*
*16 November 1678*²

However, I desire them to believe that the church of England will allwayes distinguish them from the papists, and make a difference of them who may be possibly charged with some personall fault, and those others whose very principles are intolerable, whose very faith is faction and whose religion is rebellion. They are the words of (the—*del.*) our church and part of the solemn office for the 8th of November, and therefor I need not fear to use them.

If there be any who thinke it impossible to prevent the danger which hangeth over our heads, and by a single thread, (which if it be not cut out, must wear out—*del.*) that all remedies are vain, and therefore we have nothing to do but to digg our owne graves and ly downe in them, let those men consider that it was never thought the part of a good citizen desperare de Republica; that while the King, the parliament, and the people are well disposed we can not say the infection is epidemicall (nor while—*del.*) that if we cannot find remedies, we may yet find that we are yet 200 to one at least, I speake of profest papist[s], and if we have but (the power—*del.*) arms in our hands and the law on our side, it will not be easie for any open force to cut our religion, and for fore[ig]n play, we fear it not.

If there be any that apprehend their owne personall danger by the example of Sir Edmund Godfrey, let them not be frightened, for first to dy in doing one's duty, and for doing it is as doubtlesse this gentleman did, is a degree of martyrdom, and so not to be reckond among the intolerable calamities that may befall us. But beside that, I thinke the more loudly we express ourselves against poperie, the safer we are. If the death of one man terrify us, two or 3 more such strokes will do their worke, and upon whom that may fall we can not foresee. But if we proceed [f.59v] to express (the—*del.*) our resentment [of] that terrible fact as we ought to do, the terror will reflect back upon themselves, since we that vindicate this first attempt with so just severitie, may well be thought this second may end in a finall extirpacion of the author and fountin of it.

I speake this as stating the act assuredly to be contri[buted] not by

¹ Dering used at least some of the material of this draft in his speech in the Commons on 16 Nov. (G., vi, 204).
² This is either another section of no. 35 above, or more likely a subsequent draft which Dering followed when speaking in the House on 16 Nov. (G, vi, 204).

one single enemie, but by a consult of severall papists, meerly for (religion—*del.*) some advantage they proposed to themselves, thereby to their religion. All circumstances seemed to lead plainly to it and to justify that opinion, and even without witnesses it would have been (most—*del.*). I should have laid it at their door, for wherever I find crueltie and secrecie, I suspect the Jesuits.

All this I have said to remove in some measure such motive as I would imagine might hinder men from speaking their minds freely, and that every one might resolve to bear his share, for what is a burthen would break any one mans back (would—*del.*) will prove very light and easie, if we all set our shoulders unto it.

And now, Sir, I would sit downe, but that I would not have it said that I would ingage others and skip out myselfe, and shall therefore (make—*del.*) for a beginning offer one thing.

The enemies of all laws [*sic*]

All power is radically in the King, and is desined from him to such persons as he thinks fit to commission. The judges have a great power, the interpreting the laws [f.60] that are made remaining in them. Next to them, the justices of peace, who are the great body of the gentry of this Kingdome, and like the veins distribute the nourishment through the body of the Kingdom[1], both these act by virtue of a commission from the King and subsist but by his pleasure, and in case of his death they fall, so there is a kind of [*illegible*] to bring a stop of all proceedings till the new King is pleased to commission them or others.

I think, Sir, it would be of very good use if these were continued quam diu bene se gesserint, nor is this any violacion of the prerogative, which will still have libertie to put whom in they shall think fit, but being in, it is but reasonable they should not be put out, without their misbehaviour, and for the judges, it was allwayes as I have heard of former times, and the alteracion made long since the King came in. [rest of folio blank]

[f.60v] I did not thinke it would have fallen to my share to have stood [illegible] in this matter. I expected from those who speake more frequently and much better than I can do, that they would (not have been ready—*del.*) to (have—*del.*) they have laid open the danger, would have opened the cure and the remedies also, and I should have been thankfull to them for it.

We (it is—*del.*) have voted and unanimously that there is a popish plot carying on against the King, our country and our religion, that the danger is great and present, that the foundacions of our government shake under us, and ruine and desolacion hover round about us. The King hath invited and [illegible] us, and yet we sit still, and if we do

---

[1] Mr Blake has suggested that this simile may derive from Dr William Harvey, discoverer of the circulation of the blood, and Mary Dering's uncle.

nothing in it, the world will justly say either we have no religion, or no resolucion.

We are now coming to propose the meanes, and this I would have every man take to heart, for it is certain, if nothing is done this session, there is an end of the protestant religion.[1]

If any man shall propose something even[2] that may [3]be thought to[3] go too far, something that borders on severitie, yet the greatness of the concerne and the danger that concerne is in, will render him excusable and he is much more to be commended whose zeale carries him a little, than he who sits still and offreth nothing at all.

On the other hand, if any man offer something that may seem [3]to others[3] too tender and not proporcioned enough to the present danger, yet even that is to be favourably read, for it is not any one thing that can secure us, it must be many severall particulars, and how made up as inevitably they were of many severall particulars, of which we have some resemblance in the late act past against frauds and perjuries,[4] and whatever tendeth that way, ought to be wellcome.

If any one believes that when we have reduced the papists to be inconsiderable and weake, our zeale for our church will find out some other object, and possibly leane a little heavily on dissenting protestants, I desire them not to be discouraged from joining with us against the common enemie, for first I do really believe, that when all fears of poperie be rooted out, one halfe of the dissenting protestants will really come into us, and those that will remain will be men of such condicion in severall respects as not to give any jealousie to the government.

HLRO Hist Coll 85/1

37. *Heads for bill against Papists*
[*n.d. ?1678-9*]

[This and the following paper are drafts by Dering of a bill similar in some respects to that considered in the Lords 'for freeing the City of London and parts adjacent from Popish inhabitants, and providing against other dangers that may arise from Papists', and passed by them on 2 May 1679.[5] This was amended in the Commons, but was dropped with the prorogation.[6] A similar bill was passed by the Lords but laid aside in the Commons in the autumn session of 1680.[7]]

[1] The whole of this paragraph is deleted.
[2] This word is interlineated.
[3] . . . [3] Interlineated.
[4] Statute of Frauds, 29 Cha. II, c. 3, passed 16 April 1677.
[5] HMC *HL MSS*, 1678-88, 105-10.
[6] *ibid.*, 130-2.
[7] *ibid.*, 159-60.

[f.45]

1. That all papists shall within 3 moneths register themselves as such in one of the 4 courts of Westminster and with the bishop of the diocese where they shall reside.
2. That they shall also within 3 months chuse to themselves some place of habitacion, the same not to be within 30 miles of London, nor in any towne sending burgesses to parliament.
3. Being so setled they shall not remove out of such countie without leave had from the chiefe judge of that court and from the bishop of the diocese, expressing the occasion and limiting the time of their stay.
4. That such papists so registred shall be esteemed popish recusants convict, and shall pay to the state a [blank] part of their estate.
5. They shall also register all their estates.
6. If any person shall heareafter by the lawes of this land, be convicted of popish recusansie, not being registred as above, or the son of one that is registred, he shall suffer imprisonment during life and forfeit all his estate during his life.
7. No papist registred or not to keep either sword or fire armes in his house, nor to weare any.
8. All privy councellers, bishops, justices of the peace, constables and churchwardens, when sworne into their severall offices to have it part of their oath to put this present law in execution.
9. Some breviat of the laws against papists to be made by publique authoritie, and printed and read twice a yeare in churches and at sessions.
10. All judges, justices of peace and (officers—*del.*) lord lieutenants and deputy lieutenants and officers of the militia, as farr as captains, to hold their severall places Quam diu se gesserint.
11. The act of militia to be reviewed and amended, and the [blank]
12. All papists to come once a yeare to heare a sermon at a day to be appointed by the diocesan, for their convercion.
13. Severe penalties to be inflicted on such who shall take the oathes of allegeance and supremacie and tests and shall afterwards be found at masse or maintaining the pope's authoritie, or doing anything for which they may be convicted as papists.
14. All that shall heareafter reconcile or be reconciled, to forfeit 2 thirds of their estates for life and suffer imprisonment for life, and if they have not estate left to maintain them, to be maintaind by their labour.
15. All seminarie priests to be imprisoned for life.

HLRO Hist Coll 85/1

[ff.43-4]   38. *Heads for bill against popery* [*n.d. ?1678-9*]

[Cf. no. 37 above. This text follows that of 37 quite closely, but adds the heads printed below.]

  8. All constables and churchwardens to have it part of their oath to present at the session all that they know or suspect to be papists, [not bein—*del.*] and the justices if they find them not registred shall summon them and tender them the oathes and tests.

12. All Jesuits and seminarie priests, and all persons who shall hereafter reconcile or be reconciled to incurr a praemunire. The imprisonment to be at least 30 miles from London and not to be discharged upon any pretence, till conformitie.

13. In all cases of forfeiture, the King to have one moietie and the informer the other.

HLRO Hist Coll 85/1

39. *Dering's Abstract of accounts of excise*
24 June 1678-24 June 1679

Excise for all England and Wales   —673,271—10—8

paid one yeares rent in money   —560,000

one yeares charge of management

                per covenants   —070,000

For disbursements extraordinary

         allowed by his Majestie   —001,000

For money paid by order of the

                Treasurie   —000,420

Allowances to brewers for beer

              exported   —002,665—13

Allowance by Commissioners of

         Excise for brewers   —000,132— 2—6

                           634,217—15—6

Item demanded for poundage of

    39,053—15—2 at 1^s per £   —001,952— 2—9

Interest [blank] Remaines   —037,101—12—5

Interest of the said 37,101—12—5

    from 24 June 1679 till such time

    as the overplus will be due by   003,895—13—5

    command at 7 per cent

            so remaines due   — 33,205—19

[*endorsed*] Memoranda of the £11,000 in Mr Kent's last accompt Mr Godolphin

HLRO Hist Coll 85/9

40. *Draft of grant of the excise to George Dashwood et al., ante 27 February 1679*[1]

[f.1] The King grants Geo. Dashwood etc. for 270,000 to be advanced the excise for 3 yeares from midsummer 1680 for 3 yeares, paying 560,000 per annum if addicionall excise continued, and 446,000 per annum if not continued.

	if addicionall continued				if not continued		
for London	16,666	13	4	per mensem	12,166	13	4
Kent	25,000	per annum			18,750		
Yorke	30,000				22,500		
Norfolk	21,000				15,750		
Essex	14,000				10,500		
Suffolk	12,000				9,000		
Bedford	3,300				2,475		
Berks	5,600				4,200		
Bucks	4,500				3,375		
Cambridge	8,200				6,150		
Hertford	9,200				6,900		
Somerset	9,000				6,750		
For all the rest	218,200				193,650		

The advance to be repaid

if addicionall continued	if not continued
45,000 at Lady day 1682	22,000 at Michaelmas 80
45,000 at Midsummer 82	22,000 at Xmas 80
45,000 at Michaelmas 82	22,000 at Lady 81
45,000 at Xmas 82	22,000 at Mids. 81
45,000 at Lady day 83	22,000 at Mich. 81
45,000 at Mich. 83	22,000 at Xmas 81
	22,000 at Lady 82
	22,000 at Mids 82
	22,000 at Mich 82
	22,000 at Xmas 82
	25,000 at Lady 83
	35,000 at Mids 83

[1] The draft is in Dering's hand. Cf. the grant under the privy seal, *CTB*, 1676-9, 1250-1.

[f.1v] If the present prohibicion of brandy do continue after midsummer 1680 the farmers are to have a defalcation. A defalcation for exporting beere. Farmers every 6 weekes to transmit all vouchers to the generall office. If the monthly rent not paid within 40 dayes, or the whole quarter ten dayes before the next quarter, farmers to forfeit the interest of 87,500 for that quarter. If the monthly rent not paid within 54 dayes, or the whole within 3 moneths and 8 dayes, the King may entr[*ms. torn*]. In case of warr plague or pestilence or fire or such generall calamitie, they to have defalcacions. Farmers to pay their dayly cash to the Committee of Excise having 6 per cent to the dayes of payments. Libertie to subfarme excise of Wales and of the 4 northern counties unto Turner and Leyford. If the revenue arise to more than the rente reserved the farmers shall be allowed out of the overplus 56,000 per annum for charges of management, 5,000 per annum in recompense of bad debts, and 10,000 per annum for their reward. The farmers are to accompt within 6 moneths after each yeare and to pay the overplus to the commissioners for his Majestie's use, deducting 12d per pound to themselves.

HLRO Hist Coll 85/3

[f.1v]   41. *Dering's draft 'Estimate of what may be received From 31 December 1679 to 31 December 1680'*[1] [*1679*]

1	Imprimis	from the customes neat	500,000
2	Item	from the excise	500,000
3	Item	from the hearth money at 3000 per moneth	036,000
4	Item	the farmers advance due at Lady Day '80	050,000
			1,086,000

Last year

5	Item	petty branches Viz.		
		Tenths and first fruits	015,000	11,372
		Dutchy of Cornwall	003,000	2,415
		Amerciaments and forfeitures	005,000	3,600
		Alienacion office	2,000	0,577
		petty farmers of the customes	2,000	1,200
		4½ per cent from Barbados	[blank]	

[1] *Endorsed* by Dering on f. 2r: Estimate for the yeare 25 December [16]79 to 25 October 1680.

Wine licences	4,000	000
Recusants	5,000	960
Sheriffes	2,000	1,584
Receivers of the revenue	2,000	325
	40,000	22,033

1,086,000

1,126,000

[f.2]

1	To the Navy and Ordnance (at the least)	350,000
2	To the houshold	054,000
3	To the Forces (not exceeding)	200,000
4	To Tangier	057,000
5	To the Judges	012,000
6	To Banquiers interest	082,000
7	To the King and Duke	036,209
8	Treasurers of the Chamber, great wardrobe, stable, works and foreign ministers	060,000
		851,409

[for
851,209]

	To which must be added	
9	Tallies on the excise at 2000 per weeke	104,000
10	Tallies on the customes at 2000 per weeke	104,000
11	Privy purse per annum	20,000
12	Secret service	20,000
13	Farmers deteiner before midsummer	140,000
14	Farmers deteiner after midsummer	[blank]
15	Band of pencioners; Herrion, gards, Audly end, Irwells, robes, Liberates, Tower, impost bills, masters of chancerie, requests, disbanded judges, etc., post defalcacions	20,000
16	Interest money	50,000
17	Arreares now due to the Navy for ships Tangier, chest at Chatham	50,000
18	Pencions to the king's children	25,000
19	Salaries to Lord Chancellor, P[rivy] S[eal], Lord President, ourselves, [illegible], Bedchamber, etc.	25,000

20	Pencions to those who assisted the king's escape and to some others of great merit or great want	10,000
21	To Mr. Kent and Duncomb to repay (I suppose) one moietie of their just debt	40,000

	508,000[1]
Totall is	1,359,409
which exceeds the expected income by	233,409

HLRO Hist Coll 85/15

42. *Dering's note concerning prohibited goods,*
12 January 1680

1. charge of officers in all parts, especially in Dorset and Devon
2. the King's proclamacion, to command all sheriffes justices and civill officers to be assisting
3. the third part of the custome on dry goods seised to go to the informer
4. a smack to have its station off Torbay
5. the King to be moved to give directions in this matter to the judges in their severall circuits

KAO U1107/14/10

43. *Dering's draft of a bill for the ease of dissenting Protestants,*
November 1680[2]

[f.61]

Whereas it is manifest that the statutes made in primo of Eliz. cap. 23, (28—*del.*) 29, 35, and tertio Jacobi, cap. 4, whereby certain pecuniary mulcts are laid upon such persons as shall forbeare to repaire to their parish churches and there heare divine service, were intended only against popish recusants, as by the said statutes themselves and by the constant practice ever since the making of the same doth plainly appear, and yet neverthelesse within these few yeares last past a great number of protestants have been vexed and troubled (the said st—*del.*) indicted

---

[1] Dering has written 5,008,000, and clearly meant 508,000, but the total is 608,000.

[2] On 6 Nov. 1680 the Commons appointed a committee to prepare a bill for the repeal of 35 Eliz. c. 1; Dering's draft may have been written in or for this committee. The bill was passed on 26 Nov. and agreed, with amendments, by the Lords, but there were no further proceedings (*CJ*, ix, 647 et seq.; *HL MSS*, 1678-88, 214). A similar bill failed in 1681 (cf. *HL MSS*, 1678-88, 269). Cf. H. Horwitz, 'Protestant Reconciliation in the Exclusion Crisis', *Journal of Ecclesiastical History*, xv (1964), 205 and G, vii, 424-5.

and prosecuted upon colour of the said recusants, now it being thought fit to prohibit (*deletion*) all vexacious prosecutions of any protestants for the future upon the said laws or any of them, and unite as far as maybe all protestants and induce them (to defend and propagate—*del.*) to the unanimous and common defence of the true protestant religion as it is established by law, against the subtle machinacions and open malice of the (all—*del.*) papists and of the see of Rome, the constant and implacable enemie of our King, religion and government (Be it ena—*del.*) And to the end no protestant whatsoever may be subjected to those penalties which (were—*del.*) are and allways were intended solely against the papists and popish recusants Be it enacted that from and after the 23 day (Dec—*written above and del.*) of March (which shall be in the yeare of our Lord according—*del.*) the next ensuing, no protestant shall be indicted prosecuted or any wayes troubled by or upon any of the said above mencioned statutes nor upon any other law or statute whatsoever, for not coming to his parish church or not hearing divine service (but st—*del.*) nor shall pay any summe or summes of money, nor forfeit two thirds or any part of their estates, for forbearing so to do.

And if any shall be indicted informed against or prosecuted contrary to the true intent or meaning of this act he or they so prosecuted shall and may have their action

[f.68v] and shall (and may—*del.*) being found upon triall of that single issue of (protestant—*del.*) papist or not papist, to be no papist receive his or their double costs.

And to prevent that no papist or popish recusant shall by colour heareof escape due prosecution be it enacted

That before any constable churchwarden or other person (informer— *del.*) shall indict prosecute or exhibit [1]any bill[1] or informacion in any court ecclesiasticall or civill against any person, upon any of the statutes aforesaid, the said informer shall take his corporall oath before some justice of the peace of the countie where the person complained against doth inhabit, that he doth believe in his conscience the said person complained against [1]for not coming to church and hearing divine service[1] is a popish recusant, whereupon the said justice of peace shall issue his warrant to the said person to appeare at the next generall quarter sessions to be held for that [ms. damaged] citie place or divicion, which said warrant or a true copie thereof shall be left with the person complained of ten days at least before the said sessions. And if the said person complained of shall appeare accordingly (and sha—*del.*) at these said quarter sessions [1]make and[1] subscribe the declaracion hearein mencioned, and shall likewise produce in open (companie—*del.*) court three credible and substantiall witnesses who shall openly testify that [1]that they believe[1] the person complained of (to be a protestant—*del.*) is no

---

[1] . . . [1] interlineated.

papist nor commonly so reputed, and if the [ms. damaged] required by that court shall testify their said beliefe upon their corporall oathes (then the—*del.*) then the said complaint shall be dismist and entry shall be made thereof upon the (roll of the—*del.*) by the clerke of the peace *for which he shall take the fee of 12d and no more*[1] and a copie of the said entry shall be given the person complained of attested by the clerke of the peace for which 12d shall be given and no more
An [*sic*]
[f.67v] which said copie so attested shall be allowed as his full discharge of and from (the—*del.*) all penalties of 12d per Sunday or £20 per mensem or forfeiture of 2/3ds of the profits of his land which shall be incurrd from the said 25th day of (December—partially *del.*) month next. Provided nevertheless that upon any new informacion to be brought (before—*del.*) against any such person, the justice of peace of the same divicion where such discharge shall be given, may if they [illegible] Provided that if any new informacion shall be given afterwards against any person who hath received such discharge the justice of peace at the general quarter sessions shall and may if they find the said second prosecucion to be unreasonable and vexacious, malicious, inflict upon the informer or prosecute for the first offence (the—*del.*) any summe not exceeding [blank] and upon the second offence (the said informer[2] shall forfeit the summe of [blank] and also be disabled to hold the office of clerke of the—*del.*)
Provided that no person shall be troubled or sued for any prosecucion upon the said statutes above mencioned (had—*del.*) against any protestant had made order before the 25 of December next

HLRO Hist Coll 85/1

44. *Submission to the King prepared by Dering on behalf of the contractors for a new Irish farm, c. 4 November 1681*

[f.1] The proposers of the new contract for Ireland being apprehensive that the scope and designe of the said contract by reason of the length of time since the same was offered to his Majestie being now more than six moneths,[3] may not be fully kept in remembrance, do in all humilitie take leave once more to represent the same to his Majestie laying the same together with their utmost endeavours in his service at his Majestie's feet, to be disposed as he shall think fit.

1. First the contractors are to have all that his Majestie may or can graunt or receive out of the revenue or profits of Ireland or Tangier

---

[1] The italicised words are underlined.
[2] any summe in their di—interlineated and then deleted at this point.
[3] The King had received the outline contract on 20 May 1681 (cf. p. 25 above).

for 9 yeares from May 1681, new aids to be given by parliament excepted, and with a saving to all men's rights.

2. They are to have all necessarie powers for the managing receiving and improving the said revenue and profits.

3. The particular uses to which these profits and rents shall be applyed, are particularly set downe in an establishment annexed. But in generall they are to defray the whole charge of his Majestie's government civill and military in Ireland and Tangier, and to maintain six men of warr, which will come by the said establishment to at least £48,000 p.a. more than ever the said revenue was let for, and all this beside their owne charges and their officers, which will come to at least £56,000 more.

4. They are to deposit £84,000 (lending the—*del.*) at their entrance on their undertaking as a securitie for their performance.

5. That if the contractors improve the revenue never so much (and it is their duty and interest to do it as farr as fairly and lawfully they can) they can have for all their charges paines and hazard but barely their poundage, the rest being to be accompted for to his Majestie.

[f.1v] 6. But on the contrary if it fall short, their £84,000 advance, their poundage and all allowances to the[i]r officers under them, must all go to the supplying and making good their undertaking. Besides their estates and their persons will be at his Majestie's mercie.

7. The King is to be freed from all defalcations before the first of May 1681 which may be found of considerable use to his Majestie.

8. Lastly the method of taking and inspecting the accompts of the receipts and payments of the contractors is so exact, that it seemes impossible that the money which comes in can either be delayed or diverted from the uses to which it is appropriated. And the power setled in the trustees doth secure the King from any considerable failure.

These things being all of them (very—*del.*) as we humbly conceive very good, and not only justifiable but really commendable and advantageous to the King beyond what hath been agreed in any former contract, we did not expect so many objections to the undertaking as it hath since met withall.

[f.2] We shall not presume to instance in any particulars, untill they shall be transmitted to us by order of the Lords to whom your Majestie hath referred the consideracion thereof.

But we humbly conceive whatever hath been or can be said may be reduced to one of these fouer heads

1. Either the contractors are not able to perform their contract but must faile in a short time. To which we answer

   1. This hath been frequently objected against others who have yet held on and performed their bargain.

2. That by the £84,000 advance and the frequent ¹monthly and quarterly¹ accompts and the power placed in the trustees to re-enter your Majestie is fully secured and better than ever before.

2. That the bargain is too good, and the revenue more worth.

    1. This is is [*sic*] just quite contrary to the former objection which saith the bargain will ruin us.

    2. Persons of great knowledge in affairs of Ireland have affirmed, the grosse produce of the receipt out of which all charges must be borne, never yet made amounted to £300,000, which reckoning the charges we must unavoidably be at (with great losse—*del.*) is £50,000 per annum lesse than we must make of it to save ourselves. If it come to never so much, the contractors can never have more than their poundage.

3. That the contractors aske such things as are not fit or can not legally be graunted.

    1. The contractors are apprehensive etc. as in the paper.²

[f.2v] 2. The method hitherto hath been, that the summe or scope of such contracts as these hath been first approved of by the Treasurie and such other Lords as your Majestie thinkes fit to appoint thereunto, and the drawing up and wording it in proper and legall clauses and termes, left to your Majestie's councell learned.³

    2. That provided the scope and main part of the proposall be approved by your Majestie, we are willing to leave the drawing up the same in proper and legall clauses and termes to your Majestie's councell learned to whom your Majestie hath referred it, and shall acquiesce in what he shall judge reasonable and fit for us (to have—*del.*)

4. That the contractors by searching into old arreares and long concealed rents, will harrass the people, ruine the kingdome, at least anger and provoke the parliament.

    1. That it is the interest of the contractors to please, incourage and enrich the nacion, not to beggar it.

    2. That the whole scope of the contract hath a plain bent and tendencie to advantaging the kingdome and incouraging trade.

    3. These things have been granted allready and no complaint thereof.

    4. There is an express clause that no man shall be troubled on this accompt but by consent of 2 of your Majestie's judges, or councell learned.

5. That your Majestie's graunt to the contractors will overthrow and

---

¹ . . . ¹ interlineated.

² Dering is presumably here referring to the paper sent to him by the contractors.

³ Dering has deleted the whole of this para. 2 and added the substitute paragraph following.

avoid a great many former graunts and invade the rights of many private persons.[1]

HLRO Hist Coll 85/6

45. *Draft letter from Dering to ?Edward Roberts, 4 November [1681]*

Sir

I send you heare a draught[2] which I thinke will now come into two sides of your paper, as you will judge by seeing what I have marked to be left out upon your paper. The last clause of all, you will find to be new, but I thinke it reasonable to be added, you may give those answers I have made, or what others you thinke fit.

You may if you will add some conclusion to it to this purpose, that these things being so clearly laid before his majesty, it is humbly begged that his majesty will please to continue his favourable opinion both of the contractors and the contract which will encourage them in persisting in doing his majesty service therein, (*notwithstanding the delay of six moneths since May last is exceedingly to your prejudice*).[3]

And that you do not doubt, of giving full cleare and satisfactory answers to whatever shall be objected by the Lord Rannelagh or any other.[4]

[*Ms. torn*] that line concerning the 6 months delay you may put it in or leave it out as you like best, as also add whatsoever you shall judge best, not exceeding still what may be fair written in two sides of paper.

HLRO Hist Coll 85/5

46. *Dering's draft letter to ?Edward Roberts, c. 22 November 1681*

It seemes to me all things are loose again and my Lord Rannelagh having libertie to reply and not being tide to any time when, leaves the matter as farr from a conclusion as ever.

I know no use of a meeting at present, but if you will come to me to morrow night about eight, I shall then have spoke with my Lord and have his opinion.

---

[1] The whole of para. 5 is deleted by Dering.

[2] The draft has not survived, but the previous paper (no. 45) seems to contain Dering's rough notes for the draft.

[3] L. Hyde, Finch and Dering had taken the outline contract to the King on 20 May 1681 (cf. p. 25 above). The proposed contract, moreover, was to run from 1 May 1681 (cf. p. 205 below). The sentence in italics was underlined by Dering.

[4] The letter was sent as L. Ranelagh began his attack on the proposals for a new farm (cf. *Ormonde MSS*, vi, 219-20, 222-3).

I send you heare my notes, which are not very materiall: more than that of about fourty objections your answer, as I judge, seems satisfactory to the bord in about thirty of them. Those which may require or at least admitt debate, I thinke are these

1. The civill establishment of Tangier not provided for.
2. Concealed lands.
3. King's restraint of pardoning fines and forfeitures.
4. The balance of accompts from Lord Rannelagh etc.
5. The time of beginning the contract, and ending.
6. The trustees to be removable and other appointed at the King's pleasure.
7. Postage and prisage and butlerage to be comprehended.
8. The delay of judges to grant processe, to be a ground for defalcacions.
9. The 700 per annum the King hath power in the present farme to remitt.

47. *Memoranda concerning the Irish farm* *10-12 December 1681, etc.*

[f.2v] Commissioners of Accompts[1]   10 December 1681
Having required the deputy Auditor and deputy Receiver Generall to appeare before us they did acquaint them with the substance of your Grace's (letter—*del.*) order, and delivered them a copie therof as also a copie of the Lords Commissioners letters to your Grace dated the 22 November last, and required them to observe the contents of both. In answer to which the said deputy Receiver Generall after some few dayes debate in the presence of the deputy Auditor Generall and the farmers did give in the annexed certificat, which we humbly offer and submit to your Grace's consideracion, being the only way we had to informe ourselves concerning the particulars in your Grace's said order.

The letter to the Duke of Ormond referred to, viz. 22 November 1681, is to desire his Grace to send to the commissioners of accompts to know whether the farme rent be paid up to the last of April 81, and the civill cost to 25 March 81 and what is wanting to either and whether the payments have been by money due (since—*del.*) before 1 Aprill 81 inclusive.

[f.1]   12 December 1681
Commissioners of inspection are only able to make cleare discoverie of this matter, viz. whether there have been any anticipations of the revenue since 1 May 81 to payment of (charge—*del.*) sent before that time.

---

[1] The following paragraph is the draft of a letter from Dering to Ormonde. On 7 December Arran reported to Ormonde that the auditors were not agreeing on any report. (*Ormonde MSS.*, vi, 252.)

September (*sic*) 20, 1681. Commissioners of accompts

They have often called upon Sir John Champante for accompt of all money received by him as deputy vice treasurer from any other persons (viz. than the farmers) or upon other accompt since December 1675 (being the farme rent and advance—*del.*) Sir John Champante answered that such other money as hath been received since 25 December 75 on any accompt beside the farm rent and advance money hath been received by him as instructed by the Lord Rannelagh and partners upon accompt of their undertaking and as deputy vice Treasurer, and that he conceives himselfe only lyable to give them accompt thereof. But in conclusion told them he would write to the Earl of Rannelagh and his partners about it and would in the meantime prepare the accompt of which they will send a copie when received.

HLRO Hist Coll 85/10

48. *Dering's memorandum of a meeting of the Irish committee concerning the proposed farm, 12 December 1681*

The Trustees will certainly understand all that is received and paid in the chequer. And one 6th part is allwayes paid in money into the exchequer. And it is better than ever it was, for the contractors are lyable to have their farmes seised by the Trustees and the King is immediately in possession.

The deputy being named by the King, the Trustees are not lyable for his misbehaviour, but it seemes better for the King that he should name the deputy than that the Trustees should name it, but Mr. Roberts leaves it to the King either to name the deputy himselfe, or to leave it to the Trustees.

The deputy of the Trustees giving exchequer acquittances, what have the Trustees to do?

Lord President, that the Trustees ought to reside in Ireland; that the Trustees ought to be the principal officers of the state in Ireland; that the Trustees should be alterable at the King's pleasure; that they should not be answerable for the deputy.

The Sollicitor to think of a clause whereby the King may be secured by the deputy in case the King do name the deputy.

The Trustees not to be grauntees of the revenue.

Looke into Sir James Shaen's farme and see whether he be entitled to the arreares before May 81.

HLRO Hist Coll 85/16

49. *Dering's memoranda concerning a meeting of the Irish Committee, 20 December 1681*

[f.1] From 31 December to 1st of May but 4 months. If there were £76,000 in arrear yet that could not be a compensation to exempt 6 months payment which is £150,000. The farmers know they had themselves paid this arrear and so the mistake will fall on them.

Letter of the 5th March 80.

£69,000 of assignments the farmers have credit for upon that letter, many of which are yet unpaid. They ensure the payment of £40,000 by assignments in the accompt of the first of May. No arreare but £9,000, sed quaere what shall be allowed for defalcacens, for that is equall to an arrear. If the King will cleare them from all arrears they will pay in 9 yeare £2,700,000. The farmers desire to have the same defalcacens which my Lord Rannelagh had.

If any arreare, so much as shall be paid his arrear must be discompted out of the rent, but such arreares only to be paid as are arreares at the beginning of the contract and shall be discovered during the contract. Such arrears—only as the present men are bound to pay which be allowed by the Court of Exchequer, are to be reckend as arrears

Auditers of the Imprest. Reports of my Lord Rannelagh, 2 papers. The first of November 1679 appeares by the following clause to be vitium scriptum, and should be the last. The farme to be accompted at 250,000 per annum from 31 December 1682 for the residue of the farme. The £10,000 per annum towards Tangier and shipping may be saved, for the contract doth allow 4-6 per weeke, which is 4d per weeke per head more than now. What the victuallers undertake for 6 per diem the King may do for 5d; and what can be done in England for 5d may be done in Ireland for 4d. Beefe at 3 farthings per pound in Ireland. So one 3d may be saved (that is of the victualls).

2d a day for provisen for a horse, which is more than the King allows now so in seamens.

Nor can it be said, if anything can be saved, the King shall have the benefit, for if £10,000 be saved the contracters will have £2,000 of it for their poundage.

But all this is to be accompted as part of the King's revenue, and the farmers will bring it to accompt as part of their rent, and so the King will not have it.

Mr Roberts. 6d per diem to Tangier is a mistake, for the victualls are furnished for 365 dayes whereas they do reckon to be paid but for 12 months at 28 dayes per mensem.

[f.1v] The victualls to be debited to Tangier for 365 dayes. The contractors to have no allowance for any savings till the full rent be paid up, and the King may assigne such savings to any publique use for Ireland or Tangier, and this every yeare during the farme.

Mr Roberts desires that no discourse nor persuasions of his may be conclusive to the contractors, but he will represent it to the persons concerned.

Lord President. Lord Rannelagh to have allowance of £40,000 for their entry upon the farme at Christmas and ending at May. He demands also £2,500 per annum for Tangier. The clause for not abating the summe of shipping tyes up the King's hands.

The King judgeth this reasonable. Postage of letters. What is meant by this. Leave it out.

Prisage of wines. This is my Lord of Ormond's inheritance let by him for £2,000 per annum, and the King is not to allow it. Wine to the Privy Councell valued at £1,000 per annum.

Impresting [*sic*, incomplete].

KAO U1107/14/15

50. *Memorandum by Dering on clauses in the proposed Irish contract* [*1681*]

[f.1] The cashier must be answerable for his deputy unlesse the King appoint the deputy, and in that case deputy must be answerable for what he receives, and both of them ought to give good securitie for faithfull discharging and duly accompting and to be sworn also (as I thinke).

A clause to give a yearly accompt to the commissioners of the Treasurie and the Lord Treasurer in England and to the commissioner of accompts there of all the receipts issues and payments of the yeare preceding, distinguishing (the same—*del.*) as well the receipts as item under the severall proper heads, and the same not to be allowed by our (*illegible*) and commissioner of accompts there, before they have them 6 weekes heare

[f.2] The office of vice-Treasurer is an auncient office, taken notice of by many acts of parliament, and I thinke can not be supprest.

But it hath aunciently been, and may well again be separated from the other two.

Some question may be how farr the King can erect a new officer by law, and give him power to take fees of the subject, though I suppose in this case he may do it.

Yet Mr Kent in his pattent by which he is erected cashier hath no power to take anything from the subject, but hath a salarie from the King.

If there be any doubt hearein, the King may do what is desired by determining Lord Rannelagh's grant, and constituting when he thinkes fit Receivers Generall and Treasurers at warr, with the power to receive the fee of 6d per pound, which in that case will not be a new fee but the old. And the vice Treasurers place may be given where [f.1v] the King please, either separately by itselfe or jointly with the other two.

I do doubt whether this cashier as such can give exchequer acquittances or issue the money, one part being annexed to the office of Receiver Generall, the other to that of Treasurer at warr. And therefore still it seemes best to me to retain the old [deletion] meanes known in the law and Court of Exchequer. Much lesse can this cashier give Exchequer acquittances alone, there being other officers, I take it, as the clerke of the Pells the chamberlain of the Exchequer, who do joine to make it a chequer acquittance.

Heare is no authoritie for him to pay any money by order of the commissioners of the revenue, nor possibly there needs not. He can not possibly do all things which the vice Treasurer can do, because severall things are annexed by act of parliament to the office of vice Treasurer.

Fill the blank up with (Monday)

HLRO Hist Coll 85/8

[f.65]   51. *Dering's copy of the Deputy Vice-Treasurer's Account (Ireland) [n.d., c. 1681]*

1. In case all the assignments which by the farmers have been issued toward clering the payments to the said last of Aprill 81 have been complyed with and paid, and the interest of the advance money to that time allowed, then the farme rent to the said last of April inclusive without dayes of grace is paid up and cloased.
2. The civill establishment is fully paid up to the 25 March last and the military list to the last of April, 81, excepting 5083—17—8$\frac{3}{8}$ which remaines unpaid, for which assignments are and will be immediatly sent to, the farmers to be by them signed.
3. The payments which have been made and remaine to be made, for which assignments are and will be immediatly sent to the farmers, to be by them signed to cleare and pay up the establishments to the said times, have and will be made by the farme rent done before the said last day of Aprill, that moneth being including excepting 9100—4—11$\frac{7}{8}$; which remaine is occasiond by some necessary and extraordinary payments which have been made, not included in the establishments. In this compute what may heareafter be allowed to the farmers by the Court of Exchequer for rents respited and remitted is not considered.
4. The farmers having not prepared the lists by which that matter is to be adjusted, no answer can be given at present to the fourth question, viz. what part of the assignments for payments due for and untill the last of Aprill 81 do remain unpaid.

John Champante

HLRO Hist Coll 85/1

52. *Dering's draft submission to the King concerning the Irish farm, ?February 1682*

[f.1] May it please your Majestie

It is now about 9 months since your Majestie was pleased to approve of the scope of a contract for your revenue of Ireland and Tangier for 9 yeares commencing from 1 May 1681.

The draught of (that—*del.*) which contract hath in pursuance of your Majestie's Warrant been prepared, and establishments correspondent therewith have been drawn up, all which have been severall times debated in your royall presence, by which method the contractors did humbly hope your Majestie and the Lords of the Councell and Treasurie would receive such satisfaction that the contract might (before this time—*del.*) by your Majestie's full approbacion (might—*del.*) before this time have past under your Great Seale.

The contractors do not find that any thing alledged by the Lord R[anelagh], Mr Sheriden or others hath either discoveredy our Majestie's revenues to be of greater value then the contractors have estimated them and were bona fide to have paid for them, or that the produce thereof can be better applyed than for the discharge of the establishments of Ireland Tangier and shipping as they have proposed, but rather that these endeavors discourses and computacions tend to perplex imbarras and misrepresent the true state and value of the revenue, and to impose greater burthens and hardships upon the contractors then they or any other can discharge with all the produce thereof, and to persuade your Majestie to restrain and diminish your government, without the least prospect of any reall benefit to accrue to your Majestie thereby, but rather barring limiting and extinguishing your Majestie's unquestionable rights, which will prove in the end much more to your Majestie's damage than to the contractors.

All which delayes and discouragements notwithstanding the contractors do say, they are yet willing [f.1v] to make good (their proposall —*del.*) to the utmost that they have offered in their contract, and proposalls, the substance whereof is

1. To pay your Majestie £282,000 per annum for 9 yeares by monthly payments net
2. To secure your Majestie against all defalcacions by the present farmers
3. if the revenue shall amount to more than £282,000 (and their poundage of 4s per pound to pay—*del.*) to be accomptable for the same to your Majestie
4. To advance £84,000 as a caution for their performance or what greater or lesser summe your Majestie desires

To which we shall only add at this time, that understanding the second proposall, viz. of securing your Majestie from defalcacions, is valued at nothing at all, if your Majestie shall thinke fit to leave out that clause, we will give your Majestie £3,000 per annum more for every of the 9 years.

But if after all these things so cleare as we conceive in themselves, and after 22 severall dayes of examinacion of the said particulars in your Majestie's royall presence and before the Lords of your Councell and Treasurie, the advantage of the proposals and the integrity of the proposers in serving your Majestie to the utmost of their power be not evident and manifest to your Majestie and your ministers, they know no thing now left wherein they can express their duty, than by withdrawing their papers and thereby leaving the field open to some better or at least more fortunate undertakers, which they have reason to hope your Majestie will speedily (receive—*del.*) see, Mr Sheridan having affirmed (to the Lords of the Treasurie—*interlineated*) that he knew that (bett—*del.*) a greater rent will be offered your Majestie, if it might be received. And the contractors [f.2] will be so farr from obstructing or discouraging such new proposers, that they shall be ready to give them any informacion or assistance that may inable them the better to performe any service to your Majestie. And they do entirely acquiesce in what your Majestie shall declare to be your pleasure either for closing with or dismissing their proposals.

And if your Majestie shall thinke fit to dismisse them, they most humbly cast themselves at your Majestie's feet, for such allowances and (satisfaction—*del.*) consideracion for their great paines and charges in attending this affaire, and for the improvement of your Majestie's revenue which upon the foundacion of their proposals, may arise to your Majestie, as your Majestie in your royall bountie and clemencie shall thinke fit.

KAO U1107/14/14

53. *Dering's memorandum on the final submission by the contractors,*[1] *28 July 1682*

[f.1]

1. Indenture formerly tripartite now made quadripartite: King, lessees, assignees, contractors. Contractors the same persons with the old farmers.
2. £169,000 advance money, to ly to the end of the farme and as caution for performance.

---

[1] The meeting of the Lords Commissioners at Whitehall on 28 July before whom Shaen, Roberts and the Solicitor appeared is described by Ormonde in his letter of 28 July to Arran (*Ormonde*, vi, 407-8). Ormonde recorded that 'Sunday last [6 August, 1682] has put a final period' to the contractors' proposals (*op. cit.*, 418).

3. They to pay £300,000 per annum but out of that to take £18,000 per annum for management.
4. £17,000 per mensem to Ireland, £3,000 to ships, £3,500 to Tangier, in all £23,500 per mensem.
5. the caution money to be divided.
6. the £70,000 which was to be paid by May 83 they are now to pay by August 1683 (£164,000), and they to have 4 moneths after the end of the farme to pay their arreares which will be still 4 moneths behind.
7. The trustees which were to execute the offices of vice treasurer, treasurer at warr
    now (Lessees to execute office of vice treasurer
        (Assignees to be receivers generall
        (contractors to be treasurers at warr
    assignees and contractors to have the fees and to pay the lessees as they agree, and these 2 alteracions they thinke indispensable.
8. The wine warrants to be abated to the farmers.
9. 1900 payable at Tangier to be limited to so much as they shall receive, and what they shall pay, they to be reimbursed out of surplus.
10. What the contractors are to pay of my Lord Rannelagh's balance, they desire to be limited to so much as they shall receive of my Lord Rannelagh and that to be reimbursed out of the surplus or out of the savings.
[f.2v] 11. Clauses concerning the releifs to be the same as in the present farme, one was not to levy without the King's leave, the other is (not—*del.*) to levy, but the King may forbid.
12. Lands unlet. The farmers to have the quit rents and the lands to be disposed by the King and to have nothing before May 81. Now they would have the mean profits before May 81
13. Where before the King was to satisfy them for the quit rents of the concealed lands not worth quit rent, now they will take the lands and let them out as they can, reserving the quit rent upon the whole one with another and they to have no defalcacions for it. They to have power to abate £700 per annum out of the quit rents, grauntees to have libertie to place deficiencies.
14. In my Lord Rannelagh's clause they say they will only indemnify the King, and leave out the words shall pay, and I thinke that part which indemnifies Lord Rannelagh and his partners.
15. In the clause of the shipping, they will maintain 6 ships for £36,000, but they mencion the rates which are not to be exceeded, and if they do exceed £36,000 they must be reimbursed out of the surplus.
16. They desire the King will declare the contractors to be justices of peace.
17. The clause for the Attorney and Sollicitor's consent to such to be any two of the King's councell.

18. All money due from any persons for the £60,000 advance money to be graunted to the contractors.
[f.1v] 19. The contractors to have all things which were in charge 4 September 1675 except such quit rents as have been abated.
20. The contractors to have defalcacions for all things which are due (since—*del.*) to be defalcted to the present farmers since 1st May 1681 to (May—*del.*) December 1682.
21. What is paid by the present farmers since 1 May 1681 is to be allowed the contractors, but in the former draught, it was so in case the payment since May 81 were not made for rent due before.
22. Surplus is to go to pay the contractors what they have paid more than received, and then to be divided in 3 parts
     1. to pay the King's debts to his subjects in Ireland
     2. To the publique uses mencioned in the act or others the King shall thinke fit
     3. To such persons (as have been or—*del.*) as shall be instrumentall in bringing anything into charge other than the contractors or their servants.
     This to be a limited summe, the super surplus to be to the contractors. This is the surplus of the arrears before May 1687.
23. So that the payment of the debts upon the King or establishment proposed by the Treasurie out of these arreares is heare omitted.
[f.2] 24. Trustees were to suspend them if 4 moneths in arreare, now it is that the trustees shall not enter upon nor receive any debts then in arrear but only the growing rents and profits.
25. The contractors do leave out the clause that no forfeitures shall be unlesse the trustees shall first certify that it is by the willfull default of the contractors.
26. The land souldiers if on shipbord to have no defalcacion for their dyet, now they say, defalt but one third.
27. The contractors insist to have the nominacion of the agents for the armie.

HLRO Hist Coll 85/11

54. *Will of Sir Edward Dering, 24 February 1683*[1]

In the name of God, amen. I, Sir Edward Dering now of the parish of St Martins in the Feilds in the county of Middlesex Baronet doe make and ordaine this my last Will and Testament resigning my soule to God that gave it and my body to the dust from whence it came neverthelesse in hope of a joyfull resurrection at the last day through the merits and intercession of the blessed Jesus my only Saviour and Redeemer to whom be glory forever Amen. Imprimis I give to Mary, Anne and

---

[1] Dering's first will had been made on 19 August 1681, cf. AB1, p. 82.

Katherine my three marryed daughters and to Helena Southwell eldest daughter of my daughter Southwell and to Elizabeth wife of my eldest sonne and to Jane my unmarryed daughter to each of them thirty pounds to be laid out in a ring or what else they like to keep in memory of me. Item I give to Charles Daniel John and Robert my foure younger sonns the debt of fower thousand pounds owing me by Sir Hugh Cholmeley Baronet and secured to me by mortgage upon parte of his estate the said fower thousand pounds to be divided equally between my said fower sonns. Item I give to Jane Dering my unmarryed daughter for her porcion and to her executors administrators and assignes my two houses scituate in great Russell streete in Bloomsbury which I hold for many yeares yet to come of the Right Honourable the Lady Russell one of which houses is in lease to John Hampden Esq. and the other in lease to Edward Vaughan Esq. Item I give to Edward Dering Esq. my eldest sonne and to his heires for ever the two fee farme rents which I have purchased in revercion after the death of the Queen's Majesty hee paying and dischargeing the debt of one thousand pounds for which they stand engaged to Sir John Percivall or soe much thereof as shall remaine undischarged at the time of my death. Item I give to my said sonne Edward Dering his executors and administrators my lease of Long-beech Woods in Kent hee or they paying and dischargeing all such debts as at the time of my death I shall stand bound in for the proper debts of my said eldest sonne and alsoe clearing and indempnifying my executors from all debts or summes of money due to any of the younger children of Mr Francis Bettenham deceased for their porcions out of the lands of Sherland in Plunckley [*sic*] in Kent. Item I give to my eldest sonne the right which I have to the summe of one thousand pounds out of the estate of Sir Hugh Cholmeley in case the said Sir Hugh shall happen to departe this life without issue male. Item I give to my daughter Knatchbull the summe of three hundred pounds. Item I give to my old servant Rolfe twenty pounds, to the poore of the parish of Pluckley five pounds, to the poore of the parish or towne of Hyth five pounds, to five poore ministers or ministers widowes to be nominated by my wife to each tenne pounds. All the rest of my personall estate being leases of houses chattells goods debts ready money stock arreares of rent other than arreares of rents or debts of my eldest sonne which if any such shall be I doe hereby [1]release unto him or otherwise I doe hereby[1] give and bequeath to Mary my loving and beloved wife my debts other than such as are herein mencioned to be paid and discharged by my eldest sonne and the porcions and legacies herein given and bequeathed being first paid and discharged by her. And I make my said wife my sole executrix of this my last will and testament. And revoking all other former wills and being in sound mind and memory and recommending to all my children piety humility and mutuall affection and a dutifull

[1] . . . [1] entered in margin.

obedience to a most deserving mother I have hereunto set my hand and seale at my dwelling house in Gerard Streete in the parish of St Martins in the Feilds above named this four and twentyeth day of February in the yeare of our Lord according to the computacion of the Church of England one thousand six hundred eighty and two 1682. Ed. Dering. Signed and sealed and published by the above named Sir Edward Dering Baronet at his house in Gerard Street as his last will in presence of Henry Dering William Briggs John Brookes. [The text of the grant of probate on 4 July 1684 follows.][1]

PRO PROB 11 376 C/10357
(Photocopy, HLRO Hist Coll 85/17)

55. *Dering's draft letter to Sir Hugh Cholmley, 27 November 1683*

London

Sir

I have suffered yours of the 5th instant to ly by me some dayes resolving by my answer to give you an accompt of the dispatch of your affaire now before us at the Treasurie.[2] As soon as I received yours I called upon Mr Lownes to finish it, who in few dayes after brought it to the board, and having soon after received the approbacion of the board, there hath wanted nothing for all this weeke past but the King's hand, which I were very confident would have been had upon Fryday last, but opportunitie not serving then, I nothing doubt but it will be done tomorrow, and shall take care to see it put up in my Lord's bundle of papers which are to be presented to the King for his hand, so that you may certainly rely upon it that either tomorrow or allowing one day for accidents, at very farthest on Fryday next, it will be done. However I would not deferr any longer assuring you of my humble service and of my heartie congratulacions and good wishes for the happinesse of yourself and all your family in the disposall of your daughter. My money being now of no longer use to you I am very willing to take it in this next terme, which is much more commodious for me than at any longer distance. I believe it may be so also to you, but desire to heare from you your resolucion in that point by the first opportunitie.

I am sir,

Your most faithfull servant
Ed. Dering

BM Stowe 746, f. 78

[1] A copy of the will is calendared by Miss Anderson in *DS Corr*, 31.

[2] Sir Hugh Cholmley had been appointed contractor for building the mole at Tangier, and then Surveyor-General at Tangier. Sums were owing to him for these works and also for a loan of £5000 on the credit of the Customs. A royal warrant for a privy seal to pay him passed on 5 Dec. 1683 (*CTB*, 1681-5, 976)

56. *Speech by Dering concerning accusations,* [*n.d., ?26 April 1675*]
[f.53]

I shall for my part be allwayes ready to bring offenders not only to light but to punishment also, and that great offences when they are fully proved may have great and proporcionale punishments. But I do not think that everything which is actionable in Westminster Hall is a proper businesse for this house or that every complaint or dissatisfaction which a private person may have against a publique minister or officer of the crowne ought justly to be treated among the ardua regni, the great affaires of Church and State, which we are summoned to consult about.

If ever sober councells were in season, if ever wisdome and moderacion did dwell together, it is now.

There is no man but knows that the reputacion of the King abroad, and in some measure the safetie of the nation too, depends upon the opinion the world have of a good correspondence between his Majestie and the 2 houses.

If after all we are still as complaining and distrustfull as we were, will not [it] be said our jealousies are incurable, that our honour is not to be sweetened, and especially what is helplesse must be carelesse too, and other councells and other councillors must be thought of, and what the consequence of that may be, I had rather fear than feele.

Propertie is to be considered not only as it is to be secured against the prerogative but as it comprehend trade both at home and abroad, especially in relacion to a neighbouring nacion, which seemes to grow fast upon us.

If this session end in disgust, I believe we shall have Te Deum sung at R[ome].

Let us not allwayes sit heare to find faults and never to mend them.

I think truly there is great weight to be laid upon the difference between impeachments of treason and those which are only for misdemeanour.

In cases of treason where the King's person and safetie are concerned, we can not proceed too speedily nor too secretly, and it is better in cases of that supreme importance that an innocent should be put to the trouble and the reproach of a publique triall than that a guilty person should escape by absence or by practice upon the witnesses or other means.

It is more for the honour of the King and the interest of the (government—*del.*) people that the persons intrusted by his Majestie in the government should appear men of honour and integrity every way worthy of the great trust reposed in them than persons unjust, oppressors, deserters or betrayers of that trust.

[illegible] are not charged upon their oath to present who doth well, who come to church, or who liveth virtuously at home, but who breake the laws.

No man will say that we sit heare for no other purpose but to enquire into the errors and miscarriages of the government, or that to be a good patriot, there needs no other qualification than to be a bold accuser.

HLRO Hist Coll 85/1

57. *Draft calculations by Dering* [*n.d.*]

2ff. of sums paid or owed by 'Mrs Sheldon' and various other individuals, perhaps noted by Dering as Commissioner of the Treasury, with other rough calculations.

HLRO Hist Coll 85/18

58. *'Heads for a bill for constituting a fisherie'* [*n.d.*]

[f.1v]
1. The trade of the fisherie to be managed by a new companie to be established by his majestie and carried on by a publique stock
2. This publique stock to be of 100,000 to be raised by voluntarie sub-scripcion.
3. Out of the subscribers [blank in ms.] to be chosen by themselves to be a standing committee to manage the interest and affaires of the companie.
4. Foreigne and Scotch salt to be prohibited by imposing a large dutie upon it.
5. ob. per gallon excise to be laid upon all English made salt; which is supposed will raise about 36,000 per annum.
6. Of this revenue one third part to be repaid by his Majestie to the companie for 7 yeares to come, toward the carrying on and incouragement of the fisherie.
7. A considerable imposicion to be put upon foreigne cordage, for the incouragement of our owne.
8. The company to contract with his Majestie to deliver in so much cordage and so much canvas as shall be agreed on and at certain prices, for incouragement of those manufactures heare.
9. It to breed up so many seamen, etc.
[f.2v] Ob. per gallon on english salt will produce per annum £36,000.

HLRO Hist Coll 85/19

59. *Dering's draft of part of a speech concerning witnesses and
the defence at trials [n.d., post 17 August 1681]*

[f.61]

6. That there must be two credible witnesses, but I have hardly seen any
witnesses for the King refused, nothing making him incapable but the
pillory, and if the prisoner can be so lucky as to foresee who are witnesses
against him, and can prove great crimes in his life and conversacion,
yet the jury must heare him, and then one being upon oath and the
other not, the inclinacion of beliefe bends toward the former.

Besides it hath been held by some that the King's witnesses, though
they be forsworn, are not lyable to the pillory, which may make them
the more confident.

But as witnesses of another nacion, alltogether foreigners to the partie
and to the jury too, how shall any objections be made soudainly upon
the place to them?

The being papists, though a most evident reason to take off, as things
now stand, the credibilitie of their testimonie against a protestant, is
yet no excepcion against their being legall witnesses, though in a matter
of religion, and where the interest of parties are concerned, no man as it
seemes to me can think them credible, their principles of not keeping
faith with hereticks, of not being bound to speake truth but before a
lawfull magistrate.

That no person excommunicate, or who derives his authoritie from
one that is so, can be a lawfull magistrate. That the good of their church
is to be prefered before all other consideracions, and that a private
injury may be done for the publick good, being considered, and that
they doubtlesse be easier absolved by their confessor for bearing false
witness for the good of their church, than for telling truth to their
prejudice.

And this at least while the present heate and animositie do last, is very
worthy to be considered.

[f.61v] 7: That the indictment must be proved modo et forma as they
are laid in the record, otherwise the prisoner is not guilty.

This is allwayes said, but never regarded. I speake as to the two main
circumstances of all humane actions, which is time and place. This I
confess is ancient, but it seemes unreasonable, taking away the prisoner's
just defence, as I can (tell—*del.*) recollect where I were and in what
companie the 10 of May, and perhaps bring the same persons to prove
myselfe, 50 mile of where it is said I did the robbery or said the treasonous
words. But when it comes to the triall, it is said and witnesses come to
prove it, upon the 30th day, and though I could prove as much on that
day, yet I have neither time nor meanes, and the same thing may be
said of the place, for I speake not of such things as cannot alter the case,
as whether it be a musket or carbine the man was (shot—*del.*) hurt with,

with a knife or dagger, whether the sword were 3 or 5 inches long or the like. And for this reason, among some others, I have been allwayes very unwilling to be of any jury, they being allwayes charged to consider if he be guilty modo et forma as in the indictment.

8: That no artifice of pleading, no oratory of the King's councell, no consideracion of partie nor of other crimes than what are laid in the indictment, and those positively proved, ought to sway with the jury.

This indeed is the law, and this was not only fairly opened and repeated to the jury at [f.62] Oxford, but very worthily and clearly the Lord Chief Justice left out the witnesses Sir W. J[ennings] and Mr M[aster]s in summing up the evidence to the jury, they having indeed said nothing materiall as to the particular treason then in issue.

But nobody can doubt but that those vile and odious words testified by Mr Masters, a gentleman of good credit and colledge, his justifying the most impious fact that hath been committed these 1,000 yeares, in the (death—*del.*) murther of the last King, moved an indignacion against him in the breasts of a loyall jury. I am sure it did in all those who either heard or read it, and whether it might not animate them a little against a man who appeared to be of principles bad enough to do the fact laid to his charge, and consequently add something to the credibility of the legall proofes made against him, may be considered. I speake this without any offence or reflexion to the jury, for to my judgment there were two plain witnesses enough to justify their sentence, but my meaning only is, that our trialls are not matter of oratory as in the rostrum and forum of the Romans, but upon plain matters of fact which ought not to be amplified or valued by any thing that is not it selfe a legall proof, and so much the more because the attorney commands the attendance of what witnesses he please, but the prisoner can only intreat and if they will not come, I think he is without remedy.

[f.62v] 8: That there must be two credible witnesses. This is the law, but the word credible in the (narrow—*del.*) large legall significacion signifies every man in effect who hath not been in the pillorie, nothing else making him infamous, unlesse attaint of perjury or felony, nor that neither after a pardon obtained. So that the prisoner hath little benefit by this word, which yet is materiall to his life, and doubtlesse, it is intended that the witnesses should be men of credit, such men as the neighbours knowing their life and conversacion do believe upon their word and (which makes—*del.*) wherefore men of abominable lives, known lyars, profest enemies to the prisoner and others, as circumstances may be, to be justly suspected in their testimonie, and the jury are commanded to look upon the witnesses and upon the prisoner, that their owne knowledge may guide them in such things as it can informe them in.

9: That we have no rack in England, and this is true, and a great blessing surely, but I am told Capt. Richardson hath a hole in Newgate which never any man could endure two dayes without confessing any thing laid to his charge. I believe it is very seldome made use of, but that is the dominion of the King (dome—*del.*) and of the government, for I do not see how any man is secure from it if highly charged and maliciously prosecuted.

[f.63] 10: that the prisoner at the barr must have no councell, and the reason is given, because the judge is bound to be his councell.

This is an old thredbare saying, but I could hardly ever heare it alledged with patience, for I demand of all men living if they ever yet found the judge of councell to the prisoner. Nay, all that I have seen have affected to show their authoritie more than their clemencie, rating and reviling the prisoner, discountering his witnesses, taking pleasure to shew their skill or memorie in trapping (up—*del.*) them in their evidence, letting the King's councell say what they will, and manage in effect the whole triall, and summing up the evidence at the last, perhaps partially, and yet not suffering the prisoner to reply upon them.

The things particularly I observe:

1. That the judges do plainly refuse to suggest any plea in law, any matter of just excepcions to the matter or forme, unlesse the illiterate prisoner can chop upon it himselfe.

2. No judge ever yet did find fault or flaw in any indictment brought before them, that certainly oftentimes may and ought to be done, and they would do if they thought what they say, that they are indeed bound to be of councell with the criminall.

3. The admitting indictments for (treason—*del.*) life to run contra formam statuti, on purpose to delude the prisoner, that he may not know upon what statute he is prosecuted, whereas an indictment ought to be certain.

HLRO Hist Coll 85/1

Index

Printed in England for Her Majesty's Stationery Office at the Alden Press, Oxford
Dd 288701 K16 1/76